THE
ROBERT GORE
UNIVERSIT
ABERDEEN

The Robert Gordon University
- A History

by

Professor Henry Ellington

THE ROBERT GORDON UNIVERSITY ABERDEEN

The Author

Professor Henry Ellington is a native Aberdonian. Educated at Robert Gordon's College and Aberdeen University, he graduated with First Class Honours in Natural Philosophy in 1963. After a spell as a research scientist at AERE, Harwell, he returned to Aberdeen in 1965 to train as a teacher. He joined RGIT in 1966, lecturing in physics and completing a Ph.D. in gaseous electronics at Aberdeen University. In 1973, he became Head of RGIT's newly-established Educational Technology Unit, a post that he held until he retired in 2001, although his Department underwent two changes of name during the intervening period. After changing career in 1973, he established an international reputation as an educational developer and consultant, making numerous invited foreign visits and producing well over 300 publications, including 15 books. In 1990, he became Britain's first Professor of Educational Development when he was awarded a professorial title by RGIT. In 1996, he became the first recipient of a higher doctorate (a D.Litt.) from RGU, where he is now an Emeritus Professor. He is married with two grown-up children - both graduates of The Robert Gordon University.

First published in the United Kingdom

in 2002 by

The Robert Gordon University

Schoolhill

Aberdeen

AB10 1FR

Tel. 01224 262000

ISBN 1901 085 72 4

A CIP catalogue for this book is available from the British Library

Printed in Great Britain by Polestar

Contents

Foreword

Aberdeen has for centuries prospered in an area rich in agriculture, famous for its cattle and for the grain and water that make its whisky - a product consumed throughout the world. Blessed with a natural port, Aberdeen is a long-established centre for the fishing industry. This association with the sea has continued through the twentieth century and beyond, with the growth of the North Sea oil industry.

The success in harvesting this wealth must be attributed to the people of Aberdeen, who have developed an understanding of the science of their natural resources and the competence to manage them. Thus, the provision of the best possible education for its future citizens has always been a high priority in the city.

The Gordon family, with its many branches, has long been spread throughout the North East of Scotland. Robert Gordon's grandfather was recognised as a leader of the community, and was asked by the King in the early 17th century to study the absence of population in the area. In a growing economy, every person counted, and it made sense for every person to have the opportunity to contribute. So it was not surprising, some years later, that his grandson Robert Gordon, a merchant venturer, should endow a school for disadvantaged children.

It was natural as the centuries passed that this small school should grow, meeting the demands of developing technologies in all local industries from agriculture through to the state-of-the-art needs of the modern offshore oil industry. Home-grown has its pride, but hints at limitation. No such limitation applied to the educational institution that had been founded by Robert Gordon, as it moved easily to university status and widened its remit to incorporate societal as well as economic needs. The medical needs of Northern Scotland are now met in great part by the products of The Robert Gordon University.

This book tells the story not just of an institution but also of the people of the North East of Scotland - building their own future, taking their opportunities, and making the most of them. It shows, above all, the positive use of education and the fulfilment of the potential of individual people, whatever their circumstances and whatever part of the world they came from. It is not the end of the story; it is only its first chapters. More is to come, as the University faces the new challenges of the 21st century, building bridges and alliances for the future.

Sir Bob Reid
Chancellor,
The Robert Gordon University
August 2002

Introduction

This book describes the history of the institution that is now known as The Robert Gordon University - at least for the time being. Although it has only had this name for ten years, the institution itself is very much older. Its roots can in fact be traced back to 1729, when the Aberdeen merchant adventurer Robert Gordon founded a residential Hospital for the upbringing and education of local boys from poor families. In 1881, Robert Gordon's Hospital was transformed into Robert Gordon's College. This served both as a day school for boys and as an adult education institution, eventually taking over all the work in this area that had been carried out by the Aberdeen Mechanics' Institution since 1824. In 1903, the adult-education branch of Robert Gordon's College was granted the status of a 'Central Institution for specialised instruction', and, in 1910 became Robert Gordon's Technical College. This, in turn, became Robert Gordon's Institute of Technology in 1965 and The Robert Gordon Institute of Technology in 1991, before becoming The Robert Gordon University in 1992.

It can be seen from this brief summary of the history of The Robert Gordon University that there is some uncertainty about what should be regarded as its actual date of foundation. Some say 1729, the year in which Robert Gordon's Hospital was founded, some 1750, the year in which it became operational, some 1881, the year in which it became Robert Gordon's College and started running evening classes for adults, and so on down through the various key dates in its development. Indeed, a strong case has also been made for 1883, the year in which the local industrialist John Gray offered to build a 'School of Science and Art' in the grounds of Robert Gordon's College. He intended that the entire educational programme then being run by the Mechanics' Institution should be transferred to this new School, but, in the event, there was only room for the teaching of art and related subjects. It therefore became known as Gray's School of Art rather than Gray's School of Science and Art, with the other parts of the Mechanics' Institution programme being taught elsewhere in Robert Gordon's College. If pressed on the matter of the founding date, the author would probably opt for 1881 as having the strongest case, since this was the date when the institution first became involved in post-school education. Readers will no doubt make up their own minds on the matter once they have read the book, however.

The author is extremely grateful to Professor William Stevely, current Principal and Vice-Chancellor of The Robert Gordon University, for being given the opportunity to write the official history of the institution. He had certainly never expected to do so when he retired in July 2001. He had, however, been made an Emeritus Professor in recognition of his 35 years of service, and had a meeting with Professor Stevely shortly afterwards, in order to ask what he could do for the University in his new role. The outcome of the meeting was an invitation to write this book, an invitation that the author was absolutely delighted to accept. Although he was not a trained historian, the author hoped that his extensive experience as a writer and academic researcher, together with his first-hand knowledge of the institution over a long period of time, would enable him to make a reasonable fist of the job. Whether or not he has succeeded in doing so is up to readers to judge.

During the next few months, the author carried out preliminary background research on the project, and had several discussions with Professor Stevely regarding the approach that should be adopted to the work, the outline structure of the book, and so on. It was eventually agreed that the main body of the book should contain four sections, respectively covering the early history of the institution, its time as a Technical College, its time as an Institute of Technology, and its time as a University. It was also agreed that each section should include both a broad review of the period being covered and more detailed examination of any specific topics that were felt to be of particular importance, with a separate chapter being devoted to each major topic. This approach would enable the author to explain *why* the institution developed in the way it did, as well as describe *how* it did so. In terms of style, it was agreed that the book should be written with the general reader in mind rather than the student of history, so that the approach should not be too academic and off-putting. Once again, the author leaves it to readers to judge whether he has got the balance about right.

With regards to the methodology that he adopted when actually writing the book, the author felt that it was best to tackle the four sections in chronological order, since this made cross-referencing between chapters very much easier. Producing each section first involved carrying out all the preliminary research needed to gather the relevant background information. The amount of research required, and the time taken, varied considerably from chapter to chapter, but readers can get an idea of what was involved from Appendix D, which lists the author's main sources of information in each case. The author then produced the first drafts of all the chapters in the section on which he was working, and had these read by several different people. In the case of Sections 1 and 2, these included people with specialist knowledge of the period being covered; in the case of Sections 3 and 4, they included people who were actually involved in the events being described wherever possible. The drafts were then amended in the light of the comments received, a process that continued until everyone was happy with the material. Needless to say, this all took some considerable time.

Section 1 of the book deals with 'The origins of the institution', and covers the period from 1729 to 1909. It contains three chapters, dealing respectively with 'Robert Gordon, and the foundation of Robert Gordon's Hospital', 'The transformation into Robert Gordon's College', and 'John Gray, and the foundation of Gray's School of Art'. As we saw earlier, John Gray's offer to build a 'School of Science and Art' at Schoolhill was one of the most important events in the early history of the institution that was eventually to become The Robert Gordon University - so much so that a number of people consider that he has a stronger claim to be regarded as its real 'founder' than Robert Gordon himself. Readers will be able to form their own opinions on this issue once they have read Section 1 of the book.

Section 2 deals with 'Robert Gordon's Technical College', and covers the period from 1910 to 1965. It again contains three chapters, the first of which gives a 'Review of the Technical College years'. The next two chapters deal respectively with 'The incorporation of the School of Domestic Economy', and with 'Tom Scott Sutherland and the Garthdee bequest'. Both were highly significant events, with the latter being so important that Tom Scott Sutherland is now generally regarded as one of the three main founders of The Robert Gordon University, along with Robert Gordon and John Gray.

Section 3 deals with 'Robert Gordon's Institute of Technology', covering the period from 1965 to 1992. This is by far the longest section of the book, and contains seven chapters. The first is a 'Review of the RGIT years'. The next five chapters then look in detail at specific topics relating to this period, dealing respectively with 'The impact of the offshore oil industry', 'The growth of social and management-related teaching', 'The growth of health-related teaching', 'Changes in educational methodology', and 'Research, consultancy and external collaboration'. The final chapter in this section deals with 'The achievement of university status', giving a blow-by-blow account of the events that led to this highly-important transition.

Section 4 deals with 'The Robert Gordon University' over the first ten years of its life, and again contains three chapters. The first of these gives a 'Review of RGU's first ten years', with the final two chapters of the book taking a detailed look at specific topics relating to this period - 'New buildings for a new University', and 'Moving the University into the electronic age'. The section also contains a 'Postscript', which describes the outcome of discussions with the University of Aberdeen regarding possible merger that only became available to the author after the main body of the book had been written.

The book also contains five appendices, containing supplementary material which it is hoped will be of interest to readers. Appendix A provides an annotated list of some of the key dates in the history of the University. Appendix B shows how the organisational structure of the institution has evolved over the years. Appendix C provides some key facts and figures relating to the present University. Appendix D provides notes on the sources of information that the author used when writing the different chapters of the book, and takes the place of a conventional bibliography. Appendix E provides an annotated list of the photographs and other figures that are included in the book, together with acknowledgements of their sources.

A Keyword Index is also included for the convenience of readers; this lists the main topics covered in Sections 1-4 of the book and in the Postscript.

The author would like to end this 'Introduction' by thanking all the many people who have helped him in different ways. These include the following - and the author apologises if he has missed anyone out, or has failed to give anyone proper credit for their contribution to the project:

• Professor William Stevely, who commissioned the book, helped in its planning, provided key material relating to Section 4, and checked the entire manuscript prior to publication; his advice, help and constant encouragement were greatly appreciated, as was the help received from his Acting Secretary, Mrs Janet Lawson.

• Sir Bob Reid, first Chancellor of The Robert Gordon University, for writing the 'Foreword' to the book.

• Mr. Jim Fiddes, Keeper of the Antiquarian Collection in RGU's Georgina Scott Sutherland Library at Garthdee, for providing practically all the source material used in writing Sections 1 and 2 of the book and checking these for factual accuracy; these two sections could not have been written without his help.

• Mr. Brian Lockhart, Headmaster of Robert Gordon's College and authority on the history of same, for checking the early chapters of the book for factual accuracy and providing many of the illustrations in these; the help of the College's Archive Librarian, Mrs. Penny Hartley, is also gratefully acknowledged.

• Dr. Peter Clarke, former Principal of RGIT, for providing invaluable background information, for checking Section 3 of the book for factual accuracy, and for his many helpful comments on the material.

• Dr. David Kennedy, former Principal of RGIT and RGU, for providing invaluable background information, for checking Sections 3 and 4 of the book for factual accuracy, and for his many helpful comments on the material.

• Mr. Gavin Ross, former Vice Principal of RGIT and RGU, for providing invaluable background information, for checking Sections 3 and 4 of the book for factual accuracy, and for his many helpful comments and suggestions.

• Mrs. Doreen Alexander, Secretary of RGU's Centre for the Enhancement of Learning and Teaching (CELT), for processing the manuscript and providing clerical and administrative support throughout the project; her contribution has been immense, and is greatly appreciated.

• Mr. Bill Black, AV and Digital Imaging Manager in CELT, for providing original photographs, scanning in all the illustrations in the book, and integrating the figures with the typed text.

• Mr. Martin Parker, Senior Designer in RGU's Graphics and Printing Department, for providing original photographs, designing the cover for the book, and producing the final electronic version of the document for delivery to the printer.

• Mr. Graham Ironside, former colleague at RGU, for reading the entire manuscript to check it for spelling, punctuation, grammar, style and self-consistency; a heroic task indeed!

• The author's own long-suffering wife Lindsay, for supporting and encouraging him through what turned out to be one of the biggest projects of his life - after she thought he had retired!

• All the many other past and present members of RGU staff who helped the author in so many different ways, eg, by providing information, advice, material or technical support, or by checking specific chapters for factual accuracy; these include the following: Dr. Eric Addinall; Mr. Roger Bond; Mr. David Briggs; Mrs. Pat Briggs; Mr. David Bryan, Mr. George Cheyne; Mr. Dave Cumming; Mr. Darren Davies; Mr. Hector Douglas; Mrs. Hilary Douglas; Mrs. Elaine Dunphy; Mr. Roy Glennie; Dr. Douglas Gourlay; Dr. Adrian Graves; Mr. Simon Hall; Professor John Harper; Dr. Vicky Houston; Professor David Lines; Professor Joyce Lishman; Professor Ann Lowis; Mr. Andrew McCreath; Ms. Gillian McLaren; Dr. Alastair McLeish; Professor Bill McIntosh; Mr. Sid Merrakech; Mr. Andy Mullen; Mrs. Jennie Parry; Professor Jim Penman; Mrs. Gillie Reith; Mr. Jonathan Shackleton; Miss Judith Smith; Ms. Jill Smith; Mr. Les Tarr; Mrs. Margaret Timms;

Mr. Bill Walker; Mrs. June Wells; Ms. Fiona Whyte; Mrs Anne Wilson.

The above people have helped the author to make the book as accurate and comprehensive as possible, but he would like to stress that responsibility for any errors or omissions rests solely with him.

Finally, the author would like to dedicate this history of The Robert Gordon University to his first grandchild, Claire Morag Gourlay, who was born at the same time as the idea for the book; it deals with the past, but she represents the future.

Section 1

The Origins of the Institution

(1729-1909)

Chapter 1

Robert Gordon, and the foundation of Robert Gordon's Hospital

ROBERT GORDON - HIS LIFE AND LEGACY

In beginning this history of The Robert Gordon University, it behoves the author to say something about the man who founded the institution from which it eventually developed, and whose name it still bears at the time of writing. Such a task is, however, made somewhat difficult by the almost complete lack of historically-verifiable information about Robert Gordon. No contemporary accounts of his life have survived, and, as a result, several of his early biographers chose to supplement the few hard facts that *were* available with a great deal of highly dubious material drawn from 'floating legend and tradition' (to quote Robert Anderson, a later and - in the opinion of the author - somewhat more reliable biographer). According to Anderson, these writers were 'apparently more bent on circulating "good stories" than on limiting themselves to ascertained and accurate facts', and were largely responsible for promulgating the picture of Robert Gordon as a 'notorious miser' that has survived to the present day in popular folklore.

For over 200 years, it was generally believed that Robert Gordon was born in Edinburgh in 1665 - a 'fact' that was duly presented in all his early biographies. Towards the end of the 19th century, however, examination of the register of baptisms (then the only accurate record of births) established that he was actually born in Aberdeen in 1668. He belonged to a well-known Aberdeenshire family, the Gordons of Pitlurg - a branch of the Huntly Gordons. He was the only son of Arthur Gordon, a member of the Edinburgh bar and 'an advocate of some repute', and his wife Isobel, daughter of Thomas Menzies of Balgownie. His paternal grandfather was Robert Gordon of Straloch, who is said to have been the first graduate of Marischal College. His parents moved from Edinburgh to Aberdeen shortly before he was born, and provided him with a good, liberal education. His father died in 1680, leaving the young Robert Gordon with a patrimony of 20,000 merks (equivalent to £1,100 sterling - a not inconsiderable sum at the time). In 1684, at the early age of 16, he was enrolled as a Burgess of Guild of the City of Aberdeen. In 1685, he went to Marischal College, graduating from there in 1689.

Of Robert Gordon's adult life, very little is known for certain. There is a story that he visited the Continent and 'wasted his substance in riotous living'. There is a further story that he 'was jilted by a lady, and ever afterwards bore a most unreasonable hatred to the whole gender'. These and other stories about Robert Gordon should, according to Robert Anderson, 'be received with a good deal of caution and reservation', since they are entirely uncorroborated by proper historical evidence. What *is* well established is that Robert Gordon spent most of his adult life operating as a highly successful merchant in the Baltic state of Danzig, where he not only became a very wealthy man, but periodically lent out money on the security of landed estates in Aberdeenshire. There is evidence that he handled both his business and his loans in a cautious and hard-headed way that probably laid the foundations for his subsequent reputation as a miser. Apart from this, however, virtually nothing is known about the 'Danzig period' of his life.

It is believed that Robert Gordon returned to Aberdeen in 1720 or thereabouts, although the exact date is not known. For the remainder of his life, he engaged in no further business, but, according to one of his biographers (James Bruce) 'waxed more miserly every day'. Certainly, most of the stories about his supposed miserliness relate to this period. It is, for example, alleged that he:

- lived very sparingly on cheap food, limiting his expenditure on this by helping himself to free 'samples' as he strolled round the market;
- owned gloves, but ensured that they did not wear out by carrying them in his hand rather than wearing them;
- did not light a candle when a friend called because they could 'see to speak in the dark';
- kept warm by walking up and down the room with a 'birn' of coals on his back rather than burning them in the fire.

As Robert Anderson observes, we should 'accept these stories with a very large pinch of salt', since 'they have a suspicious likeness to the common tales told of reputed misers in all times and climes'. While there seems little doubt that Robert Gordon was 'careful with his money' (a general characteristic of the citizens of Aberdeen, so it is commonly held!), reports of his miserliness are - like that of the death of Mark Twain - probably 'greatly exaggerated'.

Despite this reputation, it is generally acknowledged by his biographers that Robert Gordon was 'intelligent and well-informed, fond of reading and of rational conversation, a man of good taste'. This image of a cultured 'Enlightenment Man' is certainly corroborated by his main surviving portrait, painted posthumously by William Mossman in 1758; this is based on a bust portrait, by an unknown artist, evidently painted during his lifetime. The Mossman portrait (which is hung in the MacRobert Hall, at Schoolhill and is shown in Figure 1.1) depicts Robert Gordon standing before shelves packed with impressive volumes, with a globe of the world at his feet and his right hand resting on a front elevation of his proposed Hospital. His collection of fine coins, medals, prints and engravings, which seems to have survived with relatively few losses, further endorses this picture of a man of taste and culture. The collection is still in the possession of Robert Gordon's College.

During the latter years of his life, it appears that Robert Gordon devoted a large part of his time and energy to preparing the plans for the endowment of a Hospital for Boys similar to that which George Heriot ('Jingling Georgie') had set up in Edinburgh roughly 100 years earlier. He had decided to devote the whole of his considerable fortune to this highly-ambitious project, and, according to some biographers, denied himself 'many of the enjoyments of life to which he was so well entitled' in order to ensure that the bequest would be maximised. One of his earliest biographers, Francis Douglas, also

Figure 1.1 : William Mossman's 1758 portrait of Robert Gordon

reports that he turned down a request by one of the Lord Provosts of Aberdeen to provide
financial help to his sister's family, who had fallen upon hard times (he himself had
never married, and had no children). Needless to say this (unsubstantiated) story is
cited as further evidence of his miserliness.

Robert Gordon died in April, 1731 - allegedly 'as a result of overeating at a friend's
house'! His body lay in state in Marischal College, and he was honoured with a public
funeral - what Francis Douglas called 'a princely burial'. Douglas added sardonically
that 'the expense was great, but it was out of time for Mr. Gordon to object to it.' He was
buried in Drum's Aisle in St Nicholas Church, Aberdeen, although the precise site of his
grave is not known. On the west wall of the Aisle there is a plain white marble tablet

carrying the following inscription:

> Within this Aisle
> are interred the remains of
> ROBERT GORDON
> Merchant,
> who founded in this City and
> liberally endowed
> THE HOSPITAL
> piously designed for him
> for
> the maintenance and education
> of youth.

The tablet is surmounted by the Hospital coat of arms - a pelican plucking flesh from its own breast to feed its young, with its motto: *'Imperat Hoc Natura Potens'*. (The motto is taken from the 'Satires of Horace', 2.1.51, and, literally translated, means: *'this is the bidding of nature, whose will is law'*.) The staff and pupils of Robert Gordon's College still make an annual pilgrimage to St. Nicholas Church on 'Founder's Day' to pay tribute to Robert Gordon. He has certainly not been forgotten by them, and, like the above-mentioned Horace, can indeed be said to have 'created a monument more lasting than bronze'. It is for this that he deserves to be remembered by us.

THE ESTABLISHMENT OF ROBERT GORDON'S HOSPITAL

Robert Gordon's Hospital was formally constituted by a Deed of Mortification and Disposition executed by Robert Gordon on 13th December, 1729, and in an Appendix (or Codicil) thereto, dated 19th September, 1730. As stated earlier, it seems highly likely that he got the idea for his Hospital from his knowledge of the great success of George Heriot's Hospital in Edinburgh, which had been fully operational since 1659. His own Deed of Mortification certainly bore a close resemblance to that which had been produced by George Heriot. Through this, the sum of £10,000 sterling was 'specifically mortified and disponed in trust to the Provost, Baillies and Town Council of the Burgh of Aberdeen, and to the town's four ministers' (then the ministers of East and West St. Nicholas, Greyfriars and St. Clements). In reality, however, *all* his property and effects were made over to these trustees, who were nominated his sole executors. The money derived therefrom was to be used for 'the erection and maintenance of an Hospital, to be called, in all succeeding generations, Robert Gordon's Hospital, to be governed under Statutes and Rules embodied in the Deed of Mortification, the trustees named to be the Governors of the Hospital'.

The purpose of the Hospital was the 'Maintenance, Aliment, Entertainment and

Education of young Boys whose parents are poor and indigent, and not able to maintain them at Schools, and to put them to Trades and Employments'. The Deed of Mortification specified that the boys to be so favoured were to be:

1. Indigent sons or grandsons of decayed (*sic*) Burgesses of Guild, preference being given to

   (a)   Relations of the founder of the name of Gordon;

   (b)   Relations of the name of Menzies (the name of the founder's mother);

   (c)   Any other boys of the name of Gordon;

   (d)   Any other boys of the name of Menzies;

   (e)   Any other relations of the founder of whatever name, all, however, to possess the major qualification of being sons or grandsons of Burgesses of Guild;

2. Failing these, indigent sons or grandsons of decayed Burgesses of Trade, with the same preferences;

3. Failing these, indigent sons or grandsons of residenters in the burgh, with the same preferences.

All such boys were to be aged between eight and eleven, and were to be allowed to remain in the Hospital until they were fourteen, fifteen or, at the most, sixteen. Thereafter, they were to be 'put to Merchandizing, or lawful Trades and Employments, according as their Genius and Inclination leads them'. They were to be so apprenticed for five years, during which they would receive 'an apprentice fee of £10 sterling if bound to a merchant and £5 sterling if bound to a tradesman'. At the end of their apprenticeship, they were to receive from the Hospital '200 or 100 pounds Scots according as they had been bound to a merchant or a tradesman'. (At the time, the pound Scots was worth less than one twelfth of the pound sterling.)

The Deed also laid down the curriculum that was to be followed, stipulating that the boys were to be taught 'to read English and the Latin Tongue', as well as 'Writing, Arithmetic in all its parts, Book-keeping, and the common parts of Vocal Musick'. It specified that the Governors should appoint 'one or two Schoolmasters as the number of boys in the Hospital may require', who should be capable of teaching all these various subjects. It recognised, however, that obtaining such all-round teachers might prove difficult, and that it might be necessary to employ subject specialists. All teachers would be required to reside within the Hospital, as would the other House officials - a Steward and a Cook (both to be unmarried men or widowers) plus two or more men-servants (to whom this condition of celibacy did not apply).

This rigorous exclusion of women from the Hospital has led some of Robert Gordon's biographers - notably James Bruce - to reach the conclusion that he must have been an inveterate misogynist - possibly as a result of the alleged 'jilting' alluded to earlier. Robert Anderson (who, as we have seen, appears to be one of Robert Gordon's more credible biographers) strongly refutes this allegation, however. Not only does he dismiss the 'jilting' story as 'purely apocryphal', but he shows that the exclusion of women from institutions of this type was standard practice at the time. As we have seen, the Deed of Mortification of Robert Gordon's Hospital was closely based on that of George

Heriot's Hospital in Edinburgh - an institution that was itself an imitation of Christ's Hospital in London, which had been founded even earlier. Both operated under the same 'monastic' conditions as were subsequently decreed for Robert Gordon's Hospital.

As we have seen, Robert Gordon began planning the creation of his Hospital long before his death in 1731. He had identified a suitable site - part of the ground 'between Schoolhill and the Loch' that had once been occupied by a convent of the Black Friars or Dominicans - and had made formal application to the Town Council for the right to build there. A feu was duly granted to him on the 21st September, 1730, for an annual payment of £10. Once his estate had been realised and the resulting money (£10,300 in total) passed on to his trustees, work on the design of the building was started almost immediately. Although some early chroniclers stated that the plans were drawn up by James Gibbs, a well-known Aberdeen-born architect who had designed the West Church of St Nicholas, it is now generally agreed that they were actually produced by William Adam of Edinburgh - father of John and Robert Adam, the famous London architects. The Deed of Mortification stipulated that the total cost of erecting the building was not to exceed £2000.

Figure 1.2 : The original Robert Gordon's Hospital building (the 'Auld Hoose')

Work on the exterior of the 'Auld Hoose' (as the original Robert Gordon's Hospital building is affectionately known to Gordonians all over the world) was completed by the end of 1732, but work on the interior continued for several years thereafter. One of the stipulations in the Deed of Mortification was that the trust fund should be restored to the original £10,000 before the financing of the scholars could commence. This took some time, and, as a result, the Hospital was still unoccupied when the Duke of Cumberland entered Aberdeen in 1746, on his way north to confront the Jacobite army at

Culloden. Cumberland billeted his troops in the Auld Hoose, and proceeded to build extensive fortifications in the surrounding grounds - producing what became known as 'Fort Cumberland'. The troops did considerable damage to the new building, and it was not until 1750 that it was in a fit state for the first boys to be enrolled. Figure 1.2 shows how the building looked at the time.

The history of the Hospital until 1881

Robert Gordon's Hospital was officially opened on 10th July, 1750, with an initial cohort of 14 boys being admitted. The first Headmaster - or 'Master' as he was originally titled - was the Rev. George Abercrombie, minister at Footdee. It is recorded that he received a special dispensation from the Governors from attending church with the boys in order to fulfil his preaching obligations at Footdee. Mr. James Mitchell, a minister at Old Aberdeen, was appointed the first Schoolmaster. A steward, a cook and one servant formed the initial domestic staff of the establishment, but two other servants were added within a month due to the high workload on the latter.

Twelve more boys were admitted in 1751, and a second Schoolmaster - Mr. Robert Abercrombie, son of the minister of Leslie - was appointed to handle the additional teaching that this entailed. A further ten boys were admitted in 1752, bringing the total enrolment to 36. The first 'dismissal' of boys took place in November, 1754, when eight left the Hospital. Two were apprenticed to merchants, two to square wrights, one to a wright or cooper, one to a saddler, one to a watchmaker and one to a silversmith. This pattern continued over the next few decades, with the total number of boys enrolled in the Hospital at any one time eventually rising to over 90.

In 1772, the Governors applied for a Charter of Incorporation. The petition for the Charter pointed out that the Governors had set up and operated the Hospital purely in their capacity as trustees of Robert Gordon's estate. The funds available to them had greatly increased over the years, however, and doubts had also arisen over their legal right, as trustees of a private endowment, to acquire lands and raise and defend actions. In order to clarify and safeguard their position, they requested the granting of a Royal Charter incorporating them and their successors in office under the name of 'The President and Governors of Robert Gordon's Hospital in Aberdeen', with 'all the powers usually given to bodies corporate of a like nature'. Such a Charter was duly granted, constituting the Governors and their successors in office as 'a Corporation with perpetual succession'. By a subsequent Royal Charter, granted in 1792, the original Charter was confirmed, and the powers of the President and Governors with respect to holding lands extended. These were highly significant developments in the history of the Hospital and its successors, laying the foundations for many of the changes that took place over the next 200 years.

Another significant development during the latter part of the 18th century was the institution of what became known as the 'College Boy' system. This resulted from an approach by one of the Governors to Professors Hamilton and Copeland of Marischal

College, one of the two universities in Aberdeen at the time (the other was King's College, which amalgamated with Marischal College to form the University of Aberdeen in 1860). It resulted in an arrangement whereby a limited number of Hospital boys could attend the College's classes in Mathematics and Natural Philosophy (Physics), without paying fees, in return for the Governors subscribing to a fund for the purchase of astronomical and other equipment for the College. The Governors made a one-off payment of £50 for this purpose, thereby securing 'a title for all time coming to recommend yearly four of the boys who are educating or have been educated in the Hospital to be received into the Mathematical or Natural Philosophy class or both'. Thus began the tradition whereby Robert Gordon's Hospital (and later Robert Gordon's College) sent many of its most able pupils on to Marischal College and Aberdeen University to study these particular subjects. Readers may be interested to know that this tradition was still very much alive during the 1950's, when the author attended Robert Gordon's College as a 'foundationer'; as top physics pupil in the school, he was strongly encouraged to read Natural Philosophy at Aberdeen University, and did indeed do so.

During the early decades of the 19th Century, the Hospital continued to expand and grow in reputation. A major boost to this expansion took place in 1821, when the Trustees of Mr. Alexander Simpson of Collyhill intimated to the Governors that Mr. Simpson had 'conveyed the lands of Crichie, Easter Barrack, and others in Old Deer and New Deer in trust to the four ministers of Aberdeen and the Principal and Professors of Marischal College, for the board and education of an additional number of boys in Gordon's Hospital'. As a result, an agreement was reached between the Hospital Governors and the Collyhill Trustees that 'an additional building be erected at the Hospital and twenty six boys gradually admitted under the Collyhill Trust'. Plans for this 'new building', which eventually took the form of a series of extensions to the original Hospital, were drawn up during the late 1820's, with the extension work being carried out over the period 1830-33. A number of alternative schemes had been considered by the Governors, the one eventually put into practice being that produced by the local architect John Smith. The most notable features were the addition of two major wings to the 'Auld Hoose', executed in classical style, and the replacement of the original rounded roof pediments of the latter with the more classical ones that we see today (compare Figure 1.2, which shows the original Hospital building, with Figure 1.3, which depicts the Hospital after the 1830-33 expansion).

Before leaving the subject of the Collyhill bequest and the very significant expansion of the Hospital that it brought about, one further point requires to be made. Under his Deed of Mortification, Robert Gordon specified that anyone who subsequently mortified a sum of money to his Hospital would have their name 'honourably recorded in the Books, and also put up in gilded Letters upon a Wall within the Hospital'. Furthermore, anyone who mortified a sum of over £2000 sterling to the Hospital would be 'assumed and conjoined, in all time thereafter, with Me, the said Robert Gordon, in the Name and Title of the said Hospital, and be reckoned a Founder of the same with Me'. Since the value of the Collyhill Bequest was considerably in excess of this figure,

Figure 1.3 : Robert Gordon's Hospital, as enlarged in 1830-33

Mr. Alexander Simpson should, under the terms of the Deed of Mortification, have been regarded as a co-founder of the Hospital, and should have had his name added to the title of same. For reasons known only to the Governors of the Hospital, this never happened - possibly because the Collyhill Trust remained legally separate from Robert Gordon's own endowment until 1881, when the two were merged during the transformation of Robert Gordon's Hospital into Robert Gordon's College. Had it done so, the author might well now be writing the history of The Robert Gordon/Alexander Simpson University!

During the final 50 years of its existence, a number of further significant developments took place within the Hospital. These included a radical revision of the teaching system in 1834, with masters being largely limited to the teaching of a single subject rather than working across the curriculum, as had hitherto been the case. A half-yearly distribution of prizes was initiated in the same year. The 'monastic' conditions of service for teachers were also progressively relaxed during the mid-1800's, with reforms in Robert Gordon's Hospital generally following those being made in George Heriot's Hospital - which continued to have a considerable influence on the way in which the former operated. (It is interesting to note that Robert Gordon's specification of an all-male staff had been abandoned virtually as soon as the Hospital opened, and that more and more female employees were taken on as it expanded, including, in due course, a Matron. In his excellent and often amusing account of the history of Robert Gordon's Hospital, Robert Anderson records that one of the holders of this post engaged in 'a deep and long-seated feud' with the Headmaster and teachers, a feud that so disrupted the work of the Hospital that the Governors finally lost patience, and, in 1841, sacked both the Matron and the Headmaster!)

The Hospital also continued to expand during this period, with the number of boys in residence rising to 180 by 1872 - partly as a result of an increase in the number funded by the Collyhill Trust from 26 to 40. Figure 1.4 shows the out-going class of 1874 with their Headmaster, Dr. Alexander Ogilvie (of whom we will hear much more in Chapter 2).

Figure 1.4 : The outgoing Hospital class of 1874 with their Headmaster, Dr. Alexander Ogilvie.

As we will see in the next chapter, the progressive changes that took place during the 19th century eventually brought about the complete transformation of Robert Gordon's residential Hospital into the combined day and evening school that became known as Robert Gordon's College. Before ending this brief history of the Hospital, however, it would be appropriate to attempt to appraise its success as a charitable and educational institution during its 131 years of active operation between 1750 and 1881, when the above transformation was implemented. First, let us look at the total number of pupils involved - roughly 2500 over the period in question. All of these (or at least the ones who did not leave prematurely for various reasons) were maintained and educated, at the Hospital's expense, for between four and six years, and were then given a considerable amount of assistance in learning a useful trade or moving on to higher education. Thus, on these grounds alone, it can fairly be claimed that the Hospital made a very significant contribution to social and economic development in Aberdeen, giving a large number of boys from the poorer sections of society an excellent start in life. Indeed, this was Robert Gordon's main aim in founding the Hospital, the relief of poverty and the maintenance of the boys being much more important to him than the provision of education. But what can we say about the quality of that education? Here, we simply quote, in full, the verdict given by Robert Anderson, who attended the Hospital from 1857-1862 and wrote the following in 1894:

'I am not disposed to rate the general education offered very high; yet I think a diligent youth, of fair parts, was bound to leave the Hospital at the end of his five years with a tolerably good education - at least for those days. The notion, however, that Gordon's Hospital was a kind of secondary school must - except, perhaps for a little higher Arithmetic, a little Mathematics, a little Natural Philosophy, a little Latin, (not extended much beyond Ruddiman's Rudiments, if at all), and a little - a very little - French - this notion, I am afraid, cannot be seriously entertained. But if someone with the requisite knowledge would institute a fair and unbiased comparison between the education imparted in Gordon's Hospital and in the ordinary public schools in Aberdeen in the "Dark Ages" prior to 1872, I rather think that Gordon's Hospital would not suffer in the comparison'.

Chapter 2 : The transformation into Robert Gordon's College

THE BACKGROUND TO THE TRANSFORMATION

With the benefit of historical hindsight, it is now clear that the decision of the Governors of Robert Gordon's Hospital in 1881 to transform the institution into a combined day and evening school was the logical culmination of a chain of events that stretched back for over 300 years. It had its origins in the development of the modern scientific world picture by men like Bacon, Galileo and Newton, and the increasing realisation that natural phenomena could be explained in terms of a few basic laws. This, in turn, eventually led to the Industrial Revolution, which began in Britain in the middle of the 18th century, and, over the next 100 years, brought about the greatest social changes since the invention of agriculture at the end of the last Ice Age. As the advantages that the practical application of science could bestow became more and more apparent, it was gradually realised that Britain's educational system would have to change, with the content of that education being expanded to include science and technology, and its benefits being extended to a larger proportion of the population. This led inexorably to the progressive build up of technical education during the 19th century, and also to the great educational reforms that took place during the 1870's. Let us now take a detailed look at each of these last two developments, and show how they led to the abovementioned transformation of Robert Gordon's Hospital into Robert Gordon's College.

The build up of technical education

With the spread of the Industrial Revolution throughout Britain during the latter part of the 18th century and the early decades of the 19th century, the need for a more technically-trained population became progressively more apparent. Prior to the Industrial Revolution, Britain's educational system had been largely geared towards the provision of a broad, liberal education for the upper and middle classes, together with the training of professionals such as clergymen, lawyers, doctors and academics, of whom strictly limited numbers were required. Education of the masses beyond a very basic level was generally considered to be neither necessary nor desirable, and such education as *was* provided was generally run by the Church. Now, however, there was a steadily-increasing demand for people who were familiar both with the new technologies that were so transforming society and with the principles on which they were based. As a result, Britain's schools and universities had to find ways in which to include the teaching of science and technology - not as a replacement for the classics, liberal arts and professional training, but as equal partners to these. An increasing desire for information on such matters also developed among the more thoughtful members of the working classes, eventually giving birth to the Adult Education movement, which aimed at providing instruction in these areas, as well in more traditional subjects such as literature.

One of the early pioneers of the Adult Education movement was Dr. George Birkbeck. After studying and practising medicine in both Edinburgh and London, he was, at the early age of 23, appointed Professor of Natural Philosophy at Glasgow University. There, in 1800, he gave a course of lectures on science to which working men were admitted on payment of a small fee. After a long and successful period of growth, his University Department became, in 1823, the Glasgow Mechanics' Institute. Professor Birkbeck is remembered not only as the person who first brought science within the reach of the working man, but also for playing a major part in the foundation of the London institution that later became known as Birkbeck College. From 1823 onwards, Mechanics' Institutes were formed in many other industrial centres throughout Britain. During this period, books and periodicals also became increasingly available at reasonable prices, and were also made widely available through the public libraries that started to be set up later in the 19th century. These libraries eventually placed such literature within the reach of the majority of the working population.

In Aberdeen, which entered a period of rapid industrial growth during the early years of the 19th century, the increasing numbers of engineers, mechanics and other workmen felt the same need for scientific and technical knowledge as their colleagues in other parts of Britain. Key events in the provision of technical education for such people were the formation in 1818 of Aberdeen Academy (which provided classes in art, literary subjects and technical subjects), and the foundation in 1824 of a Mechanics' Institute similar to that which had been formed in Glasgow the previous year. The Aberdeen Mechanics' Institution began by organising public lectures on philosophical, technical and scientific subjects. For the first few years, such lectures proved highly popular, with as many as 500 tickets being sold in some cases, and many free places being allocated to apprentices. By 1828, however, interest had waned, and the programme was phased out, although the Institution's library continued to function. By the early 1830's, the Institution was largely moribund, but, in 1835, interest revived under the dynamic Secretaryship of Alexander Bain. A building fund of £270 was accumulated, but no suitable site was found for a permanent home. In 1844, by strenuous efforts on the part of the Directors, the building fund was increased to £1500, and a site was found in Market Street, adjoining Adelphi Lane. The new building, which is shown in Figure 2.1, was opened in 1848 - in time for the 1848-49 winter programme. It is now occupied by the Metro Hotel and Restaurant.

After the opening of the new building, the work of the Institution was able to expand considerably. Alongside the original classes in Natural Philosophy, Mathematics, Chemistry and Art, it also began to offer courses in English, French, Arithmetic, Book-keeping and Writing. As befitted a sea-faring community, classes in Navigation were subsequently introduced, and proved extremely popular. Another difficulty soon presented itself, however. Although the classes had been organised on the most economical lines, they had never paid their way. The Directors came to the conclusion that the extensive programmes of day and evening classes that they wished to provide for the benefit of the community would only be viable with assistance from national funds. Following the success of the Great Exhibition of 1851, the Board of Trade became interested in the establishment of Schools of Science throughout Britain. Sensing that the time was opportune, the Directors informed the Department of Education that they wished to establish a 'School of Science and Art' specifically geared to meeting the requirements of the citizens of Aberdeen and its surrounding neighbourhood. Captain Owen, one of the Department's representatives, visited Aberdeen in order to look into the matter, and subsequently submitted to the Lords of the Privy Council a 'Report on the Formation of a School of Science and Art for the Operative Classes of Aberdeen'. The scheme proposed in the Report was approved on a trial basis for the year ending in March, 1855, in order to ascertain the willingness of the industrial classes to avail themselves of the educational opportunities on offer. It is to the credit of Aberdeen that the project proved extremely successful - so successful, in fact, that similar Schools of Science and Art started to be established throughout the country.

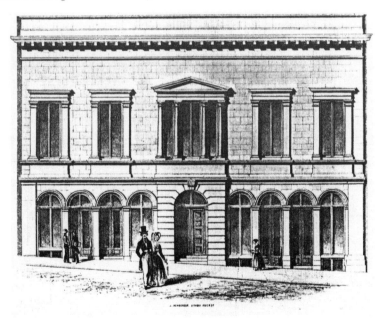

Figure 2.1 : The Aberdeen Mechanics' Institution in Market Street

The following year, the Directors submitted a similar scheme for the establishment of an English, Trade and Navigation School, and the national authorities appear 'to have had such faith in the sagacity of the Aberdonians' that the project was almost immediately approved and put into force. The aim of the new School was to provide practical training 'in technical and mechanical draughtsmanship, for shipbuilding, engineering and other such branches of industry as were to be found in progress in the city'. The new Technical School was opened in 1857, and was also well supported by the young people of the town. In 1858, however, the local shipowners decided that they no longer wished to have the training of their staff take place under the aegis of the Mechanics' Institution. They therefore withdrew the School of Navigation from the Technical School, and put it under the control of the local Marine Board. Thus, from 1858 onwards, Aberdeen had no fewer than three technical education establishments providing courses of various types for the benefit of its citizens - the School of Science and Art, the Technical School, and the School of Navigation. These laid the foundations for the even more ambitious developments that were to take place towards the end of the 19th century, as we will see later.

The Educational Reform Acts of the 1870's

During the second half of the 19th century, a number of Acts of Parliament had a considerable impact on the educational systems on both sides of the border. The first was the (Second) Reform Act of 1867, through which the franchise was extended to the working classes, thus enabling them to bring direct pressure to bear on Parliament and its members. It was also becoming increasingly recognised that education was a matter of strategic national importance, and was no longer something that could be left to the churches and other voluntary organisations. This culminated in the Education Act of 1870, which enabled the establishment of Elementary Schools that would, for the first time, provide universal elementary education throughout the country. Since Scotland had long gone its own way in educational matters, and wished to continue to do so, a separate Education (Scotland) Act was successfully piloted through the House of Commons by Lord Advocate Young in 1872. This Act was the great educational watershed in 19th century Scotland. Among other things, it transferred the work of administering education from the churches to secular authorities, in the form of School Boards elected by the people in all parishes and burghs. Thus, for the very first time, the ordinary people of Scotland had some control over the type of education their children received. As a result, the quality of this education immediately started to improve.

The Education (Scotland) Act of 1872 also had an immediate impact on post-school education. It gave the School Boards powers to establish and maintain evening classes - both general and vocational - for young people over the age of compulsory school attendance (13), and also for the adult population in so far as they chose to avail themselves of it. The 1870 and 1872 Education Acts also played a significant part in bringing about a radical reform of the 'Hospital' system that had developed over the previous centuries. This had been under attack for some time, partly because it was free, and thus undermined the fee-paying educational system, and partly because of the 'monastic' nature of such institutions, which was becoming increasingly regarded as un-natural and socially undesirable. These criticisms eventually led to the Endowed Institutions (Scotland) Act of 1878, which had wide-ranging ramifications for all institutions of this type. In Edinburgh, for example, it brought the Watt Institute (then one of the most successful Mechanics' Institutes in the country) under the control of the Governors of George Heriot's

Trust as the Heriot-Watt College (now the Heriot-Watt University). Similar changes took place in Glasgow, where a number of hitherto- independent educational institutions such as Anderson's College and the College of Science and Arts were combined with the Young Chair of Technical Chemistry to form the Glasgow and West of Scotland Technical College (now Strathclyde University). Under the same scheme, Alan Glen's Institution came under the control of the Governors of a new combined college as Alan Glen's School. And in Aberdeen, the 1878 Act led directly to the transformation of Robert Gordon's Hospital into Robert Gordon's College, as we will now show.

THE ESTABLISHMENT OF ROBERT GORDON'S COLLEGE

Even prior to the Endowed Institutions (Scotland) Act of 1878, the Governors of Robert Gordon's Hospital were becoming increasingly aware of the need to change the nature of the Hospital in a fairly radical way. As far back as 1856 Mr. (later Baillie) Oswald proposed that the Governors should set up a Committee to consider 'whether, and how far, it would be beneficial to relax the system which presently obtains in this institution known as the "Hospital system", and to adopt in its place the Free Day School system of education, or a modification thereof'. His motion was in fact carried by nine votes to five, and the proposed inquiry into the feasibility of the changes was subsequently carried out. Mr. Oswald did not take the matter further, however, probably being deterred (according to Robert Anderson, the 'official historian' of the Hospital) 'by that practically insuperable obstacle, the difficulty of securing a three-fourths majority'.

The subject of reform of the Hospital was revived in 1868, when Lord Provost Nicol submitted to the attention of the Governors 'Reports on the Hospitals under the administration of the Merchant Company, Edinburgh, and General Remarks on Hospital Training', by Simon S. Laurie. In 1869, the Governors, at a special meeting, 'unanimously approved of the Educational Endowments Bill for Scotland that was then before Parliament', which made provision for changes of the type envisaged. Matters were taken even further in 1871, when Lord Provost Leslie moved -

'That it is expedient that provision should be made for the better government and administration of the Hospital and the application of the revenues thereof, whereby the usefulness and efficiency of the Hospital may be increased and the benefits thereof extended; and that an application shall be made to the Secretary of State for a Provisional Order'.

This motion was carried by fifteen votes to three, but the proposal was subsequently dropped because the above-mentioned Act never actually passed into law in its original form. (Apparently, the Liberal Government of the day developed 'cold feet' after the changes to George Watson's Hospital in 1870, and decided not to pursue any further the opening up of Hospitals at that time.)

During the next few years, however, the Governors did make a number of significant changes to the way in which the Hospital operated under the existing Charter, these being largely instigated by Peter Esslemont, one of the leading advocates of the need to reform the institution. They included the enlargement of the area of selection of boys for admission to 'all classes of the community within the municipal boundary of Aberdeen' (July, 1872), and the increase of the number of boys in the House to 180, as already mentioned in Chapter 1 (August, 1872). Matters were then put on hold for a few years while a second Government Endowed Schools Commission deliberated on how the reform of charitable institutions such as Robert Gordon's Hospital should proceed. This reported in 1875, making a number of recommendations that greatly influenced the Governors in their subsequent reflections. They were also greatly influenced by a Schools Inspectorate report on the examination of the Hospital which advocated 'the bringing of the Hospital into contact with the University on its classical as well as its mathematical side'.

As a result of these various developments, a number of alternative schemes for the reorganisation of the Hospital were formulated by different members of the Governors later in the same year (1875). That prepared by the now Baillie Esslemont proposed: to convert the Hospital into a day school for elementary and secondary education; to reduce the number of 'foundationers' (boys financed by the Robert Gordon and Collyhill Trusts) to 100, or further if thought desirable; to board out the foundationers with their parents, near relations or others; to receive scholars into the day school, free of charge or on payment of moderate fees; to establish evening classes; and to establish bursaries. No further progress was made during the next three years, but, in 1878, the passing of the final version of the Endowed Institutions (Scotland) Act provided the Governors with the opportunity to carry out the radical review of the Hospital that they had in mind. Accordingly, in August, 1879, they adopted the following motion:

'1st. That, in consideration of the changes which have taken place since Robert Gordon's Hospital was instituted, and in respect to the position which primary education now occupies by legislative enactment, it is expedient that advantage be taken of the Endowed Institutions (Scotland) Act, 1878, and that an application be made for a Provisional Order under the same.

2nd. That, with this view, a remit be made to the Educational Committee to take into consideration the whole matter, and to formulate a scheme stating the provisions for the better government and administration of the Hospital which it is desirable to have sanctioned, to be laid before a future meeting of the Governors with a view to said application being made to the Secretary of State; that the said Committee be also authorised to communicate with the Collyhill Trustees on the subject'.

Such a Committee was duly constituted, and, in addition to talking to the Collyhill Trustees, entered into serious discussions with the Directors of the Mechanics' Institution. The latter were extremely interested in the changes that were being contemplated by the Governors, particularly with their proposal to become involved in adult education by providing evening classes. The Directors had felt strongly for some time that there should be in the city 'an endowed institution comprising schools for science and art training, with both day and evening classes, a museum and picture gallery to illustrate the principles taught in the schools, and a free library, with both reading and reference departments'. To cut a long story short, a detailed proposal for the reform of Robert Gordon's Hospital was eventually drawn up much on the lines of the scheme that had been recommended by Baillie Esslemont in 1875, a scheme that also addressed most of the aspirations of the Directors of the Mechanics' Institution. It was approved by the Secretary of State, Sir William Harcourt on 10th June, 1881, as a Provisional Order under the Endowed Institutions (Scotland) Act of 1878.

Under the terms of the above Provisional Order, the Governors were empowered 'to convert the then existing foundation known as Robert Gordon's Hospital in Aberdeen wholly or partly into a College or Day School to be known as Robert Gordon's College in Aberdeen', in which the chief subjects of instruction were to be English language and literature, history and geography, classics, modern languages, mathematics and the elements of physical science. They were also empowered 'to institute day and evening classes for boys, girls and adult persons for instruction in primary, secondary, mechanical, physical or other subjects as the existing Governors may think proper and under such rules and regulations as they may from time to time make and establish provided no boys or girls under 13 years of age shall be admitted to any of the day classes so to be established'. The Governors were further given powers 'to combine with the Managers, Trustees or Directors of any Mechanics' Institute or Scientific or Technical College or School or other Educational Institution or Institutions in Aberdeen or elsewhere' with a view to the transfer of their classes to the new College. The Order also made provision for the Collyhill Trust that had been established by Alexander Simpson in 1816 (see Chapter 1) to be 'merged into that of Robert Gordon'.

The final meeting of the Governors of Robert Gordon's Hospital was held on 30th July, 1881, two days before the Provisional Order came into force on 1st August. In order to reflect its wider remit, the new Governing Body was constituted as follows:

- The Lord Provost of Aberdeen, President (ie, Chairman) *ex officio*.
- The Dean of Guild, Principal of Aberdeen University and Chairman of Aberdeen School Board (all *ex officiis*).
- Nine members of Aberdeen Town Council, appointed by same.
- Two persons 'appointed by the Principal and Professors of the University'.
- Two persons 'appointed by the ministers of the six city charges'.

The new Governors met for the first time on 15th August, 1881, thus ushering in a new era for the institution that Robert Gordon had founded 152 years earlier. In view of the key role that he had played in bringing about the transformation of the Hospital, it was fitting that Peter Esslemont (by now Lord Provost of Aberdeen) chaired both the final meeting of the old Governing Body and the inaugural meeting of the new Governors. He must have derived great personal satisfaction from the proceedings. Figure 2.2 shows the teaching staff at around the time of the transformation. Dr. Ogilvie, the Headmaster, can be seen in the centre - complete with splendid 'lum hat'!

The Governors also adopted a new Coat of Arms at the time of the transformation, replacing the pelican that had represented the Hospital with a shield incorporating the arms of the Gordon Family and the City of Aberdeen. They also adopted a new motto : *'Omni Nunc Arte Magistra'*. This was taken from Virgil's Aeneid (VII; 441), and, literally translated, means : *'now (there is need of) all masterly arts'*. This is still the motto of Robert Gordon's College.

Figure 2.2 : The teaching staff at around the time of the transformation from Robert Gordon's Hospital to Robert Gordon's College.

HOW THE WORK OF THE COLLEGE SUBSEQUENTLY DEVELOPED

The new Robert Gordon's College was extremely fortunate in that the Headmaster at the time of the transformation was Dr. Alexander Ogilvie. He was a man of considerable vision and drive, and, before being appointed to 'Gordon's' in 1872, had been Headmaster at Monymusk, where he had introduced elementary science into the curriculum. This was something of an innovation at the time, and, when he came to the Hospital, he continued to encourage the teaching of the sciences. In 1876, he put forward a wide-ranging scheme to improve the quality of the education provided by the Hospital. As part of this scheme, he proposed that 'with a view to stimulating all and of providing for those who have shown capacity for more advanced education, arrangements shall be made for maintaining classes for a further period for technical and classical education, and that admission to these shall be by examination'. When the Hospital was reorganised under the 1881 Provisional Order, Dr. Ogilvie was given responsibility for designing and implementing the new curriculum, and for 'supervising the many intricate details of this far-reaching change'. In addition to being responsible for the work of the Secondary School, he was appointed Superintendent of Evening Classes, so that he was also responsible for the adult education work of the new College. Figure 2.3 shows the portrait that was painted of him shortly before he retired; it can still be seen in the MacRobert Hall.

It is clear that Dr. Ogilvie fulfilled his mandate in respect of the reorganisation of the Secondary School in an exemplary manner. At a graduate dinner in Edinburgh, he spelled out his aims, which were 'to give practical demonstration of the truth of the contention and belief that advanced Greek and Latin classes, Science and Technology, together with the various subjects of a good general and commercial education, could all be effectually taught in one and the same institution' - a revolutionary doctrine for the 19th century. In 1882, he persuaded the College Education Committee that it was necessary to appoint a Science Master immediately, in order to enable the teacher to make appropriate preparations for the coming session. His son Francis (who later became Sir Francis Ogilvie) was appointed to the post. He was a young man with very high qualifications, having obtained an M.A. at Aberdeen University and a B.Sc. at Edinburgh University. At the time of his appointment, he was assistant to Professor Charles Niven at Marischal College, where he was delivering a highly-popular programme of science classes. He was also assisting in the work of the Mechanics' Institution. Francis Ogilvie remained on the staff at 'Gordon's' until 1886, by which time science teaching had become well established. He then moved to Edinburgh to become Principal of Heriot-Watt College. Later, he held a number of appointments of national importance, including that of Principal Assistant Secretary (Technology and Higher Education, Science and Art) at the Board of Education.

Figure 2.3 : Dr Alexander Ogilvie - First Headmaster and Superintendent of Evening Classes at Robert Gordon's College

According to James Mackenzie, who wrote the 'Bicentenary Record' of the institution in 1929 -

'The success of Robert Gordon's College as an open secondary school was immediate and complete. In August, 1882, 360 boys attended; a year later, 507. By August, 1884, the limit of the then available accommodation - 600 - was reached, and we read that "many were refused admission'.

The new school had quickly gained the confidence of both town and country. Indeed, in 1884, Mr. Mundella, then the Government Minister responsible for education, referred to 'Gordon's' as a 'model of a secondary school'. It had certainly come far from the days of the 'Hospital' described in Chapter 1, and was to go even further, rapidly gaining a considerable reputation at both local and national level. This was manifested in the increasing success of its pupils in the Aberdeen University Bursary Competition, in gaining 'exhibitions' at Oxford and Cambridge, and in making their mark in the outside world. Its reputation continued to grow throughout the 20th century, when it became firmly established as one of the finest secondary schools in the country. It is still so regarded today, although the School is now co-educational - a development that probably caused the good Robert Gordon to turn in his grave. It would be interesting to see whether any notable seismic events originating in the vicinity of Drum's Aisle were recorded at the time!

Figure 2.4 shows how the front of Robert Gordon's College looked in 1910; it had not changed much since the major extensions of 1830-33 had been completed, and, indeed, still looks very much the same today. The interior has been extensively modernised, however, and the School has also been greatly extended by the addition of major new blocks constructed during the 1950's and 1990's. These are located behind the west wing shown on the left of the photograph - along Blackfriars Street.

Dr Ogilvie also fulfilled his remit to introduce a programme of evening classes in the new College, although adult day classes were not established for some time. The first evening classes started in 1882, initially on a small scale, but were soon being expanded into a wide-ranging and ambitious programme of 'scientific, technical and commercial courses for clerks, apprentices and others'. These classes were organised after full consultation with the Directors of the Mechanics' Institution, and, in 1884, the entire educational programme of the Institution was transferred to Gordon's College - apart from the work of the very active Art School (see Chapter 3). The classes were organised in three groups.

1. **Science** : mathematics; geometry; applied mechanics; magnetism and electricity; steam engines; machine construction and drawing; inorganic chemistry; botany; hygiene; human physiology; building construction.

2. **Technology** : plumbing; electrical engineering; carpentry; telegraphy; telephony.

3. **General and Commercial** : arithmetic and mensuration; book-keeping and commercial correspondence; English writing and correspondence; English language and composition; Latin; French; German; phonography; church music; songs and miscellaneous music.

Figure 2.4 : How Robert Gordon's College looked in 1910

Wherever possible, classes were taught by members of the College staff, but, where necessary, specialist teachers from outwith the College were brought in. By 1886, the total number of students enrolled in the programme had risen to 1,254, taught by no fewer than 37 teachers.

One of the most significant events during this period was the offer by Mr. John Gray, head of a prominent local engineering firm, to finance the construction of a new 'School of Science and Art' provided that the Governors made a suitable site for the building available. The offer was gratefully accepted, and the Governors provided an ideal site within the grounds of the College, facing directly on to Schoolhill. The new building, which was named Gray's School of Art, was opened in 1885. A detailed description of the foundation of the School is given in the next Chapter, which is entirely devoted to this extremely important development in the history of The Robert Gordon University.

Another highly-important development during the latter part of the 19th century was the establishment of a School of Pharmacy as part of Robert Gordon's College. This had its origins in a meeting of Aberdeen's chemists and druggists that took place in 1839, to discuss a request from the younger members of the profession that facilities should be provided to enable them 'to improve their minds'. Those present eventually resolved to establish a library 'of useful books on scientific subjects' in order to give their assistants and apprentices 'an opportunity of turning their leisure hours to good account'. A further outcome of that meeting was the formation of 'The Society of the Apothecaries, Chemists and Druggists' (which still prospers today as The Aberdeen Pharmaceutical Society). Some years later, this started to give lectures and purchase equipment to assist in the training of the apprentices. In 1881, the Society approached the Governors of the newly-established Robert Gordon's College requesting that they provide 'evening classes in chemistry and botany, and, if possible, in *materia medica* and pharmacy'. This request was favourably received, and classes were duly organised, initially under the South Kensington Science and Art regulations.

In April 1898, the Secretary of what had now become the Aberdeen Pharmaceutical Association wrote to the Governors suggesting that they set up a School of Pharmacy within the College in order to prepare students for the examination of the Pharmaceutical Society of Great Britain, the professional body that was now responsible for the accreditation of pharmacists throughout the country. The Aberdeen Pharmacists also offered to share the cost of the establishment of the proposed School, and to hand over to the College all apparatus, chemicals, etc. belonging to the Association and used in the work of their classes. After due consideration by the Education Committee, the Governors agreed to establish such a School, appointed Mr. Hugh E. Ellis, Ph.C. as a teacher, and issued a Prospectus in August, 1898 - a remarkably rapid rate of progress by any standards! Full courses were offered for the qualifying examinations of the Pharmaceutical Association of Great Britain, which students could undertake by day or evening classes. Subjects covered included organic and inorganic chemistry, physics, theoretical pharmacy, practical pharmacy and dispensing. The new School of Pharmacy, which was originally housed in the main College building, rapidly justified the hopes of its founders, and soon began to play a major role in the training of Scotland's pharmacists. It was subsequently housed in a number of temporary wooden buildings before moving, in 1928, to the new Technical College building that was being erected on the Harriet Street side of the College campus (see Chapter 4). It is still located there today, although it is now very much larger, occupying roughly half the building.

ESTABLISHMENT OF THE COLLEGE AS A CENTRAL INSTITUTION

By the end of the 19th century, Robert Gordon's College was firmly established as one of the major centres for technical education in Scotland, receiving significant annual grants from the Department of Science and Art in order to help finance such education. In 1901, a new 'Code of Regulations for Continuation Classes in Scotland' was introduced by the Department, reorganising post-school education under four divisions:

1. Classes for the completion of elementary education.
2. Elementary classes in technical subjects.
3. Full courses of technical education lasting three years or more.
4. Non-vocational courses.

With the publication of this new Code, a definite pattern began to emerge in the organisation and delivery of further education. Two main divisions of evening classes were recognised. The first, which constituted the beginning of the system of pre-apprenticeship training that was progressively developed during the 20th century, was directed towards particular trades and professions. The second, which was roughly equivalent to the two- and three-year vocational courses that were subsequently developed, was designed 'to fit students for the intelligent practice of particular crafts, industries and occupations'.

The Department realised, however, that no scheme of technical education would be complete unless it also provided high-quality instruction in applied science and art to selected students willing to undertake full-time study, and that a further differentiation of institutions from that defined in the Code would be necessary. Instead of all the institutions that provided technical education being subject to the same regulations, they decided that a few should be allowed to develop largely under their own initiative, in the hope that they would become 'worthy to rank not in numbers of students but in quality and advancement of work with the best of their kind in the country'. All such institutions would have to be well equipped for a considerable variety of work, have had an outstanding record of success in the past, and be located in centres of high population density. They would be known as 'Central Institutions', administered by independent governing bodies, but working in close relationship with the Scotch Education Department, the local Education Authorities, and local industry. The role that was envisaged for them is encapsulated in the following - as it proved, highly prophetic - statement:

'It is from such institutions and the opportunities of research and discovery which they will naturally afford that decisive advantage to the industries of the country, in so far as that is dependent on educational arrangements, is to be looked for'.

Accordingly, the Code gave the Department power to exempt any technical college, school of art or other special institution eligible for grants under the Code from its ministration, and to substitute a special Minute embodying the much-more-relaxed conditions of grant for the exempted institutions.

In 1903, an agreement was reached between the Governors of Robert Gordon's College and the Aberdeen School Board (the precursor of Aberdeen Education Authority) whereby responsibility for all Continuation Classes in the City would henceforth be divided between the Governors and the Board. In the same year, all the evening classes being conducted in the College joined the day and evening classes that were being run in Gray's School of Art in being formally recognised by the Department of Science and Art. (As we will see in the next chapter, the courses being run at Gray's were so recognised two years earlier - in 1901.) Robert Gordon's College was also granted the status of a 'Central Institution for specialised instruction'. This was undoubtedly one of the most significant events in the development of the institution that was soon to become Robert Gordon's Technical College, then Robert Gordon's Institute of Technology and (eventually) The Robert Gordon University. Indeed, it was regarded as so important that, in 1978, the (then) Robert Gordon's Institute of Technology produced a special 'Seventy Fifth Anniversary Brochure' to mark the occasion.

Chapter 3 : John Gray, and the foundation of Gray's School of Art

THE LIFE AND WORK OF JOHN GRAY

As we saw in the last chapter, the gift to the Governors of Robert Gordon's College of the building that became known as Gray's School of Art was one of the seminal events in the history of The Robert Gordon University. In this chapter, we will take a much more detailed look at the foundation of the School, beginning by reviewing the life of the man who made it possible.

John Gray was born in the small Aberdeenshire village of Cuminestown, in the Parish of Monquhitter, in 1811. He was the sixth son of George and Ann Gray (*née* Wilson). Around 1813, the family moved to Techmuiry, near Fraserburgh, where George Gray carried on business as a millwright and carpenter. He was assisted in his business by several of his sons, including John, and lived to the ripe old age of 101.

In around 1830, at the age of 19, John Gray came to Aberdeen. He decided that it would be in his own interests 'to learn the business of carpentry', and having already developed the rudiments of this trade while working for his father, soon became proficient. From time to time, he was employed as a carpenter in the works of William Mackinnon and Co., a firm of engineers and ironmongers based in Spring Garden, near the current site of Aberdeen College. Here, his energy and skill brought him to the notice of the heads of the firm, who eventually gave him a permanent job in their pattern shop. By virtue of his previous experience as a millwright with his father, he was able to extend the business of the firm, becoming a partner around 1865, and, shortly afterwards, head of the establishment - a post he held for many years. During the last few years of his life, failing health prevented him from taking a full share in the active work of the firm, but he maintained his interest in, and attendance at, the works until within a week of his death in 1891.

John Gray was married to Elizabeth Gordon Clark, who died in 1877, at the age of 55. They had no children. In private life, it was customary for him 'to speak the broad Doric of his native county'. It has been said of him that he was 'a homely, undemonstrative man, who preserved his simplicity of character to the last'. Such, indeed, is the impression that one gains from the photograph shown in Figure 3.1, and from the bust that was presented to him in 1886 by his fellow citizens, as a mark of their appreciation of his generous gift of a School of Art to Aberdeen. This bust was the work of Henry Bain Smith, a student of the School of Art that operated in the Aberdeen Mechanics' Institution prior to the opening of 'Gray's'. It was exhibited in a place of honour in the vestibule of the new School, where it remained until the School moved to its new building at Garthdee in 1967. It has since occupied a similar place of honour there.

John Gray's connection with public affairs in Aberdeen began in 1859, when he was appointed a Director of Aberdeen Mechanics' Institution. He took a keen and active interest in its affairs until its educational work was transferred to Robert Gordon's College - and to his own School of Art - over the period 1884-85. In 1869, he was elected to the Town Council as a representative of the Third Ward. He retired after serving for three years, but returned in 1880, and then held office until 1888, when he finally left the Town Council. During his period of office, he could not be prevailed upon to take a Baillie-ship, and it was only with some difficulty that he was persuaded to fill the office of Master of Guild Brethren's Hospital, and later that of Convenor of the Water Committee. He became a Governor of Robert Gordon's College in 1884, at the time when his new School of Art was being built, and continued to take an active interest in the affairs of the College and School until his death.

Figure 3.1 : John Gray, founder of Gray's School of Art

The endowment of Gray's School of Art was not his only gift to Aberdeen. He was a member of the Free South Church, and contributed £3000 towards the cost of its erection. (This Church, which is now known as St Mark's Church, stands between the Public Library and His Majesty's Theatre on Rosemount Viaduct, the three buildings being known to Aberdonians as 'Education, Salvation and Damnation'!) He also took a keen interest in the proposal to build the aforementioned Public Library, and was instrumental in obtaining a subscription of £1000 for that purpose from the industrialist-turned-philanthropist Andrew Carnegie. It was his earnest desire that the Library should be built on the site later to be occupied by the Central Secondary School, which subsequently became Aberdeen Academy (now a shopping mall opposite The Robert Gordon University and Robert Gordon's College); indeed, he was prepared to give £4000 of his own money towards the cost of erection on that site. It was, however, found that the purchase price of the properties on the site at the time 'was more than the Town Council was prepared to offer', so the library was eventually built some distance to the west (see above).

John Gray died on 11th October, 1891, and was buried in Nellfield Cemetery, Aberdeen five days later. The following is an extract from the Minutes of the Governors of Robert Gordon's College, dated 30th November, 1891:

'That the Governors record in their Minutes, their deep regret at the loss by death of Mr. John Gray, one of their number, through whose munification, the School of Art was provided, and their sympathy with his relatives in their bereavement.'

Much more could be said of this remarkable man, but we will leave the last word to the Rev. W.M. Clow, who paid the following tribute:

'He was a man of exceedingly public spirit, but without that crave for prominence and outspoken acknowledgement which so often blemishes public-spirited men. He lived with the highest interests of our City and community continually bearing in upon his heart, and even in these later days of bodily weakness, his care for the welfare of the poor and helpless, the disadvantaged and the fallen in the battle of life never flagged. He was a strong man, strongest in his gentleness and sympathy. His stewardship of the opportunities and the wealth that God had given him was as wise in its direction as it was munificent in its liberality.'

THE ESTABLISHMENT OF GRAY'S SCHOOL OF ART

As we saw in Chapter 2, the body originally responsible for organising art classes in Aberdeen was the Mechanics' Institution. One of their first classes was a drawing class conducted during the winter session of 1827-28 by William Ramage, a pupil of the famous Aberdeen architect Archibald Simpson. This class proved so successful that, in 1843, it had to be sub-divided. One section took figure drawing, sketching and principles of design under Mr. P.C. Auld; a second section, taught by William Ramage himself, studied architecture and mechanical drawing; the third section, also under William Ramage, took practical drawing and perspective. Later, painting, modelling and other aspects of art were introduced. As we have seen, these classes were not transferred to Robert Gordon's College in 1884 along with the other educational work of the Mechanics' Institution; they continued to be held in the Institution buildings until May, 1885, when they were transferred to the newly-opened Gray's School of Art.

It is believed that John Gray's reasons for offering to build a new School of Science and Art in Aberdeen stemmed partly from the difficulties that he himself had encountered during his early work as a tradesman, due to lack of proper technical training. As a Director of the Mechanics' Institution, he was fully aware of the valuable contribution that the Institution was making to such training, but felt that it could be delivered even more effectively if a new building, specially designed for the teaching of science and art, were to be built. Accordingly, on the 11th October, 1883, he wrote to Lord Provost Peter Esslemont, President of the Governors of the newly-established Robert Gordon's College, as follows:

'My Dear Lord Provost,

As I have already expressed to you on more than one occasion, I have long been of the opinion that the accommodation at present provided in the Mechanics' Institution for the School of Science and Art is very unsuitable for the purpose, and that a new school should be built in connection with, and in proximity to the Art Gallery, now in course of erection beside Gordon's College.

With regard to the Mechanics' Institution itself, I believe that if it were relieved of the School of Science and Art, the building could be converted into a public library at small expense, and I am aware that the Directors of the Institution are willing to hand over the building to the Town Council along with the valuable library attached to the Institution, should my fellow-citizens see fit to adopt the Public Libraries Act, which would be a great boon to the working classes.

Being desirous of assisting in carrying out these views, I beg to submit the following proposals, which I have to request you will be good enough to lay before the Governors of Robert Gordon's College. These are:

1. That the Governors of Robert Gordon's College shall set apart and dedicate as a site for a School of Science and Art, the ground on the east side of the College entrance from Schoolhill, on which the Old Grammar School at present stands.

2. That I shall erect, at my own cost, on said site, a School of Science and Art for behoof of the community of Aberdeen, in harmony with the design of the Art Gallery, and according to the accompanying plan prepared by Messrs. Matthews and Mackenzie, Architects.

On this plan, it will be observed that an arched Gateway is shown connecting the Art Gallery and the proposed School. This part of the scheme I should like to see carried out, but it appears to me that it more properly falls to be taken up by the Governors of Robert Gordon's College, either by themselves or in conjunction with the Art Gallery Committee.

3. That the School shall be named "Gray's School of Science and Art", and as regards the selection and appointment of teachers, the arrangement of classes, the curriculum of instruction and other details, shall be under the management of the Governors of Robert Gordon's College.

4. That the Governors of the College shall be responsible for the maintenance of the School in all time to come, it being, however, my desire that the cost of maintenance shall, as far as practicable, be defrayed out of the Revenue of the School, and that the Fees shall be so regulated, from time to time, as to make the School self-supporting.

I trust that the Governors of Robert Gordon's College will entertain these proposals favourably, and, in the event of their doing so, I shall cause plans and specifications of the building to be prepared and submitted for their approval'.

This letter was discussed at a Special Meeting of the Governors held on the 16th October, 1883, when the following resolution was unanimously adopted:

'That the Governors heartily concur in and gratefully accept the generous proposals made by Mr. Gray for the erection and establishment of a School of Art in Aberdeen, as embodied in his letter of 11th instant, reserving their opinion and decision in regard to the arched Gateway shown on the plan submitted, and remit to the Committee after-named to confer with Mr. Gray in regard to the details of his scheme, and to consider all matters relative thereto, and to report.'

Note that the Governors were now talking about building a 'School of *Art*' rather than a 'School of *Science and Art*' as proposed in John Gray's letter. The reasons for this change of name and function are made clear in the account of the opening of Gray's School of Art that appeared in the 'Aberdeen Journal' on 17th November, 1885. At the opening ceremony, Councillor Gill explained that the decision was made because there would simply not have been room in the new building to house all the scientific drawings and equipment that were then held in the Mechanics' Institution at Market Street. These were therefore housed elsewhere in Robert Gordon's College when it took over the Institution's technical-education programme in 1884 (see Chapter 2).

The abovementioned Committee met on 15th October, 1883, and submitted a Report to the Governors on the 26th November. The following is an extract from this:

1. That the most convenient site for the proposed School of Art is that occupied by part of the Old Grammar School buildings, with a strip of ground on the north side thereof, the whole forming a parallelogram lying to the east side of the entrance to the College, and bounded on the south by a line corresponding to the front of the Art Gallery now in course of erection.

2. That it appears from the evidence formerly submitted to the Governors that the teaching of Art in Aberdeen has been not only self-supporting, but also remunerative and there is reason to expect that with the advantages in prospect for the future School of Art, the teaching of that subject will become a considerable source of revenue to the College.

3. That inasmuch as the management and administration of the School of Art will be in the hands of the Governors, and the surplus revenue, whatever that may amount to, will be at their disposal, there is no barrier financially to the acceptance of Mr. Gray's generous offer.

It should be noted that the 'favourable financial prospects' for the proposed new School of Art predicted in the Report were not in fact realised, 'on account of changed circumstances'. What these 'changed circumstances' were is not recorded, however.

As indicated in John Gray's letter to Lord Provost Esslemont, Gray's School of Art was built in accordance with plans prepared by the well-known firm of architects, Messrs. Matthews and Mackenzie. It is interesting to note that James Matthews, one of the partners of the firm, was educated in Robert Gordon's Hospital (1829-34) and was Lord

Figure 3.2 : Gray's School of Art as it looked shortly after its opening in 1885

Provost of Aberdeen from 1883 to 1886, immediately after Peter Esslemont. By virtue of that office, he was President of Robert Gordon's College, and, as such, occupied the Chair at the formal opening of the School on 16th November, 1885. Figure 3.2 shows how the splendid new building must have looked shortly after this opening, once the archway connecting the School to the Art Gallery had been added in 1886 - see next section. (The photograph was actually taken roughly 30 years later, but it had not changed by then apart from growth of the trees that had been planted in the open space in front of the building.) It is believed that the total cost was 'around £5000'.

The actual opening ceremony appears to have been quite an occasion, being attended by many local worthies and other 'ladies and gentlemen interested in the progress of Art studies', invited through an advertisement which appeared in the local press early in November. As already mentioned, Lord Provost Matthews, as President *ex officio* of Robert Gordon's College, presided, and stated that they had met for the purpose of 'receiving from John Gray the conveyance of the building to the Governors of the College'. Unfortunately, the founder himself was not present, but it is not known whether this was due to indisposition or to 'the natural shyness of the man'. In any case, he sent a letter in which he said that 'he had great pleasure in expending a portion of his means in the erection of the School', and 'that it was his earnest wish that the School should be

48

taken advantage of by his fellow-citizens and others for the education of their families'.

In his speech, Lord Provost Matthews reviewed the development of the teaching of Art in Aberdeen, mainly under the auspices of the School of Science and Art that had been so successfully run by the Mechanics' Institution, 'of which Gray's School of Art might be regarded as a successor'. He also reminded his audience that the Directors of that Institution 'had been among the first, if not actually the first, to avail themselves of the facilities offered by the Science and Art Department, London' (see Chapter 2). In the first Report of that Department, issued in 1853, Aberdeen had received special mention as being 'the only town in Scotland that had purchased from the Department examples of drawings, casts and models for the equipment of their School'. The President also referred to the steps which had been taken to perpetuate the memory of John Gray by having the marble bust of him referred to earlier in this chapter placed in the vestibule of the new School. In the course of his speech, he also paid glowing tribute to John Gray himself, whom he had known 'intimately, both in business relations and as a friend, for many years'. He also referred to the 'great want of proper practical and technical education' that John Gray had experienced during his early days, and showed how his generosity had helped to ensure 'that the young men and women of this and future generations should have ample opportunity to obtain that instruction which he had found so difficult to obtain, and which is so necessary to fit them for the battle of life.'

How the School subsequently developed and evolved

The original Gray's School of Art building was built to match the new Aberdeen Art Gallery, which was under construction at the time when it was being planned. Like the latter, it was fronted with granite from Corrennie, in the Aberdeenshire Parish of Cluny. It had six classrooms. When it opened in 1885, the Mechanics' Institution transferred to the new School all the classes in Art that they had run in their own School of Science and Art. (As we saw in Chapter 2, these were not transferred to Robert Gordon's College in 1884 along with all their other technical classes.) The Institution also fulfilled its agreement to transfer to the new School all the models, materials and other accessories that it had used in its teaching of Art, together with the sum of £500 - 'to be applied to the benefit of the School of Art.' Robert Gordon's College also received the Arnott Fund of £500 which Dr. Neil Arnott had, in 1870, donated to the Institution in order to found 'an evening lecture in certain departments of Natural Philosophy'. (Dr. Arnott, a graduate in Arts and Medicine of Marischal College, wrote one of the earliest physics textbooks ('*Elements of Physics*') in 1825 - a book that was reprinted many times, and was translated into several other languages. He was also appointed Physician Extraordinary to the Queen in 1837.) It was perhaps unfortunate that the Directors of the Institution chose to present the Legros collection of etchings and engravings to the Art Gallery rather than to Gray's School of Art. (Professor Alphonse Legros (1837-1911) was a Frenchman who came to England in 1863. He was celebrated for his etchings and drawings, and taught at the South Kensington

School of Art before being appointed Slade Professor at University College, London. He lectured in Aberdeen in 1880, and presented the Mechanics' Institution with 'a fine collection of his works'.)

When Gray's School of Art opened in 1885, its students were prepared for the examinations of the Science and Art Department, South Kensington, London. Part of the Prospectus for Session 1885-86 is reproduced below, and provides a fascinating picture of the work of the School at the time.

'The Course of Instruction will embrace the following Subjects:

- Freehand Drawing from Copies, Models and Casts.
- Shading from Copies, Casts and the Antique.
- Painting from the Life, Landscape and Still Life in Oil and Water Colour.
- Modelling from the Life, Casts and Drawings.
- Flower Painting in Oil and Water Colour.
- Sketching from Nature.
- Tile and China Painting; Tapestry Painting.
- Perspective and Geometrical Drawing.
- Artistic Anatomy; Etching on Copper.
- Ornamental, Architectural and Applied Design.

DAY CLASSES

Morning Class for Ladies and Gentlemen, Mondays, Wednesdays and Fridays, from 10 to 12.

Elementary Section - Subjects: Freehand Drawing from Copies and Models; Geometry and Perspective. Fee, 21 shillings per Quarter.

Advanced Section - Subjects: Drawing from the Cast in Outline, in Light and Shade; Painting in Oil and Water Colour, etc. Fee, 25 shillings per Quarter.

Life Class, on Tuesdays and Thursdays from 10 to 12. Drawing and Painting in Oil and Water Colour from the Living Model. Fee, 25 shillings per Quarter; to Students of the Morning or Afternoon Classes, 15 shillings per Quarter.

Afternoon Class for Ladies and Gentlemen, on Mondays, Wednesdays and Fridays, from 1 to 3.

Elementary Section - Subjects: Freehand Drawing from Copies and Models; Geometry and Perspective. Fee, 15 shillings per Quarter.

Advanced Section - Subjects: Drawing from the Cast in Outline, in Light and Shade; Painting in Oil and Water Colour, etc. Fee, 21 shillings per Quarter.

A Special Private Class for Ladies and Gentlemen on Tuesdays and Thursdays from 1 to 3. Subjects: Sketching from Nature; China Painting; Etching on Copper, etc. Fee, 25 shillings per Quarter.

The Quarters commence 7th September, 16th November, 1st February and 15th

April. Students may enter at any time by paying the proportion for the time of the Quarter to run, and the Fee for the following quarter.

EVENING CLASSES

Class for Ladies and Youths on Mondays, Wednesdays and Fridays, from 6 to 7.

Elementary Section - Subjects: Freehand Drawing from Copies and Models; Geometry and Perspective. Fee, 10 shillings per Session from September to May Examinations.

Advanced Section - Subjects: Drawing from the Cast in Outline, in Light and Shade; from the Antique; Painting in Monochrome. Fee, 10 shillings per Term. Terms commence 16th September and 1st February.

Class for Artisans and others on Mondays, Wednesdays and Fridays, from 7 to 9.

Elementary Section - Subjects: Freehand drawing from Copies and Models; Geometry and Perspective. Fee, 10 shillings per Session from September to May Examinations.

Advanced Section - Subjects: Drawing from the Cast in Outline, in Light and Shade; Painting from the Antique; Painting in Monochrome; Ornamental Design; Modelling in Clay from the Cast and Antique. Fee, 10 shillings per Term. Terms commence 16th September and 1st February.

Life Class, on Tuesdays and Thursdays from 7 to 9. Fee, 15 shillings per Term. Terms commence 16th September and 1st February. To Students of the Antique, 5 shillings per Session.

Class for Geometry and Perspective, on Tuesdays and Thursdays. Fee, 10 shillings per Session; free to Students of the School.'

It is recorded that a total of 249 students enrolled in Session 1885-86 - 60 for Day Classes and 189 for Evening Classes.

As we have seen, it had always been John Gray's wish that his Art School and the Art Gallery should be linked together by an artistic archway and gate, and this was done in 1886, producing the striking entrance to Robert Gordon's College and The Robert Gordon University that we have today (see Figure 3.3). The provenance of the wrought-iron gates that form part of this entrance is particularly well documented. These were paid for by the Directors of the Mechanics' Institution, as the following extracts from G.M. Fraser's history of the Institution shows.

'In October of that year (1886), by which time both the Art Gallery and the School of Art were completely finished, the Directors of the Institution had submitted to them, by Mr. John Gray, the drawing of a wrought iron gate to connect the Art Gallery with the School of Art, forming at the same time an entrance gate to Gordon's College, towards which Mr. Gray desired the Directors to appropriate £150.' (This money was part of the residue of the Institution's funds.) *'The Directors agreed, and so came into being the ornamental gate, with its inscribed bronze shields, which is so familiar an object between the Art Gallery and the School of Art. It*

was the work of a southern forge, and it was not finally accepted without encountering severe criticism on its workmanship. As a memorial of the share which the Mechanics' Institution had in all these matters, one of the bronze shields on the gate carries the inscription:

This gate
Is the gift of the
Aberdeen Mechanics' Institute
whose educational work was transferred
1882-1884
To Robert Gordon's College,
Along with a proportion
Of the Institute's Property and Funds.'

It is not known why this inscription referred to the 'Aberdeen Mechanics' *Institute*' rather than to the 'Aberdeen Mechanics' *Institution*', which was its correct name. Possibly it is due to the fact that the Institution was widely referred to by the former name - and, indeed, still is today. After exposure to the harsh Aberdeen climate for nearly a quarter of a century, it is recorded that the floral decorations on the original gates became 'much corroded', and parts of these had to be removed. The bronze shields have, unfortunately, also since been removed.

Figure 3.3 : The arched entrance to Robert Gordon's College and The Robert Gordon University, showing the School in the background (note that this photograph was taken before RGIT became a University)

After its opening in 1885, Gray's School of Art grew steadily both in size and in reputation. As we have seen, it originally had six classrooms, but, by 1896, the rising student numbers and the increasing diversity of the classes on offer led the Governors to add two further rooms, by extending the building eastwards. It is recorded that the cost of these extensions was '£600 or thereby'. Further major extensions were carried out between 1928 and 1931, when the School was part of Robert Gordon's Technical College. These in fact involved the almost complete reconstruction of the School, apart from its southern facade, and cost '£27,500 or thereby'. After this work, Gray's School of Art consisted of

- Four rooms for Design and Decorative Art.
- One room for Metal Work, Jewellery, etc.
- One room for Modelling with a room for casting adjoining.
- Four rooms for Building and Allied Trades.
- Three rooms for Architecture, with Library and Museum adjoining.
- One room for Drawing from the Antique.
- Five rooms for Drawing and Painting.

In addition to these, there were provided, in buildings adjacent to the main School, workshops for Joiners and Cabinetmakers, for Stonecutters, for Plumbers, for Painters and Decorators, and for Watchmakers and Clockmakers. The School occupied these extended premises until 1967, when it moved to a completely new building at Garthdee (see Chapter 6). Figure 3.4 shows a typical class conducted in the School during the early 1930's - a life class in drawing and painting.

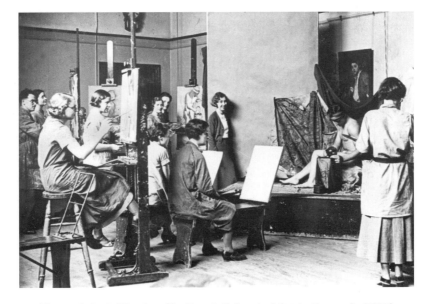

Figure 3.4 : A 'life class' in Gray's School of Art in the early 1930's

As we have seen, Gray's School of Art originally prepared students for the examinations of the South Kensington Science and Art Department in London. In 1901, however, the Scotch Education Department made Gray's School of Art one of the four Central (Art) Institutions of Scotland. (Note that this happened two years before Robert Gordon's College as a whole was designated as a 'Central Institution for specialised instruction' in respect of its adult-education work - see Chapter 2.) As a result of this change in status, the Governors became entitled to award their own diplomas and certificates to students who had successfully completed the appropriate courses of study in Art, 'under conditions approved by the Department'. Such diplomas and certificates continued to be the main awards of the School until the early 1980's, when it started to award degrees under the aegis of the Council for National Academic Awards - the CNAA (see Chapter 7). Since 1992, when the (then) Robert Gordon Institute of Technology acquired full university status, all the awards of the School have been those of The Robert Gordon University.

Before ending this chapter on Gray's School of Art, it is necessary to say something about the relationship between the School and the various umbrella organisations of which it has formed a part since its foundation in 1885. As we have seen, it was originally part of Robert Gordon's College, although it is clear that it enjoyed, from the very start, 'a considerable degree of autonomy' under its first 'Master', Mr. John P. Fraser, who remained in office until 1909. This autonomy continued throughout most of the 20th century, when Gray's School of Art was recognised as being one of Scotland's four Central Art Colleges, while still being an integral part of Robert Gordon's Technical College, Robert Gordon's Institute of Technology and The Robert Gordon University. Indeed, until comparatively late in the century, successive Heads of the School described themselves as the 'Principal' of Gray's School of Art. This caused some confusion, especially after the title of the Chief Executive of Robert Gordon's Institute of Technology was changed from 'Director' to 'Principal' in 1979 (see Chapter 7). The practice has now been discontinued, and the Head of Gray's School of Art is now simply a 'Head of School' within the University, like all the other Heads of major teaching departments.

Section 2

Robert Gordon's Technical College

(1910 - 1965)

Chapter 4 : Review of the Technical College years

BACKGROUND TO THE ESTABLISHMENT OF THE TECHNICAL COLLEGE

As we saw in Chapter 2, Robert Gordon's Hospital was converted into Robert Gordon's College in 1881, and, during the next 28 years, established a considerable reputation both as a day secondary school for boys and as an adult education college. It is to the outstanding credit of the Governors and the two Headmasters who were responsible for the educational policy of the College over this period that they were able to achieve so much, despite the limited means at their disposal. Dr. Alexander Ogilvie (Headmaster of Robert Gordon's Hospital from 1872 to 1881, and the Headmaster and Superintendent of Evening Classes at Robert Gordon's College from 1881 to 1901) was responsible for the conversion of the residential Hospital into a modern secondary school. He was also responsible for the introduction of a programme of evening classes for adults, and for making arrangements for the College to take over the entire adult education programme of the Aberdeen Mechanics' Institution over the period 1884-85. His successor, Mr. Charles Stewart (see Figure 4.1) also fulfilled the highly-demanding dual role of Headmaster and Superintendent of Evening Classes, being in charge when Robert Gordon's College attained the status of a 'Central Institution for specialised instruction' in 1903, and subsequently preparing the ground for conversion of the adult-education side of the College into a full-blown Technical College in 1910.

During the first decade of the 20th century, it became increasingly realised that evening classes alone were not capable of providing the sort of advanced technical education that the people of Aberdeen and its surrounding districts were starting to demand of Robert Gordon's College and the Aberdeen School Board. The great advances that had been brought about by the establishment of technical colleges in other parts of the country were well-known and appreciated, and the lack of such a college in Aberdeen was beginning to be widely felt. Accordingly, in 1907, the Governors of Robert Gordon's College decided that, if they were to provide similar opportunities for the young men and women of the North-East of Scotland, they must 'wholeheartedly support' the Appeal that was about to be launched for funds to establish a Technical College in the City of Aberdeen. The Appeal, which was organised by the Lord Provost of Aberdeen, the Principal of Aberdeen University, the Lord Lieutenants of the neighbouring counties and other local dignitaries, emphasised the need for such a centre of technical education in the area to augment the work 'so creditably being performed by Gordon's College in co-operation with the School Board'. In total, a sum of £70,000 was donated, including £40,000 from the Government and £15,000 from the Town Council.

At the request of the Appeal Committee, Charles Stewart drew up a detailed report on the subject, in which he put forward the idea of setting up a College in Aberdeen to provide comprehensive technical instruction in engineering, chemistry, natural science, architecture and building, including appropriate co-operation with Gray's School of Art (which, as we saw in the last chapter, was by now operating largely independently of the rest of Robert Gordon's College). The College Governors were fully aware of the situation, and 'most generously' undertook to provide a site for the main building of the proposed new college within their own grounds, subject to certain conditions, and 'so disposed as not to interfere with the amenity of the school'. This offer did pose some legal problems, however, it being uncertain whether the Governors, 'either at common law or by their constitution', were entitled to grant a site for the erection of the proposed college within the grounds on which Robert Gordon's College was built. They were subsequently advised by King's Counsel that they could legally do so 'by way of sale, feu or lease at a feu price but not gratuitously', and that, in making any such arrangement, they would also have to show 'due regard for the future requirements of the Hospital' (*sic*). The legal problems having been duly dealt with, Mr. Stewart's suggestion was approved, and the offer of the site accepted.

Figure 4.1 : Mr. Charles Stewart, Headmaster of Robert Gordon's College from 1901-1920 and first Principal of Robert Gordon's Technical College (1910 - 1921)

In 1909, a Provisional Order (Robert Gordon's Technical College and Aberdeen Endowments Trust Confirmation Act) was promoted and approved 'for establishing Robert Gordon's Technical College and the Aberdeen Endowments Trust; for constituting the Aberdeen Endowments Trust and transferring the Endowments to the Trust; and for other purposes'. The new Technical College would come under the control of the Governors of Robert Gordon's College, who would henceforth have a dual role, governing both Robert Gordon's College (the boys' school) and Robert Gordon's Technical College.

In order to reflect this even wider remit, a new, enlarged Governing Body was constituted as follows:

- The Lord Provost of Aberdeen, President (ie Chairman) *ex officio*.
- Nine members appointed by Aberdeen Town Council.
- Two members appointed by Aberdeenshire County Council.
- Three members appointed by Aberdeen School Board.
- One member appointed by Aberdeen Endowments Trust.
- Two members appointed by Aberdeen University.
- One member appointed by the Harbour Commissioners.
- One member appointed by the Incorporated Trades.
- One member appointed by the Presbytery.
- Nine members appointed by the Governors themselves.

They would also henceforth be known as the 'Governors of Robert Gordon's Colleges'.

All the existing grounds, buildings and facilities of Robert Gordon's College, including Gray's School of Art, were placed under the jurisdiction of the new Board of Governors, along with all the grounds, buildings and facilities of the hitherto-completely-separate School of Domestic Economy at King Street. (A detailed description of the early development of this School, its transfer to Robert Gordon's Technical College, and its subsequent evolution is given in Chapter 5.) At the same time, the Governors were given powers 'to acquire such additional lands and execute such street improvements as were necessary to extend and improve the site of the Technical College'. The new Robert Gordon's Technical College officially came into existence on 1st January, 1910, with Mr. Charles Stewart being appointed as its first Principal, in addition to his duties as Headmaster of Robert Gordon's College.

EXPANSION AND DEVELOPMENT UNDER CHARLES STEWART (1910 - 1921)

During the eleven years in which he was Principal of Robert Gordon's Technical College, Charles Stewart continued the excellent work that he had carried out as Superintendent of Evening Classes in Robert Gordon's College, expanding and developing its activities, and enhancing its reputation as a provider of high-quality technical education. After surveying the areas in which the new College was to operate, he and the Governors created the following three Schools:

- A **School of Engineering and Chemistry**, incorporating the
  School of Pharmacy.
- A **School of Arts and Crafts**, incorporating a new Department
  of Architecture and Building.
- A **School of Domestic Science**.

The second and third Schools already had premises of their own (Gray's School of Art at Schoolhill, and the School of Domestic Economy at King Street), but the whole of the work of the first had still to be carried out within the Secondary School buildings. This effectively limited its work to evening classes, which met most of the needs of local industry at the time. Conditions in the engineering industry, in particular, apparently made it 'impossible' for workers to be released in order to attend day classes. It was, however, realised that day classes would almost certainly have to be organised at some time in the future. Figure 4.2 shows an engineering class being held in the old gym building of Robert Gordon's College (recognisable by the cast-iron railings round the balcony) around 1913. It is interesting to note that Robert Gordon's Technical College set up its School of Engineering and Chemistry 15 years before Aberdeen University established its Chair of Engineering in 1925.

Figure 4.2 : An engineering class being held in Robert Gordon's College c 1913

Principal Stewart and the Governors also formulated highly-ambitious plans for the extension of existing buildings and the construction of new buildings in order to meet the ever-increasing need for accommodation by the different Schools that now made up Robert Gordon's Technical College. These included the extension of the King Street building of the School of Domestic Science, extension of Gray's School of Art, and - most ambitious of all - the construction of a completely new building at Schoolhill to accommodate the School of Engineering and Chemistry. Unfortunately, only the first of these projects (the extension of the School of Domestic Science) was able to be completed as planned, the new buildings being opened in 1912 - see Chapter 5. Plans for the other two projects were in fact drawn up, and, by 1914, had actually been approved by the Scottish Education Department. Before the work of erection could be started, however, the First World War had broken out, and building operations of the type proposed were prohibited by the Government. Even if there had been no such restriction, the increased cost, coupled with a shortage of cash on the part of the Governors (partly due to a fire which had destroyed sections of the College buildings in 1911) would probably have prevented the work from being started at that time. In the event, the plans were not revived until the mid-1920's (see next section).

Mention has already been made of the transfer of the School of Domestic Economy to Robert Gordon's Technical College, and of the establishment of a new Department of Architecture and Building within the School of Arts and Crafts. Both of these highly-important developments will be described in more detail in later chapters. Another extremely-important development at this time was the transfer of the Aberdeen School of Navigation to the new Technical College. As we saw in Chapter 3, classes in Navigation and related subjects were originally conducted by the Mechanics' Institution, but, in 1858, were taken over by the local Marine Board. This remained responsible for the operation of Aberdeen's School of Navigation until the Technical College Appeal was launched in 1907. The Appeal Committee felt justified in including in their scheme a proposal to construct, near the harbour, an extensive new building that would house the School of Navigation together with a new Fisheries Institute, and provisional plans were drawn up. This highly-ambitious project never came to fruition, however, and, in 1914, an agreement was reached between the Marine Board and the Governors of Robert Gordon's Colleges that the latter would take over responsibility for Navigation teaching. Captain E. Barker Thornber was appointed Head of the new School of Navigation, whose work was transferred to the main College buildings at Schoolhill. It subsequently instigated a varied programme, including:

- Preparation for Mercantile Marine Certificate examinations.
- Classes for fishermen.
- Classes in science, including marine biology.
- Vacation courses for teachers in navigation and marine biology.

During the First World War, the teaching work of the Technical College continued, although there was a great shortage of staff. Courses were provided on many topics, but mainly in subjects such as munitions, engineering and navigation that were directly geared to the war effort. Over 1000 men and women were trained to work in munitions factories, and, after discharge, over 750 disabled service men were provided with vocational training to fit them for civilian life. Much of the teaching during the war took place in temporary huts that were erected on both sides of the main avenue through the Schoolhill campus. In 1919, these temporary quarters were further extended to accommodate new engineering classes. Such classes had been conducted in the College since the establishment of the

School of Engineering and Chemistry in 1910, and had, until then, largely been restricted to civil, mechanical and marine engineering. These continued to be the main growth areas after the end of the war, since there was still very little electrical engineering industry in the Aberdeen area.

On 19th October, 1921, Charles Stewart wrote to the then President of the Board of Governors, Lord Provost Sir William Meff, intimating his resignation as Principal of Robert Gordon's Technical College. He had already retired from the post of Headmaster of Robert Gordon's College. He gave as his reason for resignation a disagreement with the Governors over a 'new policy' for the Technical College apparently being proposed by them. What this 'new policy' was is not clear, but Dr. R.B. Strathdee, historian of the period in question, believes that 'the difference of opinion might have been resolved had there not also been a clash of personalities.' Be that as it may, Mr. Stewart demitted office on 31st December, 1921, after providing 38 years of sterling service to the Governors - not only as an 'inspiring English master' and a highly-successful Headmaster, but also as Superintendent of Evening Classes and Principal of the Technical College. Indeed, it was in no small measure due to his efforts that the new Robert Gordon's Technical College achieved its undoubted early success. He would be greatly missed in future years.

THE LEADERLESS INTERREGNUM (1921 - 1944)

For reasons known only to themselves, but probably not unconnected with the unfortunate circumstances that led to Charles Stewart's resignation, the Governors decided not to fill the vacant post of Principal of Robert Gordon's Technical College. What followed, in the words of Dr. Strathdee, was 'a period of 23 years in the history of the Technical College characterised by a complete lack of imagination and initiative'. During this period, the Secretary and Registrar of Robert Gordon's Colleges, Mr. James McKenzie, was authorised to deal with all official correspondence with the Scottish Education Department, and the Heads of the various Schools within the Technical College were made directly responsible to the Board of Governors for the management of their Schools, in respect of both day and evening classes. While these arrangements no doubt enabled the individual Schools to operate reasonably effectively within their own specific remits, they meant that the College *as a whole* totally lacked strategic direction - with consequences that could have been disastrous.

In order to help readers to understand what happened next, it is necessary to say something about the way in which technical education in Britain developed between the 1870's and 1920's. As we saw in Chapter 2, the various Acts of Parliament that were passed during the 1870's provided a great stimulus to this development, leading (among other things) to a considerable expansion in the provision of technical education through bodies such as the reformed Robert Gordon's College. With the spread of such education, there gradually arose a perceived need for some sort of nationally-recognised certificate or other award for students who pursued their studies successfully. In 1878, the City and Guilds of London Institute was founded, and, in 1900, was granted a Royal Charter as an educational association for the promotion and certification of technical and scientific education. Technical and craft courses leading to the award of 'City and Guilds' Certificates soon became commonplace, enabling apprentices and industrial workers of virtually all types to advance themselves educationally. A number of such courses were introduced by Robert Gordon's Technical College.

After the end of the First World War, however, the Board of Education became increasingly dissatisfied with the way in which technical courses and examinations had developed. The pattern was difficult for employers to understand, and, as a consequence, some of the qualifications did not receive the recognition that they merited. As a major step towards overcoming the problem, the National Certificate and National Diploma systems were introduced. These enabled part-time students to work towards Certificates awarded at two levels - Ordinary National Certificates (ONC's) and more advanced Higher National Certificates (HNC's), and full-time or 'sandwich' students to work towards Diplomas also awarded at two levels - Ordinary National Diplomas (OND's) and Higher National Diplomas (HND's). The objectives of this scheme were threefold. The first was to enable students to obtain worthwhile qualifications of national standing, with the active participation of the appropriate professional bodies. The second was to provide teachers with greater flexibility in respect of the planning, delivery and assessment of certificated technical courses - a somewhat revolutionary idea at the time. The third was to help meet the growing demands of industry for well-educated technicians, and for greater numbers of qualified professionals than the few Universities in existence at the time were capable of producing.

Once the system for the award of National Certificates and Diplomas had been approved, joint committees of the Board of Education and various professional bodies started to be established in order to validate courses devised by specific colleges. The first (in Mechanical Engineering) was formed in 1920, and similar bodies dealing with courses in Chemistry, Electrical Engineering, Naval Architecture and many others soon followed. In Scotland, the first National Certificate courses - in Chemistry and in Mechanical Engineering - were approved and initiated in 1924. Unfortunately, no such developments took place in Robert Gordon's Technical College, much to the dismay both of local employers and their work forces and of the Scottish Education Department. Indeed, for six years after the resignation of Principal Stewart, there was little or no progress either in the development of new courses or in the provision of the new accommodation that the College so badly needed.

Ultimately, pressure was brought on the Governors from two different sources. In April 1924, the Scottish Education Department wrote to the College regarding the desirability of instituting National Certificate and Diploma courses in Mechanical Engineering and Chemistry. A little later, the Governors were reminded by the local Education Authorities that, in terms of the 1909 Provisional Order, Robert Gordon's Technical College had been established to provide 'technical instruction for the City and North of Scotland', and, if they continued with their present policy and failed to introduce the new National Certificate and National Diploma courses, the Authorities would have no alternative but to 'affiliate with Colleges in Edinburgh and Glasgow, where such courses were provided'. Since this would have effectively meant the end of the College as a 'major player' in local technical education, the Governors and College authorities were at last spurred into action, and took steps both to introduce courses of the type required and to improve their accommodation, so that they could deliver such courses more effectively.

With regard to courses, steps were initiated to replace Mr. Alexander Horne, who had resigned as Head of Engineering in 1922; since then, the School of Engineering had been subdivided into two Departments - Civil Engineering, and Mechanical and Marine Engineering - each with a lecturer in charge. In 1925, however, Professor W. Blackadder was appointed to the new Chair of Engineering at Aberdeen University, and was also appointed Director of the School of Engineering at Robert Gordon's Technical College. For almost 50 years thereafter, the two institutions would collaborate closely in the provision of engineering education, with virtually all of the actual teaching being carried out in the Technical College, and, later, in RGIT.   The first National Certificate course - an evening class in Mechanical Engineering - was initiated in session 1925-26. In order to comply with the National Certificate regulations, a Department of Mathematics and Physics was also created in 1925, and Dr. J.D. Stewart was appointed as its Head. From then on, National Certificate courses constituted an increasingly important part of the work of the Technical College. In 1926, a new Department of Electrical Engineering was created within the existing Engineering School, although the number of students was initially low due to the small number of local firms then involved in the electricity industry; fifty years later, the School of Electronic and Electrical Engineering would become the biggest School in Robert Gordon's Institute of Technology, and would remain so until it was overtaken by the expansion of the Business School (see Section 3).

With regard to accommodation, the Buildings Committee had, for some time, been considering the provision of new and enlarged premises for the School of Engineering. Now, however, the Governors realised that if the Technical College was to fulfil its proper function, suitable permanent accommodation would have to be provided not merely for the Engineers, but for *all* Departments that did not already have such accommodation. It was therefore essential that the use of the temporary huts referred to in the last section should be discontinued as soon as possible. Accordingly, they instructed Mr. R. Leslie Rollo, Principal Teacher of Architecture at the Technical College, to draw up plans for a new building capable of housing all Schools and Departments with the exception of the Schools of Domestic Science and Art, which were, at the time, relatively well catered for. The plans were based on the assumption that the number of day students would increase from 250 to roughly 390 over the next few years, and that the number of evening students would increase from 931 to roughly 1250.

The new building was to be a two-storied structure on the east side of and facing the main avenue through the College campus, with a frontage of just over 280 feet; it would have extensive single-storey accommodation behind it, mainly for engineering laboratories. The plans were eventually approved, and construction was carried out in three phases, beginning with the urgently-needed laboratories, then the northern half of the main building, then the southern half. At the same time, the opportunity was taken to extend Gray's School of Art in the ways described in Chapter 3. In the event, it took six years to complete the new buildings, to take down the old huts, and to re-sow the front lawns, and it was not until October 1932 that the new Technical Building was officially opened - by Sir Frank T. Smith, Secretary of the Department of Scientific and Industrial Research. It had cost a total of £125,000. Figure 4.3 shows the main building as it looked at the end of 1929, before all the temporary huts had been demolished. The back of Gray's School of Art can be seen behind these huts.

Figure 4.3 : The new Technical College building as it looked in 1929, before the temporary huts had all been demolished.

Another major new building complex was constructed on the other side of the main avenue over the same period. For some time, the question of the provision of a large hall for use by the Secondary School and Technical College had occupied the attention of the Governors. Work on this was eventually able to start in 1929, largely due to the generosity of Lady MacRobert of Douneside, who donated £5,000 towards its construction in memory of her late husband, Sir Alexander MacRobert of Cawnpore, who had at one time been intimately connected with Robert Gordon's College. The new MacRobert Hall, an architect's sketch for which is shown in Figure 4.4, was opened by Lady MacRobert in 1931. It was, at the time, one of the largest in Aberdeen, being capable of seating 800 people, and also providing adjoining accommodation on its north side for a suite of administrative rooms, and for a new Library and Reading Room for use by the School and Technical College. A few years later, these were extended northwards by erecting a two-storey building matching the new Technical College building on the other side of the avenue. This enabled the Library to be greatly enlarged, and also provided additional classroom accommodation for Robert Gordon's College. The new Central Library was officially opened by Dr. Walter Reid, Chairman of the Governors, in 1938. The College also continued to run sectional Libraries in its various Schools, catering for the more specialised interests of staff and students.

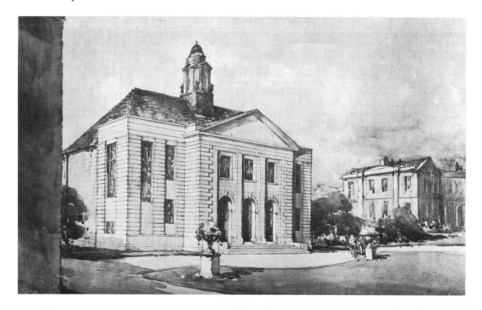

Figure 4.4 : An architect's sketch of the MacRobert Hall, opened in 1931

A further important development that took place over this period was the establishment, in 1931, of the Students' Representative Council, and its formal recognition by the Governors. Several years previously, the students of Gray's School of Art had set up such an organisation to represent their interests. With the imminent completion of the new buildings at Schoolhill, however, it was felt by the general student body that there would be a closer connection between the various Schools of the Technical College and with the Governors and Staff if a Council representing *all* the students was constituted. The new S.R.C. started to play a significant role in College affairs right from its inception, organising student activities, collaborating with the Governors in providing sporting and other recreational facilities for students, and, eventually, obtaining its own premises in Rubislaw Terrace. It continues to do so today, as the Students' Association.

Over the years since its establishment in 1910, the steady expansion of the teaching work of the Technical College had led to progressive modifications of the original School structure described in the previous section. By the early 1930's, the College consisted of the following seven Schools:

- The **School of Engineering**, with Departments of Civil, Mechanical and Electrical Engineering; this ran courses leading to the Diploma in Engineering of the Technical College and to the Degree of B.Sc. in Engineering of Aberdeen University. It also ran lower-level courses in Marine Engineering and Engineering Surveying, leading to Board of Trade Awards, together with a wide range of evening-class courses leading to National Certificates; these included courses in Civil, Mechanical and Electrical Engineering, and in Naval Architecture.

- The **School of Chemistry**, which ran day and evening classes in Inorganic, Organic and Physical Chemistry, the Chemistry of Fuels and Oils, Metallurgy and Papermaking. These led to a wide range of awards, including National Certificates and Diplomas.

- The **School of Mathematics and Physics**, which ran a range of courses in each of these subjects, as well as providing a wide range of service teaching for courses run by other Schools.

- The **School of Pharmacy**, which provided day and evening courses preparing students for the examinations of the Pharmaceutical Society of Great Britain; these consisted of the 'Preliminary Scientific Course', the 'Chemist and Druggist Qualifying Course', and the 'Pharmaceutical Chemist Course'.

- **Gray's School of Art**, with Departments of Drawing and Painting, Design, Sculpture, Architecture, and Building and Surveying. This ran a wide range of day and evening courses leading to the award of Diplomas and Certificates. The Architecture courses were recognised by the Royal Institute of British Architects, and, combined with appropriate professional experience, enabled students to obtain full professional status (see Chapter 6). The School also ran day courses in Building and Surveying, together with a wide range of evening classes.

- The **School of Domestic Science**, running Diploma courses in Cooking, Laundry Work and Housewifery, and also in Needlework, Dressmaking and Millinery. It also ran shorter courses for Housewives, Housekeepers, Cooks, Domestic Servants, Ladies' Maids, Dressmakers and Milliners, together with courses for men wishing to enter the Mercantile Marine as Ships' Cooks, the latter being recognised by the Board of Trade.

- The **School of Navigation**, which ran courses leading to Board of Trade Certificates of Competency in the Mercantile Marine for Extra Masters, Masters, First Mates and Second Mates in the Foreign Service, for Masters and Mates in the Home Service, and for Extra Skippers, Skippers and Second Hands in the Fishing Service. It also ran courses in Navigation and Seamanship, and in Boat Sailing and Rowing, for Cadets.

As was the case during the First World War, classes continued as usual throughout the Second World War, despite the shortage of staff due to military service. Total student numbers remained steady at around 1000 during most of this period, and, in addition, 16,833 men and 6,796 women were trained for war work or rehabilitation. Figure 4.5 shows a class of naval cadets undergoing engineering training. Some of the College's students also played an important part in the war effort. In answer to an appeal from the Scottish Education Department, for example, a number of Domestic Science students travelled to London in 1944. There, 'smartly dressed in white overalls and caps', they cooked for and fed 500 workmen who were engaged in repairing bomb-damaged buildings. They enjoyed the experience : as one student said, 'at the College, we used to work in ounces, but now we have to think in stones!'

Figure 4.5 : A class of naval cadets undergoing engineering training in Robert Gordon's Technical College.

RESTORATION OF VITALITY UNDER DR. ALEXANDER WEST (1944 - 1964)

Despite the considerable progress that had been made since the crisis of 1924-25, the impact of the Second World War made the Governors increasingly aware of the lack of strategic leadership within the Technical College, particularly in respect of its academic development. They therefore started to think seriously about appointing 'someone with the relevant qualifications to take charge of the academic administration of the College'. During session 1942-43, a special *ad hoc* committee was set up to consider the matter. After a number of meetings and discussions with the Scottish Education Department and the Aberdeen University authorities, this recommended that 'a Director of the Technical College should be appointed if a suitable candidate presents himself' (*sic*). At the same time, it was noted that 'the Secretary of the Colleges had expressed a desire to be relieved of his duties at an early date', thus adding to the urgency of the situation. The Secretary and Registrar in question, James Mackenzie, had been in post since 1913, and, for over 20 years, had effectively been running the College. It was therefore with some relief to all concerned that an eminently suitable candidate was eventually identified - Dr. Alexander C. West, a mechanical engineer who was Principal of Croydon Polytechnic at the time (see Figure 4.6). He took up the post of Director of Robert Gordon's Technical College on 1st March, 1944.

In his inaugural address in September 1944, Dr. West made a plea for 'a great expansion in technical education' in order that the country could 'maintain its industrial position in a competitive world, and play its part in the shaping of a new, post-war civilisation'. During his 20 years in office, he worked wholeheartedly to strengthen the links between the College and industry, and also tried, wherever possible, to rekindle the interest of former students in their *alma mater*. To this end, he instigated the formation, in December 1944, of the Robert Gordon's Technical College Former Students' Association. He was only too well aware that he had inherited an institution that had shown little initiative and imagination for over 20 years. Fortunately, the 1944 Education Act provided a much-needed stimulus for expansion, imposing on local education authorities a duty 'to secure the provision for their area of adequate facilities for further education'. In the coming years, Dr. West was to take full advantage of this.

Figure 4.6 : Dr. Alexander C. West, Director of Robert Gordon's Technical College from 1944 to 1964.

One of the very first innovations under Dr. West was the decision to look into the possibility of setting up new courses leading to the award of external degrees at London University. It was felt that there was a very real need for a part-time-day or evening course, with chemistry as its main subject, among laboratory workers in local Government research establishments, in the various medical departments of Aberdeen University, in local paper mills, and in other local industries such as farming and fishing. Plans for such a course were duly drawn up during the 1944-45 session, and approved by the Governors and Scottish Education Department. The initial chemistry-based course was later followed by a similar external degree course in engineering.

After the end of the Second World War in 1945, large numbers of young men returned to civilian life after having had their careers interrupted by war service - in some cases for five or six years. In order to assist these ex-servicemen to resume their chosen professions, the Government introduced its Business Training Scheme, and arrangements were made for the Technical College to participate in the scheme by providing training courses in Business Administration. As we will see later, this work laid the foundations for the eventual formation of a School of Business Management Studies within the institution. In addition, a close liaison was maintained between the College and the Resettlement Department of the Ministry of Labour.

Another innovation at this time was the setting up in Scotland of five Advisory Councils for Technical Education. The North-East Council was the first of these to meet, and, from the very outset, its members stressed the importance of striking a balance between theory and practice in the planning of future policy for the training of apprentices and other people who were learning a trade or profession. The Council realised that, in order to ensure success, such people would have to be released from their work to attend college by day. Furthermore, for students attending college from remote areas, release for an extended continuous period would be necessary. Dr. West believed that this would only be possible if there was a close relationship between the Technical College and industry, and if industrial managers could be convinced of the benefits *to them* of arranging such release. Accordingly, he arranged for members of his staff to make contact with and visit local firms. Such visits were greatly appreciated, and, partly as a result, day-release and 'sandwich' courses gradually gained acceptance among local employers. Later (in 1963) he would set up an Industrial Liaison service within the College.

Another area in which the new Director interested himself from the start was the corporate life of his students. Despite the formation of the Students' Representative Council in 1931, the College had hitherto done very little to encourage and support extramural student activities. Dr. West therefore held several meetings with the S.R.C. to see how he could help them to set up sports clubs and student societies, establish a refectory where they could obtain reasonably-priced meals, especially at lunch time, and, in due course, set up a Students' Union to foster the social life of the College. Discussions regarding the last of these projects eventually bore fruit in 1952, when the S.R.C. acquired premises for such a Union at 17 Rubislaw Terrace. This was the forerunner of today's splendid Student Union at Schoolhill.

In the first few years after the end of the war, numbers of both full-time and part-time students increased significantly, with the total number of students rising from 1384 in 1944-45 to 2890 in 1949-50 - an increase of over 100%. Needless to say, this placed a great strain on accommodation, particularly during the day. Dr. West eventually managed to persuade the Governors that more accommodation was essential, and that the provision of additional classrooms and laboratories on the Schoolhill site should be given top priority. Due to the lack of ground for new buildings, they decided, in March 1948, to add a third floor to the main Technical College building, thus providing 6,600 square feet of extra space. In October of the same year, Mr. David J.A. Ross of Messrs. Allan, Ross and Allan was appointed as Architect for the extension, and, after approval of the scheme by the Scottish Education Department, building commenced during the 1949-50 session. While the work was being carried out, it also proved possible to build two additional classrooms on the second floor, and these were incorporated in the plans along with some other minor alterations. The new extension, which can be seen in Figure 4.7, was officially opened in November 1951. The new third floor was taken over by the School of Mathematics and Physics in 1952, thus freeing additional rooms for the then-rapidly-expanding Electrical Engineering Department.

Figure 4.7 : The main Technical College building as it looked in 1952, after the new third floor had been added (note that this photograph was taken somewhat later, after the St. Nicholas House building seen in the background had been erected)

In the early 1950's, the Governors of Robert Gordon's Colleges received another of the substantial bequests from local citizens that have played such an important role in the development of Robert Gordon's Hospital and its successors. This time, the benefactor was Mr. Tom Scott Sutherland, a prominent local architect, businessman and public figure, who had recently purchased Garthdee House, together with over 20 acres of policies and grounds. Both the house and the grounds were gifted to the Governors so that they could establish a School of Architecture on the site. Mr. Scott Sutherland vacated Garthdee House in June, 1955, and work on conversion into the new School began soon afterwards. The Scott Sutherland School of Architecture was formally opened on 24th May, 1957 - and proved to be the first of many Schools to move to Garthdee. Much more detailed accounts of the Garthdee bequest and its aftermath are given in Chapters 6 and 15.

We have already seen how, in the aftermath of the Second World War, a number of courses were organised in conjunction with the Ministry of Labour and National Service, with which a close co-operation was maintained thereafter. Thus, when the United Kingdom Atomic Energy Authority decided to build a Fast Reactor Development Establishment at Dounreay in Caithness during the mid-1950's, Robert Gordon's Technical College was well placed to provide help in the training of the large numbers of technical staff that were required. The first students from Dounreay were admitted to the College in 1957-58, and the College also helped to set up local training facilities in Thurso, under Caithness Education Authority. When it was subsequently decided to build a Technical College in Thurso, considerable assistance was given both during the planning and during the equipping of the new College. Close collaboration with both Dounreay and Thurso Technical College has continued to the present day.

Mention has already been made of the rapid expansion of electrical-engineering-related work that began during the Second World War, and continued for a considerable time thereafter. During the war, temporary accommodation was taken over from Gray's School of Art, and converted into workshops, laboratories and classrooms for this purpose; indeed, over a period of four years, some 2000 ratings were trained as radio and radar mechanics for the Royal and Merchant Navies. After the war, the electrical engineering industry entered a period of phenomenal growth, almost doubling in size during each of the next three decades, and, despite a greatly increased output of graduates from Britain's universities, the industry was unable to recruit trained professionals in the numbers required. During the same period, the novelty and complexity of electrical-engineering products such as power sources, communication systems, weapon systems and computers presented Britain's universities and colleges with serious challenges. Not only had electrical and electronic engineers to be produced in ever-greater numbers, but the level of their training had to be steadily increased, and opportunities for post-graduate study and research also had to be provided.

We have already seen how the constant demands for additional space by the College's Electrical Engineering Department were partly met by the release of space made possible by the move of the School of Mathematics and Physics to the new third floor of the main Schoolhill building in 1952. This was still not enough to meet their seemingly-ever-increasing accommodation requirements, however, so it was decided to move the Department to a completely new building, to be built at the back of the MacRobert Hall, facing Blackfriars Street. This four-storey building would provide the Department with over 10,000 square feet of space, including room for 'heavy' workshops and laboratories in its basement. Its top floor would also provide space for a new, much-larger Central Library for the College, which would finally be able to vacate the Library next to the MacRobert Hall that it had shared with the Secondary School since 1931. Work on the new building began in the late 1950's, and it was officially opened on 12th September, 1960. The move of the electrical engineers to the new Blackfriars Street building (which is shown in Figure 4.8) allowed a much-needed expansion of the Department of

Mechanical Engineering to take place in the main Technical College building, on the other side of the campus.

In 1961, the College inaugurated a major new training course for the paper industry, for which it had been running courses of various types for many years through its School of Chemistry. The new City and Guilds course in the 'Science and Technology of Paper and Board Making' was the only one of its type in the country, and attracted students from far and wide, as well as from the local paper mills with which the College had worked for so long. So welcome was the new course to the Scottish paper industry that it contributed £2,500 towards the purchase of equipment to be used in the teaching. The course was originally run in the main Schoolhill building, but was later transferred to St. Andrew Street (in 1972). The School of Chemistry was provided with further new facilities

Figure 4.8 : The Blackfriars Street building that was opened in 1960

in 1962, when a Radiochemistry Laboratory was set up in its premises at Schoolhill. This made use of radio isotopes provided by the United Kingdom Atomic Energy Authority's Harwell facility, and enabled students of Chemistry and Pharmacy to gain hands-on experience of the many applications of such isotopes in their respective fields. The facility was again subsequently transferred to St. Andrew Street.

Another highly significant event for the future of Robert Gordon's Technical College took place at around this time, with the publication, in 1961, of the Government White Paper '*Better Opportunities in Technical Education*'. This clearly mapped out the future direction of such education in Britain, its overall aims being to build on the strengths of the existing National Certificate and Diploma systems, and help establish an even-more-effective system that would enable people to become qualified as technicians through a wide range of courses designed to meet the needs of modern industry. Its four main objectives were: to broaden the students' education and provide maximum continuity between school and technical college; to adapt the system more closely to the specific requirements of industry; to increase the variety of courses available; and to reduce substantially the wastage resulting from the failure of many students to complete their courses successfully. One of its main effects on the Technical College was to bring about the gradual transfer of its O.N.C., and, in a few cases, of its H.N.C. courses, to Local Education Authority Colleges, in accordance with the new Scottish Education Department policy that Central Institutions should ultimately concentrate on providing full-time courses.

Under the Directorship of Dr. West, the facilities available to the School of Navigation were also significantly expanded. During the 1954-55 session, a new boathouse was built for the School on the south bank of the River Dee. This provided a wide range of facilities that had previously been lacking, including rowing, sailing and power boats along with equipment and materials for teaching all branches of practical seamanship. Another important new facility was the Radar Station at the Bridge of Don that was opened in 1961; this proved to be of great value in the training of marine students of all types. In the same year, the School was provided with a sea-going training schooner in the form of a converted Zulu-type fishing boat. This sailed under the name of 'Radium of Don', and enabled cadets to acquire a type of sea-going experience that proved invaluable for their future employment prospects. The original training schooner was eventually replaced by the 'Robert Gordon' - a two-masted stay-sail schooner that was specially built for the School in 1968. This magnificent vessel, which is shown in Figure 4.9, enabled the sea-going training work of the School to be greatly extended.

The ultimate fate of the 'Robert Gordon' might be of interest to readers. In 1978, she was transferred to the School of Mechanical and Offshore Engineering, when the School of Navigation moved to Aberdeen Technical College (see Chapter 7), and was thereafter used as a floating test bed for offshore equipment. Unfortunately, she had to be sold a few years later because of her extremely high running costs. Dr. Peter Clarke, Principal at the time, recalls what happened next.

'The Scottish Office had handled the sale - to an entrepreneur who wished to take holiday bookings in the Mediterranean. The next thing we heard was that she had run aground off the east coast of England, and that coastguards had discovered drugs aboard. It was excellent PR for us - all the more so because she took the first opportunity to run aground when she reached home waters, and was thus rescued from life as a drug-runner!'

Other significant developments during the latter part of Dr. West's highly-productive Directorship included the construction of a completely new building for the School of Domestic Science at Kepplestone, on the corner of Queen's Road and Anderson Drive.The reasons for the move, the rationale for the design of the building, and the way in which the School evolved after its move to Kepplestone in 1963 will be described in some detail in the next chapter. This move also eased the pressure on accommodation at the Schoolhill site by enabling the School of Navigation to move into the vacated King Street premises in 1964.

Figure 4.9 : The School of Navigation's training schooner 'Robert Gordon'

Dr West retired on 31st December, 1964. During his twenty years as Director of Robert Gordon's Technical College, he had played a major role in enabling the work of the College to expand, initiating many innovations from which his successors were able to benefit. He had also greatly extended the accommodation available to the College, forged strong and lasting links with local industry, and improved the relationship between the College and its students - both current and past. It could indeed be said of him that he 'builded better than he knew'. He was replaced by Dr. Gerald Bulmer, who took up office on January 1st, 1965 and brought the institution into yet another new era - that of Robert Gordon's Institute of Technology and the C.N.A.A. How this happened will be described in Section 3 of the book.

Chapter 5 : The incorporation of the School of Domestic Economy

THE ORIGINS OF THE SCHOOL OF DOMESTIC ECONOMY

As we saw in Chapter 4, the School of Domestic Economy that had hitherto been run by Aberdeen Education Trust became an integral part of the new Robert Gordon's Technical College when the latter was formally constituted in 1910. This was a major event in the history of the institution that was eventually to become the Robert Gordon University, bringing in a whole new area of activity that has (albeit with many changes) remained a significant aspect of its work right through to the present day. In this chapter, we will take a detailed look at this important development, tracing the origins of Domestic Economy teaching in Aberdeen, showing how the original School of Domestic Economy was established, describing how it was brought into Robert Gordon's Technical College, and reviewing how the 'Do-School' (pronounced *Dough*-School) subsequently evolved.

The teaching of Domestic Economy in Aberdeen began in a number of charitable institutions that were established at various times during the 19th century. One of the first was the Girls' Hospital that was set up in the Gallowgate in 1829. Here, the inmates were trained in a wide range of domestic activities, including 'washing the linen, sweeping and cleaning the house, cooking and preparing the victuals', as well as receiving instruction in 'knitting, sewing and other needlework'. The older Boys' Hospital, which had developed from the Poor's Hospital that had been founded in 1739, amalgamated with the Girls' Hospital in 1852, and, in 1871, the combined Boys' and Girls' Hospital moved into a new building in King Street.

Another foundation of a similar type was the Hospital for Orphan and Destitute Female Children that was established in Huntly Street in 1850. Here, 'friendless and destitute orphans' from Aberdeen and the surrounding area were accommodated between the ages of 6 and 14-16. They were maintained, and 'properly instructed in all kinds of female housework, including plain cooking', so that they became 'qualified for earning their livelihood as domestic servants, or by any other industrious and respectable employment'. On leaving the Hospital, they were all placed with 'respectable families'. Other institutions, such as Sherriff Watson's Female School of Industry, provided similar training, its aims being to help girls to become 'useful and obedient servants, dutiful wives and judicious mothers'; feminism was clearly not active at the time!

The best known - and most influential - institution of this type was undoubtedly the Female Orphan Asylum, which was founded by Mary Emslie (see Figure 5.1). The daughter of an Aberdeen wine merchant, she was born in 1780, married James Emslie, a merchant in Gibraltar, and was widowed in 1833. In 1839, she purchased 'nearly two imperial acres of ground in Albyn Place and erected a handsome building thereon' for the institution that she also handsomely endowed. Her Asylum opened on 19th

November, 1840, and took in orphans from 'parishes in the city and surrounding area'. Her stated aim in founding the Asylum was 'to bestow a portion of the abundance which God has placed in my hands, as a supply for the wants of those little beings who are the objects of his particular care and fatherly promises'.

Figure 5.1 : Mary Emslie, founder of Aberdeen's Female Orphan Asylum

The Female Orphan Asylum provided its 46 inmates with a 'general education' as well as instruction in various aspects of Domestic Economy. It was staffed by a Matron, two Teachers and two 'Pupil Teachers'. The daily timetable included 6 hours of lessons and practical instruction in 'needlework and knitting with making and mending of clothes and linen and the business of the house and kitchen', plus 4 or 5 hours of recreation. Work might be 'taken in', but there was a provision that 'the educational work and leisure time of the girls should not be sacrificed'. Mary Emslie maintained an active interest in the Asylum for many years. She died in 1868, and is commemorated by a memorial plaque to her and her husband that was subsequently mounted on the wall of the School of Domestic Economy at King Street. It can be seen there to this day, showing that her work as the founder of the main institution from which the School developed has not been forgotten.

THE ESTABLISHMENT OF ABERDEEN SCHOOL OF DOMESTIC ECONOMY

As we saw in Chapter 2, the climate of opinion regarding the desirability of educating children in residential charitable hospitals such as Robert Gordon's Hospital and the Female Orphan Asylum had undergone a considerable change by the latter part of the 19th century. When they were founded, they were regarded as 'agencies for good'; by the time Mary Emslie died in 1868, however, they were being denounced as 'monastic institutions' and even 'hotbeds of evils'! Whether or not this was the case, there was certainly a strong feeling that such institutions were ripe for reform. As we have seen, one result of this was the conversion of Robert Gordon's Hospital into Robert Gordon's College in 1881. Another was the amalgamation of a number of other charitable institutions, including the Female Orphan Asylum and the Hospitals in King Street and Huntly Street, under the auspices of the Aberdeen Educational Trust, which was formed in 1888. Like those of Robert Gordon's College, the Trust's Governors represented a wide range of local interests - the Town Council, the School Board, Aberdeen University and the Churches - and included one particularly notable figure. This was William Milligan, a Professor of Biblical Criticism, a former Moderator of the General Assembly of the Church of Scotland, and an active participant in local affairs. He was to play a key role in formulating and implementing the Trust's future policy.

The Trust had its first meeting in January 1889, and soon came up with a radical plan for the reorganisation of the various charitable bodies for which it had been made responsible. This involved closing many of the institutions immediately, and concentrating its activities in the King Street building of the Boys' and Girls' Hospital. This would become Aberdeen's School of Domestic Economy. The Albyn Place building of the Female Orphan Asylum would be kept open on a temporary basis, but would eventually be disposed of. (In 1891, it was sold to Aberdeen School Board for £4,500, to become the High School for Girls - now Harlaw Academy.) Since it soon became apparent that the existing buildings on the King Street site were, as they stood, insufficient for the Trust's requirements for its new School of Domestic Economy, it was decided to carry out fairly extensive modifications in order to provide, *inter alia*, a demonstration room, a practice kitchen and a laundry. Further extensions were carried out in 1903 and in 1909, prior to the School being incorporated in the new Robert Gordon's Technical College. The frontage of the building is shown in Figure 5.2

William Milligan played a prominent role in the planning of the new School of Domestic Economy, making visits to London, Glasgow and Edinburgh in connection with this. An early decision was that the School's main purpose would be 'to train girls for the duties of their own future homes and families' rather than prepare them for careers in domestic service. As the Chairman of the Trust said at the official opening of the School on 7th October, 1891:

'The daughter of many a rich professional man leaves her costly boarding school no better fitted for her life's work in regard to the science of domestic economy than is the millworker's child; both are disgracefully ignorant of what they ought to know. The one who gets a house and costly servants, knows not whether her work is well or ill done; the other can often do nothing, not even boil a potato or make her husband's porridge. Good Mrs. Emslie has every way the credit of creating the Girls' Home and School of Domestic Economy. Her own institution and its conduct has largely influenced the creation of the scheme.'

Figure 5.2 : The School of Domestic Economy building at King Street

It is reported that the new School was opened 'with a flourish, and including a brass band!' Its first Head (or Lady Superintendent, as the post was initially designated) was Miss Helen Johnston.

Although enrolments for the new School were slow at first, they soon picked up as its reputation grew. It also very quickly extended its original brief by becoming involved in the education of teachers of Cookery and other aspects of Domestic Economy. In 1892, the School's Cookery Diploma was recognised by the (then) Scotch Education Department for this purpose, and, by 1894, students from both of Aberdeen's teacher-training colleges were attending classes at the School. (These had been set up during the mid-1870's in order to meet the increased need for teachers that had resulted from the 1870 Education Act and the 1872 Education (Scotland) Act, which, as we saw in Chapter 2, brought about the establishment of Elementary Schools throughout the country. One was run by the Church of Scotland and the other by the Free Church.) Indeed, the training of teachers was soon to become one the School's main activities, as is clear from the 1896-97 Prospectus, which listed its work as:

- The training of pupils to become Teachers of Cookery.
- The training of Elementary School Teachers, Students in Normal College, and others to be Teachers of Cookery in Elementary Schools.
- Provision of instruction in high-class, plain and household cookery.
- Provision of instruction in dressmaking for teachers and others.
- Provision of instruction in laundry work for teachers and others.

This dual role for the School - provision of training both for teachers of Domestic Economy and for the housewives of the future - continued for the remainder of the 19th century and during the first six years of the 20th century. In 1906, however, the School Governors decided to 'discontinue the training of intending teachers of cookery and laundrywork' because of a 'changed official policy towards the teacher-training colleges'. For a time, those aspects of its activities variously described as the 'Cookery School' or 'Training School' closed down, but the work of the School of Domestic Economy continued for other students, including the Foundationers of the Girls' Home. A report by Helen Johnston in 1907 described their busy routine of work, including providing help with public demonstrations of cookery and other activities, and 'occasional music and a happy evening'.

THE TRANSFER TO ROBERT GORDON'S TECHNICAL COLLEGE

The events that led to the transformation of the adult-education branch of Robert Gordon's College into Robert Gordon's Technical College in 1910 have already been described in detail in Chapter 4. As we saw, one of the provisions of the 1909 Provisional Order that set up the new College was the placing of Aberdeen's School of Domestic Economy, together with all its grounds, buildings and facilities, under the jurisdiction of the Governors of Robert Gordon's Colleges. Its name was also changed to the School of Domestic Science - one of the three Schools of which the new Technical College was initially composed (see Chapter 4).

As soon as the Governors took over responsibility for the School of Domestic Science, they took stock of the situation and began to plan for the future. As we have seen, the School had discontinued its work in respect of the training of teachers in 1906. It was currently running day classes in high-class, household and plain (or artisan) cookery, in dressmaking and laundry work, and in 'housewifery' - a subject that included first-aid, needlework, household-management and book-keeping. Students included 30 'Trust Foundationers', who were trained for domestic service, and some 20 girls from the 'Congested Districts Home' in Willowbank House, who were instructed in domestic economy in order to enable them 'to fill superior situations'. The fact that the School was no longer training teachers was causing a considerable amount of local concern, however, and, in June, 1910, the Principal of the Technical College, Charles Stewart wrote to the Domestic Science Committee pointing out that 'the award of the Diploma' was 'a matter of real importance', since students now 'had to go to Glasgow, Edinburgh or London for teaching diplomas'.

Helen Johnston retired in September,1910, and was replaced as Lady Superintendent by Miss Mary A. Smith, who had been educated in Liverpool (at the Liverpool School of Cookery) and in Switzerland. She had previously worked in several parts of England, latterly as Principal of the Wiltshire Training School of Cookery and Domestic Economy. Under her leadership, the training of teachers was quickly restored, and the portfolio of courses run by the School soon assumed a pattern which was to be broadly maintained for many decades:

- A two-year 'Group I' course for 'intending teachers', covering cookery, laundrywork, housekeeping, chemistry, physiology and hygiene.
- A two-year 'Group II' course, also for future teachers, covering needlework, dressmaking, and millinery.
- A one-year 'housewives' course', for potential housekeepers, matrons and house mistresses.

Professional teacher training was now organised by the Aberdeen Provincial Committee, which had taken over responsibility for such training from the two church colleges mentioned above. At the time, teaching practice was supervised by the staff of the School, being conducted both within the School at King Street and in various Board Schools. Figures 5.3 and 5.4 show typical classes during this period - a cookery demonstration and a dressmaking class. Note the uniforms that were worn by both students and staff at the time!

In order to accommodate the increased amount of teaching and new specialist classes that the above changes required, the Governors decided to carry out further major extensions of the buildings at King Street. Fortunately, these were commissioned fairly quickly, and were completed before the events described in Chapter 4 brought the other building projects being planned by the Governors to a halt. One of the extensions involved the construction of a completely new block to the east of the main building. At the opening ceremony in 1912, Lord Provost Adam Maitland, President of the Board of Governors, stated that the construction of the new building was 'the first significant step in the life of the new Technical College'. He went on to observe that 'there is no department of education that is looked on with more respect and sympathy than a thorough training in all those matters that pertain to the comfort and consequent happiness of the home, not more indeed of the poor than of the rich'. This augured well for the future of the School under its new Governors.

THE SUBSEQUENT DEVELOPMENT OF THE 'DO-SCHOOL'

Like the rest of the Technical College, the School of Domestic Science had its normal work disrupted by the onset of the First World War. Classes continued as usual, but the School also had to make its contribution to the war effort, running courses for army cooks and providing public demonstrations of 'economical cookery' such as how to prepare 'stoved potatoes and skirlie'. Staff of the School also carried out research into such matters as the nutritional value of locally-caught fish. The introduction of food rationing later in the war resulted in the School becoming even more involved in the life of the citizens of Aberdeen, providing classes in 'Economical Cookery for Housewives' for a fee of one shilling. It is recorded that the imposition of this fee caused one indignant 'east-end housewife' to write to the press complaining about the fee and the difficulties of the 'Urquhart Road ladies' who had children. A tart reply from one of the 'select West-end ladies' referred to munition workers who could afford the 'movies' - and also presumably, the classes at King

Street! After the end of the War, the School provided courses for disabled ex-servicemen and war widows, and also ran courses in 'invalid cookery' for nurses from local hospitals.

Mary Smith resigned as Lady Superintendent in 1916, and was replaced by Miss Beatrice Marshall, who had been Vice-Principal of the National Society's School at Berridge House in London. It is recorded that her appointment 'unfortunately caused a dispute in the Governing Body, with attendant newspaper publicity'. This was probably due to concerns that staff were increasingly being brought in from outside the area at the expense of local people. Indeed, in 1921, another dispute in the Governing Body about a staff appointment led to what the local newspaper headline described as an 'Unprecedented Scene at Gordon's College'. It was said that there were no Aberdonians on the staff of the School at the time, and that 'the citadel was being strengthened by the importation of alien teachers'!

Figure 5.3 : A cookery demonstration in the School of Domestic Science (1913)

The 1920's were a period of consolidation for the School. A new 'Institutional Housekeeping' course was started in 1921, but attracted an initial intake of only eight students, so 'no additional teaching staff were provided'. The work that had to be carried out by the students at this time was described as 'very hard - starching, polishing, scrubbing : specimens to sew, flat-irons to heat'. Those students who intended to become teachers moved on to the new College of Education that had been opened in St. Andrew Street, and carried out their teaching practice in local schools. One former student who was interviewed in connection with the history of the School that was produced by staff during the late 1970's (see Appendix D for details) recalled a heated dispute between the class teacher and a visiting inspector during one of her practice placements - about the best way to cook a 'clootie dumpling'! The writer Erik Linklater lectured in the School

Figure 5.4 : A dressmaking class in the School of Domestic Science (1913)

for a short period during the 1920's, and later commented on the students thus:

'They were for the most part plain and friendly creatures, country born, who for the two years of their training were crammed like Strasbourg geese with all manner of instruction from domestic economy to freehand drawing, from psychology to eurhythmics and the history of European thought'.

It was, incidentally, also at about this time that the School became generally known to Aberdonians as the 'Do-School'. The students, apparently, referred to it as 'The Tec', but everyone else called it the 'Do-School', and it was this name that stuck.

Beatrice Marshall resigned in June 1926, and was replaced by Miss Charlotte L. Dunnett at the start of 1927. She had been educated in Glasgow, Edinburgh and London, and had taught in London, and at teacher-training colleges in Preston and Bangor. More recently, she had been the Senior Cookery Lecturer in the Glasgow College. With her appointment, the term 'Lady Superintendent' was discontinued, and Miss Dunnett became the first Head of the School of Domestic Science. She held the post until her premature death in 1933, when she was replaced by Miss Annette G. Kelly, who had also been educated at Glasgow College, and had had several years experience of teaching in the Northern Counties College in Newcastle. She was to hold the post for the next 27 years, during which she was to bring about many changes in the work of the School.

One of the developments that took place during the Kelly era was the build up of work in the education of dieticians, thus laying the foundations for what was eventually to become a separate School of Nutritional Science. In January 1934, a request by the Professor of Medicine at Aberdeen University that experimental work on the diets of anaemic women should be carried out at the School was approved by the Governors. The results of this and other experiments on nutrition were published in the *'British Medical Journal'* and elsewhere, and made a significant contribution to the development of the growing field of dietetics. Indeed, the Aberdeen work on anaemia was mentioned in several successive editions of one of the standard textbooks on the subject - *'Human Nutrition and Dietetics'*, by Sir Stanley Davidson and associates. This is the earliest recorded case of top-quality collaborative research being carried out in Robert Gordon's Technical College.

Another important development during this period was the introduction of a new 'Group III' course. This covered all the subjects that had been included in the Group I and Group II Diplomas described in the previous section except millinery, and lasted for three years rather than two. The first small cohort of students began the new Group III course in 1935, eventually qualifying as fully-trained Domestic Science Teachers in 1939. Other teaching being carried out at this time included courses for cooks, advanced cooks, ships' cooks, ladies' maids, housekeepers and housewives, and in laundry work, millinery, dressmaking, and upholstery; there were also single-subject courses in such things as cleaning silver and simple household repairs. It is interesting to note that, in terms of numbers of day students, the School was by far the largest in the Technical College at the time. In 1934-35, for example, its total enrolments were 137 full-time students and 304 part-time students. It had no evening students, however, having discontinued its evening-class programmes at the end of the 1925-26 session; these were transferred to the local Education Authorities.

The onset of the Second World War in 1939 again had an immediate impact on the work of the School, with half-time working being introduced for the first few weeks. Thereafter, the School contributed to the war effort in much the same ways as it had done in the earlier conflict - providing advice and guidance on nutrition, including the careful use of 'real eggs', running special courses and classes, sending its students out to cook at voluntary agricultural camps, and so on. As we saw in the last chapter, it also sent a party of its students to London to cook for bomb-repair workers. It is recorded that a bomb fell on the grounds of the School in September 1940, causing favourable comments to be made on the 'sturdy characteristics of granite' as a building material. Sacrifices made as a result of the war included the dropping of the 'High-Class Cookery' course, presumably because it was rather difficult to carry out cooking of this type on war-time rations! Figure 5.5 shows a Group 1 Diploma cookery class in 1944.

In the years following the war, the teaching of Domestic Science in schools assumed even greater importance, partly as a result of the Education Acts of 1944-45, which, among other things, raised the school leaving age to 15 and, for the very first time, provided secondary education for all. Large numbers of additional Domestic Science teachers were therefore required, and the School made a significant contribution to the training of these. New courses also continued to be introduced, including, in 1955-56, a day-release course for hotel chefs and another for apprentice hospital cooks - forerunners of the work that was later to be carried out in the School of Hotel and Institutional

Administration. In 1960, the long-serving Annette Kelly retired as Head of the School. She was replaced by Mrs. Mary H. Gillbe, who had worked in Manchester and had recently completed a post-graduate psychology course at Cambridge. She became the first Principal of the School of Domestic Science - and also the last, as we will see in the next section.

Figure 5.5 : A Group 1 Diploma cookery class in the School of Domestic Science in 1944

THE MOVE OF THE SCHOOL TO KEPPLESTONE

By the mid-1950's, the Governors were starting to think seriously about moving the School of Domestic Science away from the King Street site that it had occupied for so long. The main buildings were now almost 100 years old, required constant repair and redecoration, and were also becoming increasingly inadequate to cope with the changing requirements of the School. Indeed, the architects were talking about the need for a massive new extension costing over £180,000! In 1957, the Scottish Education Department wrote to the Governors suggesting that it would probably be more economical in the long run to erect a completely new building on another site. A year later, a suitable site was identified at Kepplestone, to the south-west of the junction of Queen's Road and Anderson Drive. Messrs. Allan, Ross and Allan were again engaged as project architects, and, after lengthy discussions with the staff of the School regarding their various specialist needs, came up with plans for the striking modern building shown in Figure 5.6. What the nearby inhabitants of Queen's Road thought of it is a matter of conjecture, but it was certainly very different from their own traditional granite houses!

Figure 5.6 : The new College of Domestic Science opened at Kepplestone in 1963 (note that this photograph was taken somewhat later, after the top floor had been extended to the south)

On account of the ground contours on the site, a considerable proportion of the accommodation, comprising working kitchens and other specialist areas, was built on a single-storey plan, parallel to and below the level of Queen's Road. The main multi-storey block was carried on pillars at the lower ground level, and commanded a magnificent view of the West End of Aberdeen. To the east of this was a large assembly and recreation hall, with a fully-equipped stage. The building also had a tiered demonstration lecture theatre capable of seating over 100 students. Both students and staff were extremely well catered for, with excellent common room and refectory facilities, together with space for playing fields to the south of the main buildings. These enabled football, rugby and hockey pitches to be provided, and did much to stimulate the growth of student sport in the College (see Figure 5.7). The new building was officially opened by the Countess of Airlie on 24th September, 1963. It is recorded that the students of the time had 'mixed feelings' about leaving the 'small and friendly community' that had existed at King Street for the 'somewhat overwhelming splendours' of the new building, with its ultra-modern equipment and furniture. Few tears were shed for the old floors and wooden tables, however, with the lino tiles, plastic surfaces and better lighting at Kepplestone being 'well received'. The original 'Do-School' building at King Street still stands, and is one of Aberdeen's architectural treasures. It was finally vacated by The Robert Gordon University in 1998, when the two Schools still housed there moved to the new Management Building at Garthdee (see Chapter 15).

Figure 5.7 : One of the sports for which facilities were provided at the new Kepplestone playing fields.

At the time of the move to Kepplestone, the School was re-named as the 'College of Domestic Science', to make it equivalent to Scotland's other two Domestic Science Colleges, in Edinburgh and Glasgow. This change of status did not last for long, however, the 'College' returning to being a mere 'School' during a major internal restructuring of what was now Robert Gordon's Institute of Technology that took place in 1968 (see Chapter 7). During this restructuring, the School of Domestic Science also lost a significant proportion of its staff, with its specialist teachers of Physics, Chemistry, Pharmacy and Business Studies being transferred to the existing Schools of Physics. Chemistry, Pharmacy and Business Management Studies. As we will see in Chapter 7, these transfers resulted from a policy decision to make all Schools 'import' specialist service teaching in these and other areas rather than employ their own teachers of these subjects.

In 1971, the Governors took advantage of the resignation of Mrs. Gillbe as Principal of the School to carry out an even more radical restructuring. By then, the work of the School had undergone very significant changes, with the nature of Home Economics (as Domestic Science was now being called) having changed almost beyond recognition, and Nutritional Science and Institutional Administration having emerged as major fields of study in their own right. It was therefore decided to split the School into three separate parts, forming new Schools of Home Economics, of Nutritional Science, and of Hotel and Institutional Administration, all occupying the same group of buildings at Kepplestone. These Schools themselves lasted for only seventeen years, however, being recombined to form a new School of Food and Consumer Studies during a further major restructuring of RGIT that took place in 1988 (see Chapters 7 and 13). This School was itself 'deconstructed' in 1999, with the Nutrition and Dietetics staff being transferred to the School of Health Sciences, and the rest of the School being moved into the Faculty of Management as the School of Hotel, Tourism and Retail Management (see Chapter 14). Later, in 2001, the Nutrition and Dietetics staff would undergo a further transfer - joining the staff of the School of Applied Sciences to become the new School of Life Sciences (again see Chapter 14). In the immortal words of the former baseball player, Yogi Berra, it was indeed 'a case of *déjà vu* all over again'!

Chapter 6 : Tom Scott Sutherland and the Garthdee bequest.

THE EARLY DEVELOPMENT OF ARCHITECTURAL EDUCATION IN ABERDEEN

With the benefit of hindsight, it is now apparent that the gift of his Garthdee estate to the Governors of Robert Gordon's Technical College that was made by Mr. Tom Scott Sutherland in 1955 was one of the most important events in the history of The Robert Gordon University. At the time, it enabled the Governors to build the new School of Architecture that they had been wanting for so long - the magnificent Scott Sutherland School of Architecture that was opened in 1957. Ten years later, it provided a site for the equally-magnificent new building into which Gray's School of Art moved in 1967. But most important of all, it paved the way for the large-scale transfers of the University's activities to Garthdee that took place in 1998 and 2002 - into superb new buildings built on land immediately adjacent to that so generously donated by Mr. Scott Sutherland. These recent events will be described in detail in Chapter 15, but, in the meantime, let us take a closer look at the origins of architectural education in Aberdeen, the foundation of the Scott Sutherland School of Architecture, and the subsequent relocation of Gray's School of Art at Garthdee.

As we saw in Chapter 3, the teaching of architecture in Aberdeen had its origins in the classes run during the 1840's by William Ramage, as part of the work of the Aberdeen Mechanics' Institution. The Institution remained responsible for the provision of classes in architecture and related subjects until 1885, when they were transferred to the newly-opened Gray's School of Art at Schoolhill, along with all the other work of its School of Art. During the next 15 years, this aspect of the new School's work expanded steadily, and, shortly after it became part of Robert Gordon's Technical College in 1910, it was decided to open a Department of Architecture within the School of Art and Crafts, as Gray's School of Art was for a time designated. The first Head of the new Department, Mr. T. Harold Hughes, was appointed in the same year. Figure 6.1 shows a class in the new Department of Architecture shortly after its opening.

By virtue of the high standard of the teaching provided and the 'fine accomplishments of the students', the Department's main course soon received official recognition by the Royal Institute of British Architects (RIBA). In 1914, students became eligible for exemption from the Intermediate Examination of the RIBA, and, eight years later, were granted exemption from the final examination. Up to that time, only two other institutions had received such recognition - the Architectural Association in London and the Liverpool University School - thus making Robert Gordon's Technical College one of the pioneers of professional architectural education in the UK. After modifying the original course under conditions approved by the Scottish Education Department, the Governors were subsequently given authority to award their own Diplomas to students who had successfully completed their studies. In 1932, their Diploma in

Architecture was recognised for registration purposes by the Architects' Registration Council of the United Kingdom. This meant that students who had attained the Diploma could go on to become fully-qualified and registered architects provided they had met the necessary practice requirements.

Figure 6.1 : An architecture class in the School of Arts and Crafts c1913

The work of the Department of Architecture continued to expand during the next twenty years, with a progressively-wider range of classes being conducted, and student numbers rising steadily. By the late 1940's and early 1950's, however, it was becoming increasingly apparent that the limited accommodation available within Gray's School of Art was totally inadequate for the current and future needs of the Department. The Governors therefore started to look at ways of moving the Department to more spacious accommodation elsewhere, but were unable to find anything suitable. Fortunately, their problem was solved in 1955, when Mr. Scott Sutherland (see Figure 6.2) presented them with an ideal site at Garthdee, together with a large mansion on to which the new School of Architecture could be built. Let us now look at the life of the remarkable man who made all this possible.

TOM SCOTT SUTHERLAND - HIS LIFE AND BEQUEST

Tom Scott Sutherland, who has been described by his biographer Diane Morgan as 'probably the greatest entrepreneur the North East has ever known', had humble beginnings. He was born in a two-roomed tenement flat at 84 Walker Road, Torry on 13th January, 1899, the eldest son of Robert Sutherland (then a deckhand on a trawler) and his wife Annie, who 'hailed from North Shields'. Two years later, a second child, Mary, was born, and the family moved to slightly-more-commodious accommodation at 63 Fonthill Road in Ferryhill - the first step on their journey to the West End. By 1903, Robert Sutherland had become a trawl skipper, and, in the same year, his second son - Robert - was born.

Figure 6.2 : Mr. Tom Scott Sutherland photographed during the mid-1950's

Next year, while on a holiday with his relatives in North Shields, young Tommy suffered an accident which eventually led to the loss of his left leg. He fell from an apple tree in his grandfather's garden and suffered a cracked hip, an injury that was 'aggravated by the ministrations of a quack bonesetter in Newcastle'. On his return to Aberdeen, he was bedridden, unable to walk, often in severe pain, and unable to attend school. He was eventually admitted to Aberdeen Royal Infirmary, where no fewer than twelve operations were carried out in a vain attempt to save the leg. This was finally amputated through the hip joint because of a diseased bone, something that was to prevent him from being fitted with an artificial limb in later life. Tommy had by now been disabled

91

for three years, and, before his final operation, had so wasted away that he was not expected to live. Once his diseased leg had finally been amputated, however, he began to stage a rapid recovery, moving around the ward on crutches within a few weeks, and being able to return to his home within two months. His will to survive and to overcome difficulties had already been firmly established.

Tommy's education started belatedly at Ferryhill School, where he was initially placed with a class of younger children, and was taunted and bullied by other pupils. He soon learned to look after himself, however, 'lashing out with his crutch' where necessary. In 1908, his family moved to a six-roomed terraced house in Burns Road, and he transferred to the 'more select' Ashley Road School. Five years later, at the age of 14, he was enrolled at Robert Gordon's College as a fee-paying pupil - something of a gamble on his father's part since, as a 'share fisherman', his income fluctuated wildly. Despite frequently getting into trouble because of his 'misdemeanours', Tommy prospered at Gordon's, 'displaying a determination to master subjects he detested, as well as shining at those he enjoyed, such as Greek'. He also developed into an outstanding sportsman, despite his disability. He played tennis, did well at cricket both as a batsman (with a runner) and a wicket-keeper, and eventually captained the School at swimming, at which he excelled. One of the highlights of his final year at Gordon's was leading his School to victory over the 'old enemy', Aberdeen Grammar School, in the annual Grammar v Gordon's Gala at the Beach Baths. Points were level when Tommy swam last in the relay with his team well behind, but he made up the necessary ground, won the relay, and won the competition for Gordon's.

Tommy left Robert Gordon's College in 1916. He had originally 'toyed with the idea of a career in medicine', but had found that his disability precluded this. On the advice of his Headmaster, Charles Stewart, he eventually decided to study Architecture at Robert Gordon's Technical College. He was good at art, and was also offered a bursary to cover the full six-year period of the course. With no fees to pay, he and his father decided that this was 'too good an opportunity to miss', so Tommy embarked on training for the profession in which he was to make so great a mark. This involved three years of full-time study in the Department of Architecture at Gray's, two years in an architect's office, and then a further year back at College before sitting the final RIBA exams. On starting his course, he became articled to J. A. Allan, who had offices in Union Terrace; his father paid a premium of £50 for this privilege. The next six years were a hectic period of hard work, fun, and lots of romances, since Tommy was 'a great romeo'. He was also 'bitten by the motorbike bug', acquiring the first of several such machines - a lightweight Enfield. By 1922, he became a fully-qualified architect.

Once he had qualified, Tom Scott Sutherland entered into partnership with Major G.D. McAndrew - and persuaded his father to guarantee a loan of £500 (a very substantial sum in those days) to pay for the furniture and 'tide him over until some clients came along'. Initially, business was slow, but he eventually had a stroke of luck involving work on new houses being built at Broomhill being put his way by a local lawyer, E. R. Lumsden. This work soon snowballed, and Tom then entered into a lucrative profit-sharing scheme with Mr. Lumsden. As his income from this soared, he decided that it was time to get rid of his (somewhat indolent) partner, Major McAndrew. This he did with the aid of a further £500 loan from the Clydesdale Bank, astounding the manager by saying that he wanted to use part of it to buy a car! But he was now in business on his own, 'the possessor of a four-figure overdraft and a second-hand, open-two-seater 8 h.p. Rover'. By the mid-twenties, however, his business was booming. He opened branch offices in Huntly and Fraserburgh, and, in 1926, moved his main Aberdeen office to a four-roomed suite above the Clydesdale Bank at 232 Union Street. He found the four flights of stairs 'no deterrent'! Thereafter, he never looked back.

The 1930's saw Tom Scott Sutherland at 'the top of his form as an entrepreneur'. It was a boom time for speculative builders in Aberdeen, with prime sites becoming available at low prices for houses, for offices, and for that 'hallmark of the era, the super-cinema'. Unlike most of his competitors, he had 'a gift of making the right contacts', initiating projects that he knew would make money for everyone involved. In 1931, he became involved in his first 'super-cinema' project, the Regent (later to become the Odeon) in Justice Mill Lane; this had seating for 1800 people, and cost £30,000 to build. Other, equally-magnificent cinemas were to follow, including the Majestic on Union Street and the Astoria at Kittybrewster. The latter was 'one of the wonders of the age' - complete with an illuminated Compton organ that rose from the darkness to entertain the audience between films. Mr. Harold Titherington came up from Blackpool to be the cinema's 'resident organist'. The new cinema was opened in 1934, and remained an important part of the Aberdeen entertainment scene for over 30 years (the author remembers it well!) Other cinemas followed, as well as many other major building projects and business ventures, and, by the early 1950's, Tom Scott Sutherland had become one of Aberdeen's best-known and most-respected architects, businessmen and public figures. He was elected to Aberdeen Town Council in 1934, and subsequently represented the Ruthrieston Ward for well over 20 years. He also became an extremely wealthy man, eventually leaving an estate of over £1 million, of which £800,000 went in death duties.

Nor were his activities limited to his work. He was, as we have seen, a keen sportsman, and he also loved travel and the 'good life'. In 1929, he had married 19-year-old Iris Webber 'after a whirlwind aquatic courtship in the sea off Blackpool'. Her parents had 'had their reservations', but, as Tom was able to tell them, he was, at the age of 30, earning over £5000 a year - a vast income for those times. They had an eventful and action-packed marriage, but she left him six years later to work in Newcastle with an actor whom she had met through Aberdeen's amateur dramatics set. Tom admitted that he had neglected Iris because he was 'so absorbed in business and amassing wealth'. They were divorced in 1941, and Iris subsequently remarried - not to her actor friend, but to a surgeon from overseas. Tom also eventually married again, to Georgina (Ina) Buchanan, the young and attractive secretary of the Governor of Hong Kong, whom he had met 'on a slow boat' from Hong Kong to Australia during a round-the-world trip. They were married in Edzell in July, 1950, and lived happily together until his death from cancer in 1963.

Tom and Ina Scott Sutherland lived in a number of homes during their 13 year marriage, including Garthdee House, a large granite mansion with over 20 acres of grounds looking south over the River Dee that they purchased in 1953 (see Figure 6.3). During their first winter there, however, they found the house cold, draughty and unfriendly, and realised that they had made a mistake. What followed is described in detail in Tom's highly-readable autobiography: *'Life on One Leg'*.

'Early in 1954, a chance meeting with Baillie John Hall, Chairman of the Governors of Robert Gordon's College, revealed that they were badly in need of a new School of Architecture. "You know, Tom", he said, "when Garthdee House came on the market we were after it. Trouble was we were tied to a price fixed by the District Valuer. And the furniture, although wonderful, was no use to us. In your case it was different. You bid a price we couldn't look at".

"What's all this leading to, John?" I asked quizzically.

"Well Tom, we are in a fix. Can't even find a suitable site for a temporary school. What about the three-acre field on your east boundary? Are you using it?"

"No. It's let out for cattle grazing at six quid an acre. My wife likes the rural scene. But if you want the field you can have it free". That evening I sat deep in thought. If I died, what use would Garthdee be to Ina?

Next morning, I telephoned John: "Listen John. About that three-acre field. Delay having a conveyance prepared. I've decided to convey the whole property to Gordon's, subject to a life interest. That should allow you to plan ahead".

**Figure 6.3 : Garthdee House, the mansion purchased by
Tom Scott Sutherland in 1953**

A year passed, during which time plans were prepared for an eight-classroom temporary school to cost about £8,000. Then one evening as Ina and I sat shivering over dinner in the large dining room, we reached a momentous decision. It seemed nonsensical that two people should live in a house big enough to accommodate fifty. We had had two happy years at Garthdee. We had organised garden fetes for charity, thrown dinner parties and housed numerous visitors from abroad. But the fact remained that only four rooms were in regular use. After a lengthy discussion, Ina agreed to my suggestion to find another home.

Again I rang John Hall:

"Scrap the plans for a temporary school. Tell your colleagues that they can have the whole damn shooting match, apart from the furniture, as soon as Ina and I can find another home". I could almost hear John gasp, as he grasped the significance of my offer.

*Five months elapsed before I found precisely what I wanted. It was in the neighbourhood in which I had lived and worked so long. For years, 27 Albyn Place had attracted my predatory eye for property. Diagonally opposite my office, and next door to my club, it proudly exhibited a granite column porch. Ina fell in love with it at first sight. Some time after we settled in, she remarked : "Tom, **before** we had a mansion .... **Now** we have a home. This is our fourth move in five years. Please don't let's move again."'*

In 1958, Tom Scott Sutherland had a portrait of himself painted by T. Gordon Moffat, Principal Art Master at Robert Gordon's College. In 1974, his widow, Ina Scott Sutherland, presented the portrait to the School of Architecture that he had founded back in the 1950's. She did so with these words:

'Tom Scott Sutherland was a man of brilliance and tenacity of purpose, fired with ambition and determination to succeed; a man of great foresight who knew where he was going. But it wasn't easy. Few people realise the bitter disappointments that confronted him on the ladder to success. He was a fair man, a man of great compassion and feeling for his fellow men and a champion of the underdog. Such a man I knew and am glad of it.'

THE ESTABLISHMENT OF THE SCOTT SUTHERLAND SCHOOL OF ARCHITECTURE

Tom Scott Sutherland not only made a gift of his entire Garthdee estate to the Governors of Robert Gordon's College; he also arranged for his own firm of architects, T. Scott Sutherland and Partners, to produce the plans for the new School at 'net cost' (ie for no fee). Nor did his benefactions cease there, since, on his death, he bequeathed a further sum of £50,000 to the Governors 'to be used exclusively for the School of Architecture'. This fund has been used for various purposes over the years, including financing student overseas visits and sponsoring guest lectures in the School; it is still in existence today, and continues to benefit the School.

Work on the conversion of Garthdee House into Robert Gordon's Technical College's new School of Architecture started in the autumn of 1955. The main contractors were the Chairman of the Governors' own firm of builders, Messrs.

Alexander Hall and Son, who carried out the work on a 'time and material' basis (ie at no profit). The new School, which is shown in Figure 6.4, was effectively a major extension of the original house, which dated back to the late 19th century, and had a particularly fine galleried entrance hall. Care was taken to preserve its character while making the best possible use of the facilities it afforded. The administrative, research and postgraduate accommodation was located in the actual house, together with the library, criticism rooms, small lecture rooms, and the student and staff common rooms. The original galleried entrance hall was retained as a key feature. The main studios and large teaching rooms were housed in a major new wing, extending to the east of the house along the existing terrace. The basement area was allocated to the Building Science section of the School, providing demonstration and research laboratories, a darkroom, and an extensive area for the display of materials and methods of building. Most of the furniture was specially designed to meet the specific requirements of the School, and to provide individual students with optimum working space. Particular attention was paid to the lighting levels in the different work areas.

Two ceremonies were held to mark the opening of the new School. The first took place on 29th March, 1957, and involved the unveiling of a bronze plaque by the Lord Provost of Aberdeen, Dr. George Stephen. This commemorated the generosity of the donor and the name by which the School was to be known - the 'Scott Sutherland School of Architecture'. The ceremony was followed by luncheon in the Caledonian Hotel. The second was held two months later, on 24th May, when the new School was officially opened by Lord Strathclyde, Minister of State at the Scottish Office. In his speech, he said that 'the world had grown smaller in the past 100 years', and that 'the young men and women who learned their craft in the School would be more likely to leave their mark not only on Aberdeen but on many places far removed from it. Councillor T. Scott Sutherland's generous gift, therefore, was not only to Aberdeen, but to Scotland'. He also thanked Councillor Scott Sutherland and Mr. Hall for their generosity in carrying out the design and construction work for no fee or profit. This had greatly reduced the cost of the conversion - from a possible £300,000 to an actual £95,000. He hoped that there were 'men and women of means and good will in other parts of Scotland who would be stimulated to emulate this piece of munificent imagination. There was plenty of room in Scotland for comparable developments'.

Figure 6.4 : The new School of Architecture at the time of its opening in 1957

THE SUBSEQUENT DEVELOPMENT OF THE SCHOOL

At the time of the opening of the new School of Architecture, its main course was still the Diploma in Architecture that enabled students to obtain full professional qualification as Registered Architects. This was now run in two modes - a six-year course involving two years of practice combined with part-time study followed by four years of full-time study, and a five-year full-time course. The School also ran a wide range of evening courses, the most important being National Certificate courses in Building, Scottish Certificate courses in Plumbing, and City and Guilds Certificate courses in the same subject; the Building courses had been in existence since the 1930's. No extended courses in Quantity Surveying had been run up to then, however, although short courses on various aspects of the subject had been organised on an *ad hoc* basis.

During the late 1950's and early 1960's, however, two major developments caused the traditional work pattern of the School to change significantly - and its overall workload to increase dramatically. The first was a decision made at the 1958 RIBA Architectural Educational Conference to raise the standard of entry to the architectural profession;

this would involve upgrading the academic standards of courses so that they were 'compatible with established university disciplines', and also ensuring that students had the opportunity 'to study in depth a subject in which they had shown particular aptitude' during the 'advanced' part of their courses. To meet these new educational requirements, Britain's Schools of Architecture were forced to move away from the traditional craft-based approach to architectural training and make their curricula 'more technological'. This meant that they needed more accommodation, including specialist laboratories, additional seminar and tutorial rooms, and additional library facilities - and, of course, more staff.

The second development was an increased demand for courses in Quantity Surveying (Building Economics). In 1962, the School started running its first extended course in this area on a part-time basis, appointing its first full-time lecturer in the subject at the same time. As a result of the high demand for this new course and pressure from the local and Scottish branches of the Royal Institute of Chartered Surveyors (RICS), a full-time 'sandwich' course in Quantity Surveying was subsequently initiated in 1966. In 1967, a Department of Building Economics was established within the School, under a Principal Lecturer. This ran two types of courses - full-time and part-time professional courses in Quantity Surveying, and part-time courses for Building, Surveying and Architectural Technicians leading to the award of an H.N.C. in Building.

These two developments, together with the build-up of post-graduate work and research within the School, placed an intolerable pressure on the existing accommodation at Garthdee. The Governors therefore obtained Scottish Education Department approval (and £400,000 of funding) to embark on a major extension programme at the Scott Sutherland School of Architecture in order to provide the new laboratories, workshops, classrooms and staff offices that were required. This was carried out in two phases. The first, which was completed in 1969, involved building a new large lecture theatre and an L-shaped block of laboratories and workshops to the south of the existing buildings. The second, which was completed in 1971, involved adding two further large blocks to the east of the 1957 and 1969 extensions, thus completing the hollow square of buildings that we see in Figure 6.5 While this work was being carried out, the Building Economics Department had to move temporarily to the old Aberdeen College of Education building at St. Andrew Street that was taken over by the Governors in 1968 (see Chapter 7), but moved back to Garthdee as soon as the extensions had been completed.

As we will see in Chapters 7 and 14, the work of the Scott Sutherland School of Architecture continued to develop and evolve during the RGIT and RGU years, converting its main course in Architecture into an unclassified CNAA Degree in 1970 and an Honours Degree in 1974. Similar developments in Quantity Surveying followed. These various CNAA degrees were, of course, all subsequently converted into RGU degrees when full university status was acquired in 1992. With regard to its organisational structure, the School has gone through a similar process of 'dis-integration' and subsequent 're-integration' to that experienced by the School of Domestic Science. In 1983, the Building Economics Department was detached from the rest of the School to form a new School of

Surveying, later to be 'rebranded' as the School of Construction, Property and Surveying. In 2001, however, the process was reversed, with the School of Construction, Property and Surveying rejoining the Scott Sutherland School of Architecture, and the new combined unit being renamed as the 'Scott Sutherland School'.

Figure 6.5 : An aerial view of the Scott Sutherland School of Architecture, showing the major extensions that were carried out between 1967 and 1971.

THE MOVE OF GRAY'S SCHOOL OF ART TO GARTHDEE

Brief mention has already been made of the move of Gray's School of Art to Garthdee in 1967. Although the move actually took place during the 'RGIT Years' to be described in the next section of the book, it was undoubtedly a direct result of Tom Scott Sutherland's Garthdee bequest, so we will take a closer look at it here. The move was a result of the enormous pressure on accommodation at Schoolhill that built up during the 1950's and 1960's, the causes of which have already been described in Chapter 4. In 1960, the Governors sought permission from the Scottish Education Department to help relieve the pressure by moving Gray's School of Art into a new building to be constructed to the west of the School of Architecture at Garthdee. Only a small part of the land gifted to the Governors by Tom Scott Sutherland in 1955 had been taken up by the School of Architecture, so there was plenty of room for the proposed new development. Once due permission and promise of funding had been received from the S.E.D., plans for the building were drawn up by Mr. Michael Shewan, a graduate of the School of Architecture, with the aid of 'expert advice and assistance from the officers of the Department and others'. It was influenced by the world-famous and highly-acclaimed Illinois Institute of Technology, which had been designed by Mies van der Rohe a decade earlier. After a lengthy period of discussion, building commenced in 1963.

Figure 6.6 : An aerial view of the new School of Art at Garthdee

The new School of Art was erected in a secluded area of the Garthdee estate sloping down to the river Dee, bounded and screened by well-developed deciduous trees - 'undoubtedly one of the loveliest sites of any Art School in the United Kingdom'. The building itself did full justice to the site, being a fine example of contemporary modern architecture incorporating many of the latest building techniques. It has been described by Gavin Ross, Vice Principal of RGIT and RGU from 1985 to 1997 and himself an architect, as 'the finest Miesian building in the UK', and 'the best mid-20th-century building in Aberdeen'. As can be seen in Figure 6.6, an aerial photograph of the new building, it took the form of a three-storey main block running from east to west, with two lower wings extending to the south from either end. The main block was originally intended to have only two floors, but was subsequently re-designed to take a third floor to increase the accommodation available. In order to maximise the amount of light entering the building, it was built round an externally-exposed steel skeleton supporting floor-to-ceiling windows 15 feet high. This method of construction also meant that all internal walls could be made non-load-bearing, thus enabling them to be easily re-positioned should the room configuration have to be changed in later years. The building incorporated all the facilities required by a modern Art School, including specialist workrooms and workshops of various types. It was officially opened on 27th February, 1967, by Sir William MacTaggart, President of the Royal Scottish Academy. Gray's School of Art has been there ever since, and its staff have no wish to move elsewhere. Everyone who visits the School can see why!

Section 3

Robert Gordon's Institute of Technology

(1965-1992)

Chapter 7 : Review of the RGIT years

ENTERING THE CNAA ERA UNDER DR. GERALD BULMER (1965 - 1970)

As we saw in Chapter 4, Dr. Gerald Bulmer took over from Dr. Alexander West as Director of Robert Gordon's Technical College at the start of 1965. This inaugurated yet another new phase in the history of the institution that was eventually to become The Robert Gordon University - the 27 'RGIT years' for which it would first be known as Robert Gordon's Institute of Technology, and then, very briefly, as The Robert Gordon Institute of Technology. It also marked the start of the 'CNAA era', during which RGIT progressively built up a wide-ranging portfolio of degree courses under the auspices of the newly-established Council for National Academic Awards, and prepared the way for the achievement of full university status in 1992. We will now review the evolution of the institution during this period, looking at how it developed under the stewardship of Dr. Bulmer between 1965 and 1970, under Dr. Peter Clarke from 1970 to 1985, and under Dr. David Kennedy from 1985 to 1992. As we will see, all three men played crucial roles in the transition from Technical College to University.

Dr. Bulmer (see Figure 7.1) came to Robert Gordon's Technical College from West Ham College of Technology in London, where he had been Principal since 1959. He had previously been Vice Principal at Bolton Technical College. On arriving in Aberdeen, he found his new College 'straining at its frontiers both academically and physically'. Academically, it was clear that it had gone about as far as it could as a Technical College, and needed to be prepared to play its part in the massive expansion of higher education that had been recommended in the 1963 *Robbins Report* (of which we will hear more later). Physically, it was once again feeling the need for greater 'lebensraum', and, since scope for expansion on the existing Schoolhill campus was strictly limited, it was clear that this would almost certainly have to be provided elsewhere. As we will see, both of these problems were well on the way to being resolved by the time Dr. Bulmer left Aberdeen five years later.

One of Dr. Bulmer's first acts as Director was to set up a proper academic committee structure, something the Technical College had hitherto lacked. This took the form of an overarching Technical College Council and three Academic Boards which reported directly to it. The Council comprised the Director and Deputy Director, the Secretary to the Governors, all Heads of major teaching departments, and three elected staff members - one from each of the Technical College's main academic divisions (Science and Technology; Art and Architecture; Domestic Science). The new Technical College Council, which was chaired by Dr. Bulmer himself, was formally constituted by the Governors in March, 1965. It is still in existence today as the Academic Council - a name that was adopted in 1969.

Later in 1965, the Governors agreed to change the name of the Technical College to Robert Gordon's Institute of Technology in order to reflect more accurately the nature and standard of the work that was then being carried out. It was felt that this would also provide a clear signal to the outside world that the institution had ceased to be part of the further-education (FE) sector, and was now firmly established as a major player in the Scottish higher-education (HE) sector. The name change took effect from 1st October, 1965. At the same time, the Governors took the opportunity to simplify their own committee structure, reducing the number of Standing Committees from eleven to six. These now comprised the Chairman's Committee and Finance Committee (which dealt both with Robert Gordon's College and with RGIT), the College Committee (which dealt only with the boys' School) and three other Committees dealing exclusively with the three academic divisions of RGIT (see previous paragraph).

Figure 7.1 : Dr. Gerald Bulmer, Director of Robert Gordon's Technical College and Robert Gordon's Institute of Technology from 1965 - 1970

During Dr. Bulmer's five-year period of office, a number of further changes were also made to the institution's organisational structure. These included the following:

• The division of the existing School of Mathematics and Physics into separate Schools in 1965. Dr. John D. Stewart (Head of the combined School) became Head of the new School of Mathematics, and Dr. Norman Langton was appointed Head of the new School of Physics.

• The appointment of a full-time Head of the Department of Business Management Studies located at King Street in 1965, and conversion of the Department into a School in 1968. (The events that led to the establishment of the School, and its subsequent development, are described in detail in Chapter 9).

• The establishment of a completely new School of Librarianship, also located at King Street, in 1967. (Its establishment and subsequent development are also described in detail in Chapter 9.)

• The establishment of a new School of Social Studies located at Schoolhill in 1968. (Its establishment and subsequent development are again described in detail in Chapter 9.)

• The division of the existing School of Engineering into separate Schools of Mechanical Engineering (with Mr. Harry Hampson as Head) and Electrical Engineering (with Dr. John C. Earls as Head) in 1968. (Note that the name of the latter was changed to the School of *Electronic and* Electrical Engineering in 1969, in recognition of the increasing importance of this aspect of its work.)

• The adoption in 1968 of the term 'School' to describe *all* major teaching units within the Institute. (Prior to then, the terms 'Department', 'School' and 'College' had all been used, something that had caused a certain amount of confusion!)

• Discontinuation of the practice whereby some Schools employed their own staff to carry out teaching in subjects outwith their main disciplinary area, and replacement of this with an extension of the existing 'service teaching' system. (This involved a certain amount of transfer of staff between Schools, but enabled a much more rational and cost-effective overall system to be developed.)

But by far the most important and far-reaching academic development that took place during Dr. Bulmer's Directorship was the establishment of the Council for National Academic Awards (CNAA), and the initiation of the conversion of virtually all of RGIT's advanced courses to CNAA degrees. Let us therefore look at this in some detail.

The formation of the CNAA had its roots in the report of the Committee of Inquiry that the Government had set up in 1961, under Lord Robbins, in order to look into the possible future of higher education in Britain (the *Robbins Report*). This was published in 1963, and, during the next few years, led to the most radical changes in British higher education that had taken place since the 19th Century (see Chapter 13). These included the conversion of the Colleges of Advanced Technology into Universities, the creation of several completely new Universities, the establishment of the Polytechnics, and the foundation of the CNAA. This was set up in order to enable the new Polytechnics and other non-university higher-education institutions (such as the Scottish Central Institutions) to run their own programmes leading to the award of CNAA-validated degrees. It was awarded its Royal Charter in 1964, and began accepting applications to run degrees in 1965. The process involved submitting highly-detailed documentation on the proposed degree programme and undergoing a rigorous validation event organised by the CNAA Secretariat. By the beginning of 1965-66, the CNAA had over 4000 students enrolled on 89 courses in the areas of business studies, science and technology.

Since it was clear that several of the existing courses that were being run in RGIT had the potential for being upgraded to CNAA degrees, early approaches were made to the new body. The first submission was made by the School of Pharmacy, which, at the time, was running a non-degree course preparing students for the Pharmaceutical Chemist Qualifying Examination of the Pharmaceutical Society of Great Britain. In 1967, an amended version of this was validated by the CNAA as a B.Sc. in Pharmacy (see Chapter 10 for details). In 1968, a second successful submission was made - by the School of Electrical Engineering, this time for an Honours B.Sc. in Electronic Engineering. And in 1969, the Schools of Chemistry and Physics made a further successful submission - for a linked suite of B.Sc. degrees in Physical Science, Chemistry and Physics. These were only the first of a whole range of undergraduate and postgraduate courses that would be validated by the CNAA during the 28 years of its operation. Indeed, by the time RGIT achieved University status in 1992, all of its Schools had been running CNAA degrees and diplomas for many years.

Let us now turn to the considerable easing of the pressure on accommodation that took place under the Directorship of Dr. Bulmer. We have already seen (in Chapter 6) how Gray's School of Art moved to a new building at Garthdee in 1966. This enabled most of its old building at Schoolhill to be taken over by senior management and administrative staff, thus liberating additional accommodation for use by the various Schools still located at RGIT's central campus. Even more accommodation became available to these Schools in 1968, when Aberdeen College of Education moved to its new campus at Hilton. Its old premises at St. Andrew Street (see Figure 7.2) were taken over by RGIT, subject to a lease-back of roughly one-fifth of the accommodation until 1972. Over half-a-million pounds was then spent on refurbishing this fine building - which is believed to be the third-largest granite building in Europe (after the Escorial complex near Madrid and Aberdeen University's Marischal College).

**Figure 7.2 : The St. Andrew Street building that RGIT took over
from Aberdeen College of Education in1968**

Acquisition of the St. Andrew Street building enabled Schoolhill's accommodation problems to be solved at a stroke - albeit temporarily. The Schools of Physics, Chemistry, Mathematics and Social Studies were able to move into commodious, custom-designed accommodation, incorporating a wide range of specialist laboratories and other teaching facilities. These included a state-of-the-art acoustics suite for the School of Physics, and a greatly-enlarged radiochemistry suite for the School of Chemistry. RGIT's Central Library was also able to move into much-more-extensive accommodation at St. Andrew Street, occupying 11,000 square feet - five times what had been available in its old premises at Blackfriars Street. To increase space for book racks and study carrels, an open mezzanine gallery was built along the whole length of the two main rooms, which originally housed the College of Education's gymnasia (see Figure 7.3). Truly, Mr. Sidney Latham (the Chief Librarian) and his colleagues felt that they had finally arrived in the 'promised land'!

**Figure 7.3 : One of the main rooms in RGIT's new Central Library
at St. Andrew Street, showing the mezzanine gallery**

Another important development on the accommodation front was the purchase in 1969 of the adjacent extensive shop and bakery at Schoolhill and Harriet Street that had hitherto been occupied by Mitchell and Muil. For a number of years, the Students' Representative Council had been pressing the Governors for better student amenities, including a new 'Union' building to replace the inadequate premises in Rubislaw Terrace that they then occupied. Acquisition of the new accommodation at Schoolhill enabled plans to be made to move the Students' Union into the handsome granite building to the east of the former Gray's School of Art, and, although these took some time to be implemented, the new Union was eventually opened in 1974. It was also decided to demolish the old bakery buildings on Harriet Street, behind the main Schoolhill building, and construct a large new teaching block, but this project was delayed for many years, mainly for economic reasons.

Dr Bulmer resigned from the post of Director of RGIT with effect from 30th March, 1970 in order to become Rector of Liverpool Polytechnic. During his five years in office, he had guided the new Institute of Technology into the 'CNAA era', greatly eased its accommodation problems - although these were soon to return - and increased its numbers of full-time students by almost 50%, to over 1500. (He had also provided the Institute with an exceptionally talented student - his daughter, Cathy. She was part of the first cohort of students to embark on the Institute's new CNAA degree in Electronic Engineering, graduating with First-Class Honours while still in her teens. The author had the privilege of teaching this remarkable young lady, whose academic achievements are still remembered by all who were around at the time.) Dr. Bulmer handed an extremely healthy and vigorous institution over to his successor, Dr. Peter Clarke, who took up his appointment on 1st September, 1970. During the intervening period, Dr. Mearns B. Watson, Head of the School of Chemistry, served as Acting Director.

DEVELOPING AND GROWING UNDER DR. PETER CLARKE (1970 - 1985)

Dr. Peter Clarke (see Figure 7.4) came to RGIT from Huddersfield College of Technology, where he had been Vice Principal since 1965 (this became Huddersfield Polytechnic in April, 1970, while he was serving out his notice before moving to Aberdeen). He had previously been Head of the Department of Chemistry and Biology at Nottingham Regional College of Technology, and had also had considerable industrial experience - three years with ICI, and six years as Chief Chemist with British Enka. The author still remembers the highly-impressive inaugural address that he gave in the MacRobert Hall shortly after his arrival, in which he set out his vision for the future of the Institute. He envisaged a considerable expansion of tertiary education during the 1970's, particularly in the vocational area, and exhorted all members of staff to help ensure that RGIT met this challenge by 'providing new and innovative courses that met the changing needs of industry and commerce.' In order to do so, it would be necessary for us 'to consult, to explore, to choose, to innovate and to lead'. He himself certainly provided an admirable role model on how to do so during the next 15 years.

One of Dr. Clarke's first acts as Director was to establish the Course Committee system advocated by the CNAA that was to serve RGIT and RGU so well until the late 1990's. Such a Committee was set up for each substantial existing or proposed course, membership comprising the Head(s) of the School(s) responsible for running the course or their representative(s), staff in charge of main sections of the work, one senior member of staff not involved in the course, and two student members chosen by the course students. In addition, Committees were established for Academic Planning, for Publicity and Advertising, and for the Institute's Libraries. All these new Committees reported to the Academic Council, and were designed 'to provide the broadly-based knowledge, experience and agreement necessary for the conduct of all academic work, and especially at degree and similar levels'. A year later, two further Committees were established - the Staff Development Committee and the Research and Higher Degrees Committee.

Figure 7.4 : Dr. Peter Clarke, Director of RGIT from 1970 - 1979 and Principal from 1979 - 1985

During the next two years, Dr. Clarke also made a number of further changes to the Institute's School structure. These included:

• The division of the School of Domestic Science into three separate Schools (Home Economics, Hotel and Institutional Administration and Nutritional Science) that was described at the end of Chapter 5. (The establishment and subsequent development of two of these - Hotel and Institutional Administration and Nutritional Science - are described in greater detail in Chapters 9 and 10.)

• The transfer of Aberdeen City's College of Health Visiting in Willowbank House (see Figure 7.5) to RGIT as the School of Health Visiting. (This transfer, and the subsequent development of the School, are described in greater detail in Chapter 10.)

• The establishment in 1972 of a new School of Speech Therapy at St. Andrew Street. (The establishment and subsequent demise of this School are also described in greater detail in Chapter 10.)

At around this time, a number of important changes were also made to the way in which the Institute's Academic Council and Governors were organised. In order to comply with new statutory requirements for all the Scottish Central Institutions, RGIT broadened the composition of its Academic Council to include greater numbers of elected members of staff and also co-opted members, including the President of the Student Association and one other student. The powers delegated by statute to the Academic Council were also revised and enhanced. These changes were all made during the 1972-73 session. During the following session, the Governors also established an Institute Committee to deal solely with RGIT affairs. For some time, it had been felt that RGIT and Robert Gordon's College should eventually have separate Governors, and the establishment of this new Committee was seen as the first step on the road to such separation, which eventually took place in 1981, as we will see later in this chapter.

Figure 7.5 : Willowbank House, the site of the College of Health Visiting that was transferred to RGIT from Aberdeen City in 1972

In February 1973, the Institute received its first CNAA quinquennial visit. This was a standard CNAA procedure for all its associated institutions, involving a comprehensive assessment of their work and resources - staff, buildings, equipment, academic and administrative organisation - in order to determine whether they would have continued approval to offer CNAA degrees and other courses over the next quinquennium. The resulting report from the CNAA Council granted such approval, and was 'generally encouraging to Governors, staff and students'. It also highlighted a number of specific areas that required 'further consideration' by the Institute, all of which were subsequently addressed by Dr. Clarke and his colleagues.

Following the CNAA visit, it was decided that the time was now ripe for the establishment of a Faculty system within RGIT, something that had been considered previously but not implemented. This was done towards the end of the 1973-74 session, the Institute's seventeen Schools being organised in four Faculties as shown below:

Faculty of Art and Architecture (Dean: Mr.Stanley Wilkinson)
- Gray's School of Art
- Scott Sutherland School of Architecture

Faculty of Arts (Dean: Mr.Ralph T. Hart)
- School of Business Management Studies
- School of Hotel and Institutional Administration
- School of Librarianship
- School of Social Studies

Faculty of Engineering (Dean: Dr. John C. Earls)
- School of Electronic and Electrical Engineering
- School of Mathematics
- School of Mechanical Engineering
- School of Navigation

Faculty of Sciences (Dean: Dr. Norman H. Langton)
- School of Chemistry
- School of Health Visiting
- School of Home Economics
- School of Nutritional Science
- School of Pharmacy
- School of Physics
- School of Speech Therapy

The four Deans, all of whom were a Head of School within their Faculty, were initially appointed for three years, with the possibility of renewal. In order to free time for the additional work involved, an Associate Head was appointed within each of their Schools for the duration of their tenure of office. It is interesting to note that the Deans received no extra remuneration in recognition of their increased duties and responsibilities, although the Associate Heads did; one can hardly imagine this happening today!

During the first half of the 1970's, Dr. Clarke also played a key role in a number of other important developments. First, he finally disentangled the teaching of engineering in RGIT from that in Aberdeen University. During the late 1960's, an agreement had been reached between the two institutions that the former would henceforth concentrate on Mechanical and Electrical Engineering and the latter on Civil Engineering, but joint teaching of engineering, and joint staff appointments, continued for some time thereafter. Dr. Clarke phased such arrangements out, so that RGIT could be totally responsible for its own engineering courses. He was also largely instrumental in ensuring that RGIT responded to the educational and training needs arising from the discovery of North Sea oil and the subsequent establishment of Aberdeen as the 'oil capital of Western Europe'. Just how he did so is described in detail in Chapter 8, which deals exclusively with the development of the offshore oil industry and its impact on the work of RGIT.

Dr. Clarke also set up two new Central Service Units within RGIT during this period. The first was the Educational Technology Unit (ETU), which was established in 1973, with the author as its Head. During the next 29 years, this Unit and its successors were to play a significant role in several major developments within RGIT and RGU, including the introduction of new teaching/learning methods, the embedding of the educational-technology-based 'systems approach' in course and curriculum design, the training of lecturers in educational methodology, and the refinement of the institution's academic quality systems. All of these developments will be described in detail later in the book. The ETU and its successors have also provided staff with a wide range of state-of-the-art audiovisual and media services, including slide making, photography, video production and (more recently) multimedia production and digital imaging.

The second new Unit was the Computer Services Unit (CSU), which was set up in 1974, with Mr. Ian Ellis as its Head. RGIT had had its own computer since 1966, when an Elliot 4100 'second-generation' mainframe machine (costing £33,330) was installed in the former Gray's School of Art building at Schoolhill. Since then, this had been run by the School of Mathematics, but Dr. Clarke felt that computing was now becoming sufficiently important for its development to be organised on an Institute-wide basis. As we will see later, the new Unit and its successors played a major role in facilitating the spread of computing and information technology to virtually all aspects of the work of RGIT and RGU that took place during the next 28 years.

The following summer, Mr. Charles Birnie, who had been Secretary to the Governors since 1955, retired. Until then, RGIT and Robert Gordon's College had been serviced by the same group of administrative staff, under Mr. Birnie, but, with his retiral, it was decided to introduce separate administrative arrangements for the two institutions. Mr. Christopher Anderson, who had been Mr. Birnie's deputy for many years, was appointed as the new Secretary to the Governors, and also became RGIT's first Chief Administrative Officer. At the same time, specialist administrative sections were introduced in order to provide more direct communication with, and support services for, the various Schools of the Institute. Four such sections were established, namely Finance (under Mr. George M. Pattison), Personnel (under Mr. Iain Kennedy), Student Services (under Mr. Raymond A. Leslie) and Buildings (under Mr. David Wilson).

By the time of the next CNAA quinquennial visit in March 1978, a number of further changes had taken place within RGIT. On the positive side, these included the introduction of professorial titles in 1975 - something that was becoming common within the English Polytechnics at the time. The Institute's first three Professors were John C. Earls, Head of the School of Electronic and Electrical Engineering, Norman H. Langton, Head of the School of Physics and Stanley Wilkinson, Head of the Scott Sutherland School of Architecture.

The Institute had now lost one of its 17 Schools, however, and was about to lose another. The first was the School of Navigation, which became part of Aberdeen Technical College in January 1978, as a result of the on-going Scottish Education Department policy of transferring non-degree work from the Central Institutions to local-authority colleges. The second was the School of Speech Therapy, which, despite its initial promise, never succeeded in attaining the critical mass needed to make it viable - partly due to a sharp fall in job opportunities for qualified speech therapists that took place from 1974 onwards. This led to the phasing out of the School's Diploma course over the next few years, and the closing down of the School itself at the end of the 1977-78 session (see Chapter 10 for more details).

The closure of the School of Speech Therapy was in fact a direct consequence of the major recession that began in Britain in 1974, as a result of the *Yom Kippur* War in the Middle East and the subsequent oil and energy crisis. This resulted in massive economies being made right across the UK public sector, with RGIT suffering severe restriction of the expenditure that was approved annually by the Scottish Education Department. This marked the start of the progressive increases in student/staff ratio (SSR) and other cuts that were imposed on the higher-education sector during the next two decades and beyond. As we will see later, these became particularly severe during the late 1980's and early 1990's.

In its report on the 1978 visit, the CNAA Council again granted RGIT on-going approval to run courses leading to its awards, but also identified a number of major issues that it felt should be addressed. It was, for example, concerned about the extremely wide range of courses being run at the time, several of which had low numbers of students, thus necessitating long contact hours on the part of the teaching staff. It was also unhappy with some aspects of RGIT's current Faculty structure and with the role of the Deans. Finally, it queried the effectiveness of the long-standing arrangement whereby RGIT and Robert Gordon's College still had the same Board of Governors. As we saw earlier, the Governors had in fact established a separate Institute Committee early in the 1970's, but it was suggested by the CNAA that the governance of the two institutions should now be completely separated - just as their administrative systems had been separated in 1975.

In response to the CNAA report, RGIT's Academic Council immediately set up a Working Party under the Chairmanship of Dr. (later Professor) Philip Mars, Head of the School of Electronic and Electrical Engineering. This was asked to review the Institute's academic organisation and make recommendations as to how the specific issues raised by the CNAA might be addressed. As a result, a number of significant changes were made to RGIT's Faculty and Academic Committee structures, and to the way in which the Institute's academic and academic-related work was organised. They included the following:

• The reduction of the number of Faculties from four to three, by the transfer of Gray's School of Art into the Faculty of Arts, and the transfer of the Scott Sutherland School of Architecture into the Faculty of Engineering - which was re-named the Faculty of Technology.

• A change from the system whereby the Deans were appointed, and had executive responsibilities in respect of the operation of their respective Faculties, to one in which they were elected by their colleagues, and had no executive powers; their main functions would now be to chair their Faculty Board and report to Academic Council on their Faculty's operation.

• The creation of a new full-time post of Vice Principal. (Until then, the post of 'Deputy Director' had been a purely honorary one, held by senior members of the academic staff on a rotating basis. It had, however, been decided to change the title of RGIT's Chief Executive from 'Director' to 'Principal', since this term was now in almost universal use throughout the HE sector - hence the use of the term 'Vice Principal' for the new post.)

• A radical revision of the Academic Council's system of Standing Committees and the way in which these operated, with all the new Committees having considerable delegated functions.

All these various changes were intended, *inter alia*, 'to improve effective participation by academic staff in the process of decision-making and implementation'. Apart from the change of Dr. Clarke's title from Director to Principal, which took place in June, 1979, they were all implemented at the start of the 1979-80 session. The three new elected Deans were Mr. (later Professor) Alastair F. Flattely (Faculty of Arts), Professor Norman H. Langton (Faculty of Science) and Mr. Maurice Hately (Faculty of Technology). Mr. Brian Gomes da Costa, Deputy Director of Luton College of Higher Education, was appointed as RGIT's first Vice Principal, taking up his post in January 1980.

The long-running task of separating the governance of RGIT from that of Robert Gordon's College was also made a priority as a result of the report on the 1978 CNAA visit. This took some time to implement, however, because it required changes to be made to the relevant legislation. Two statutory instruments were in fact required. The first of these, The 'City of Aberdeen Educational Endowments (Amendment) Scheme 1981', provided for the transfer of the Institute's properties to the new Institute Governing Body and for the winding up of the former Institute Committee. The second instrument, the 'Central Institutions (Scotland) Amendment Regulations 1981', established the new Governing Body for RGIT and also set out the statutory functions of this new Body. Both instruments came into operation on 22nd October 1981, although the Institute and the boys' College continued to make joint use of certain facilities (eg the MacRobert Hall), and still do so to this day. The following year, RGIT received a new Coat of Arms from the Lord Lyon King of Arms. This was based on the earlier Robert Gordon's Colleges crest that had been shared with the boys' College, with the addition of heraldic symbols representing technology, learning and commerce; it was subsequently further modified by the Lord Lyon, and this new version can be seen on the cover of this book.

By the end of the 1970's, steadily-rising student numbers were again placing great pressure on the Institute's accommodation. This was partly eased by the transfer of the School of Business Management Studies to a vacant block on the Hilton site of Aberdeen College of Education (see Figure 9.2) in 1980. This enabled a major refurbishment programme costing roughly £1 million to be started at King Street, which was subsequently re-named as the Merkland Site. The work took roughly two years to complete, providing commodious new accommodation for the School of Social Studies, which had hitherto been housed at St. Andrew Street, and for the School of Health Visiting, which had previously occupied Willowbank House. The splendid new facilities at Merkland included a state-of-the-art colour television studio, which was operated by the Educational Technology Unit. This was extensively used for teaching and staff training over the next 17 years (see Figure 7.6).

Two further changes were made to RGIT's academic structure in 1983. The first was the separation of the Building Economics Department from the rest of the Scott Sutherland School of Architecture to form a new School of Surveying (see Chapter 6). Mr. (later Professor) Seaton Baxter was appointed as Head of the new School, which continued to share accommodation at Garthdee with the School of Architecture. The second was the incorporation of the (very small) School of Health Visiting into the School of Social Studies, following the early retirement, on health grounds, of Miss Alice Hay, Head of the former. It was hoped that this would help facilitate the expansion of health education within RGIT, and, as we will see in Chapter 10, this did in fact happen. Indeed, during the remainder of the 1980's and early 1990's, health education became one of the two main growth areas within the Institute, along with management.

**Figure 7.6 : The new television studio at Merkland
being used to teach Communication Studies**

Since first becoming involved with the CNAA during the late 1960's, RGIT had had two quinquennial visits - in 1973 and 1978. Because of the large number of issues that the CNAA wanted to discuss during its third quinquennial visit - scheduled for 1983 - Dr. Clarke had suggested that it would be more effective and helpful to conduct this on a 'continuous-assessment' rather than a 'big-bang' basis. The review was therefore conducted in three stages, each involving a separate visit to RGIT. The Stage I visit took place in March 1983, and led to a report expressing 'general satisfaction' with the position reached and progress made. The Stage II visit took place in March 1984, and involved a detailed examination of the Institute's course validation, monitoring and review procedures; the subsequent report again expressed 'general approval', but identified a number of areas where further work required to be done. The Stage III visit was held in March 1985, and dealt with RGIT's staff development and research policies. The resulting report again raised a number of issues requiring further consideration. All of the matters raised by the CNAA were fully addressed during the next few years, as we will see later.

Another major development during the latter years of Dr. Clarke's Principalship was the proposal by Aberdeen University that a Committee of Inquiry should be set up 'to consider a union of the University with RGIT and Aberdeen College of Education'. Dr. Clarke recalls a representative of the local press telephoning him one evening to ask what he thought of the proposal, and being 'somewhat surprised' to hear the news, since the Principal of Aberdeen University had not discussed the idea with him before making it public! He and his colleagues had found the idea 'interesting', but had felt that it might not be in RGIT's best interests, since it would almost certainly have affected its primary role as a provider of vocational courses designed to meet the needs of industry, commerce and the professions. A full merger could also have led to a considerable increase in the cost of running RGIT's courses, since Aberdeen University's unit costs were very much higher (due to the fact that it was funded for research as well as for teaching). In the event, the Secretary of State for Scotland took the view that, before any serious discussions took place regarding the proposed merger, a national review of the whole of Scottish tertiary education should be carried out. He therefore established the Scottish Tertiary Education Advisory Council (STEAC) in 1984. This eventually concluded that Central Institutions such as RGIT were fulfilling a discrete and complementary role to the Universities, and could best continue to do so by remaining independent.

The 1984-85 session was also highly eventful in that it saw the replacement, by retiral or resignation, of all three members of RGIT's Senior Management Team. Mr. Christopher Anderson, the Institute Secretary, retired during the summer of 1984, and was replaced by Mr. David Caldwell, who moved to the Institute from Aberdeen University. Later in the session, Dr. Clarke took early retirement, demitting office at the end of April, 1985, and Mr. Brian Gomes da Costa, the Vice Principal, coincidentally tendered his resignation with effect from the same date in order to become Principal of Bath College of Higher Education. During his 15 years as Director and Principal, Dr. Clarke had seen all Schools of RGIT become firmly established in running CNAA degrees and other courses, the number of full-time students more than double to over 3000, the number of students undertaking specialist short courses rise to over 15,000 a year, and the reputation of the Institute increase considerably. He was replaced by Dr. David A. Kennedy, Vice Principal of Dundee Institute of Technology, who was to be the last Principal of RGIT and the first Principal and Vice-Chancellor of The Robert Gordon University. Mr. Gomes da Costa was subsequently replaced by Mr. Gavin T.N. Ross, a qualified architect and town planner with extensive experience both as a practitioner and as an educator, who had previously been Principal of Edinburgh College of Art. Both Dundee Institute of Technology and Edinburgh College of Art were Scottish Central Institutions of long standing.

REACHING MATURITY UNDER DR. DAVID KENNEDY (1985 - 1992)

Figure 7.7 : Dr. David Kennedy, Principal of RGIT from 1985-1992, and Principal and Vice-Chancellor of RGU from 1992-1997.

As we have seen, Dr. David Kennedy (see Figure 7.7) came to RGIT from Dundee College of Technology, where he had been Vice Principal since 1976. Before that, he had obtained numerous academic and professional qualifications in chemistry and biology, worked as a Research Fellow at Newcastle University, and taught in several Colleges of Further and Higher Education. He had also developed a clear vision of how institutions like RGIT should be run, together with the drive and determination to put his ideas into practice. Although some of the changes that had to be put through during the next six years did not prove popular in some quarters, he was convinced that they were absolutely necessary if RGIT was to survive in the increasingly competitive and demanding environment in which it had to operate from the mid-1980's onwards. The author is in no doubt that, without these changes, RGIT would have found it extremely difficult to cope with the progressively-more-draconian 'efficiency savings' that were imposed upon all Higher Education Institutions during the late 1980's and for most of the 1990's. Nor, in his opinion, would it have been able to achieve a university title in 1992.

Some of the challenges that Dr. Kennedy and his colleagues had to meet during his first years in office were as follows:

• The need to ensure the future viability of RGIT by developing a sound academic plan and effective organisational structure that would enable it to cope with the increasing competition for 'good students' that was expected to develop during the next ten years, when the number of 18-year-old school leavers would fall by roughly 25% according to demographic forecasts. Later, they would also have to cope with the unprecedented expansion of higher education that resulted from the 1987 Government White Paper : 'Higher Education - Meeting the Challenge'.

• The need to improve RGIT's financial position, which had been adversely affected by changes in the system of funding its academic staffing that had recently been made by the Scottish Education Department. These made it absolutely essential for the Institute to reduce its 'unit costs' (the overall cost of educating each student), and the pressure to do so later became even greater once RGIT was made responsible for apportioning its SED income across all headings of expenditure - including staff - in 1988. Until then, expenditure under each different heading had to be approved by the SED, and virement was only allowed in exceptional circumstances.

• The need to take full advantage of the CNAA's existing 'Partnership in Validation' policy and its new 'Accreditation' scheme, which presented institutions like RGIT with the opportunity to take on progressively greater delegated responsibility for validating their own courses - if they could demonstrate that they were capable of so doing without compromising on quality. Indeed, it would be no exaggeration to say that RGIT's entire future depended on gaining delegated power to validate and review its own courses under these two schemes. It could certainly never become a full university until it did so.

The ways in which these challenges were successfully met are described in detail in Chapter 13, so we will only deal very briefly with them here. In essence, they involved the following:

• Instigating the most radical and far-reaching review of RGIT's academic structure and associated committee structure that had ever been carried out, between 1986 and 1988. This produced a completely new Faculty system, in which the Deans had unprecedented executive powers, and also became members of RGIT's Senior Management Team, with the status of Assistant Principals. The four new Faculties that resulted from this review, and their constituent Schools, were as follows:

Faculty of Design (Dean : Professor Seaton Baxter)
- Scott Sutherland School of Architecture
- Gray's School of Art
- School of Surveying

Faculty of Health and Food (Dean : Professor Ian Nowell)
- School of Food and Consumer Studies
- School of Health and Social Work
- School of Pharmacy

Faculty of Management (Dean : Mr (later Professor) Peter W. McIntosh)
- Business School
- School of Librarianship and Information Studies
- School of Public Administration and Law

Faculty of Science and Technology (Dean ; Professor Frank McIntosh)
- School of Applied Sciences
- School of Computer and Mathematical Sciences
- School of Electronic and Electrical Engineering
- School of Mechanical and Offshore Engineering

• Carrying out an equally-radical revision of RGIT's overall management and administrative systems during the early 1990's. This involved the division of RGIT into twelve separate management areas, each with its own delegated budget controlled by the member of the Senior Management Team responsible for that area. Several new departmental managers were also appointed as a result of this review.

• Implementing a series of measures designed to reduce RGIT's unit costs and improve its overall financial position. These included the introduction of new staffing policies, changing the management system in the ways just described, and an expansion of income-generating activities of all types - including the running of full-cost courses, consultancy, externally-funded research, and the increased recruitment of overseas students.

• Enhancing and refining RGIT's academic quality-assurance and quality-control systems in order to meet the exacting standards required to attain CNAA- accredited status (which was achieved for taught courses in 1989 and for research degrees in 1991), and ensuring that this was subsequently retained through constant monitoring and improvement of the systems.

• Developing a much-more-detailed academic plan for the Institute than it had had hitherto, and standardisation of its course, assessment and other regulations through the development of appropriate documentation where this did not already exist.

Let us now end this chapter on the 'RGIT years' by looking briefly at some of the other important developments that took place between 1985 and 1992. One of the most satisfying was the final completion of the new building at Harriet Street that the Institute had been wanting to construct ever since it acquired the site from Mitchell and Muil in 1969. Although provisional plans for such a building were produced during the early 1970's, the project had to be put on 'indefinite hold' in 1972, due to lack of Government funding. Dr. Clarke made repeated attempts to secure the necessary SED backing during the next 12 years, but it was only in June 1984 that they agreed that work could start. Gibson Pacitti Associates were appointed as Architects for the project. The Clarke Building (as it was very fittingly named, after the man who had done so much to ensure that it was built) was due to become operational in time for the start of the 1986-87 session, but a serious fire in its top storey caused this to be put back for a full year. (Professor Frank McIntosh, Dean of the Faculty of Science and Technology at the time, remembers this event well, since he was not only wakened up in the middle of the night to be told the bad news, but also had to find alternative accommodation to teach the very substantial intake of new engineering students who were due to start using the new building in September 1986!). The Clarke Building, which is shown in Figure 7.8, was eventually opened by the Scottish Secretary, Malcolm Rifkind, on 29th September, 1987. It provided badly-needed new accommodation for the two Engineering Schools and the School of Pharmacy, as well as general teaching facilities.

Figure 7.8 : The new Clarke Building at Harriet Street

Another extremely important development on the 'estates front' during the late 1980's and early 1990's was the erection of several large blocks of student accommodation, in partnership with a private developer, at Woolmanhill - next to the St. Andrew Street building (see Figures 7.9 and 7.10). This greatly increased the total number of students who could be offered reasonably-priced accommodation by the Institute, and thus made it very much easier to recruit students from outwith the Aberdeen area and from overseas (systematic recruitment of overseas students had begun in 1986). As Gavin Ross subsequently observed, 'it enabled RGIT to enter the extraordinary period of growth that began in the late 1980's knowing that *all* first-year and overseas students could be guaranteed accommodation - something that was unique within the Central Institution sector at the time'. This undoubtedly 'contributed enormously to the rapid growth in student numbers that RGIT was able to sustain throughout this highly-important period', and thus 'made a very significant contribution to the eventual attainment of university status' (which depended, *inter alia*, on reaching the critical number of 4,000 full-time-equivalent students).

As we have seen, RGIT received three staged visits from the CNAA during the mid-1980's, visits that had a very strong influence on the Institute's subsequent development. Another extremely important visit took place in February 1988, when the Scottish Education Department carried out a major inspection covering all aspects of RGIT's operations. Although the subsequent report was, on the whole, 'very favourable', it raised a number of matters that the Institute required to address. Many of these were already well in hand by the time the report was published, and would be dealt with through the changes that were being made to RGIT's academic structure. Most of the others would be addressed during the subsequent revision of the Institute's management and administrative systems. All the issues raised had been fully addressed by the time RGIT applied for a university title in 1991.

Figure 7.9 : Some of the new student accommodation that became available at Woolmanhill during the late 1980's and early 1990's

Other important developments during the late 1980's and early 1990's included the following:

• The revision of the composition and terms of reference of the Board of Governors in order to comply with the 'Central Institutions (Scotland) Amendment Regulations 1988'; the changes were implemented at the start of 1989.

• The establishment of a 'Centre for Enterprise' in 1988, as a result of a successful bid for funding under the Government's 'Enterprise in Higher Education' initiative. As we will see in Chapter 11, the institution received roughly £1 million from this source between 1988 and 1993, when its 'Enterprise' programme made a very significant contribution to the dissemination of innovative teaching methods.

Figure 7.10 : One of the new student study-bedrooms at Woolmanhill

• The introduction of systematic training in tertiary-level teaching methods for lecturers in 1989, through a highly-innovative open-learning course run by the Educational Development Unit (as the Educational Technology Unit had been re-named). As we will again see in Chapter 11, this also made a major contribution to the general improvement of teaching quality throughout RGIT.

• The provision (in 1989) of foreign-language teaching, which had previously only been available to overseas students, for all interested staff and students, under the auspices of the European Commission's 'Erasmus' programme. This led to the development of a sizeable Modern Languages teaching unit within RGIT, first as part of the Educational Development Unit and then within the School of Information and Media. (See Chapter 9 for more details.)

• The steady expansion of Nursing education within the School of Health and Social Work during the late 1980's and early 1990's, eventually leading to the establishment of a separate Department of Nursing. (See Chapters 10 and 14 for detailed descriptions of these and subsequent developments in Nursing education.)

• The transfer of Grampian Health Board's Schools of Occupational Therapy, Physiotherapy and Radiography to RGIT in April, 1990, to form the Centre for Professions Allied to Medicine within the Faculty of Health and Food. (Again see Chapter 10 for a detailed account of this transfer and the subsequent development of the Centre.)

• The development of a new 'corporate image' for the Institute with the aid of an internationally-recognised, London-based firm of consultants (n & n). Among other things, this resulted in its name being changed from 'Robert Gordon's Institute of Technology' to 'The Robert Gordon Institute of Technology' in 1991 - somewhat to the bemusement of the Institute's staff and students. It also produced a new RGIT tie which, if nothing else, certainly enabled its wearers to make a brave fashion statement. It did, however, provide the institution with a comprehensive Corporate Identity Manual, and brought about some very important improvements that were subsequently widely copied by other institutions.

By far the most significant development during this period was the publication, in 1991, of yet another Government White Paper on the future of British Higher Education - 'Higher Education - A New Framework'. This announced the imminent abolition of the 'binary line' between the Universities and the Polytechnics, all of which would automatically be granted full university status in 1992. Since RGIT was already effectively a 'University' in all but name as a result of the developments that had taken place during the previous six years, Dr. Kennedy immediately sought clarification if its position. When he discovered that it was by no means certain that the Institute was entitled to automatic upgrading under the provisions of the White Paper, he organised a vigorous and highly-public campaign throughout Scotland and beyond to ensure that it would be so upgraded. As everyone knows, this campaign proved successful, and RGIT became The Robert Gordon University in the summer of 1992. Because of the importance of the complex sequence of events that led to the eventual achievement of a university title, a full chapter (Chapter 13) is devoted to them. Readers who cannot wait to find out what happened might like to 'skip forward' to this chapter now!

Chapter 8 : The impact of the offshore oil industry

THE DISCOVERY OF NORTH SEA OIL AND GAS

In this chapter, we will take a detailed look at one of the most important developments that took place during the 'RGIT years' - the discovery of North Sea oil and gas and the impact of the ensuing oil-related developments on the work of the Institute. As we will see, these not only had a considerable effect on RGIT's academic work, leading to the development of new courses and research programmes, but also brought in a large amount of consultancy, and enabled several highly-profitable commercial centres and units to be established. These included the Offshore Survival Centre, which eventually grew into the World's largest provider of safety training for offshore oil and gas workers. The discovery of North Sea oil also led to the development of RGIT's most successful educational game - the 'Bruce Oil Management Game' that was run as an annual competition between 1974 and 1980.

Interest in the North Sea as a possible source of oil and gas began during the late 1950's, after the fuel shortages caused by the 1956-57 Suez crisis brought home to the countries of Western Europe the dangers of continuing to be so heavily reliant on importing oil from the Middle East. Exploration could not begin, however, until the sea-bed mineral rights had been allocated to the countries bordering the North Sea. This was done in 1958, when the 'median line' system shown in Figure 8.1 was agreed by the various interested parties. As can be seen, Britain did rather well out of this, ending up with almost half of the total area. The UK sector was divided into large 'licence blocks' bounded by lines of latitude and longitude, with each licence block being subdivided into thirty smaller 'concessions', for which interested companies were subsequently invited to bid by the British Government.

Early developments took place in three main phases. The first was the discovery of an extensive natural-gas province in the southern part of the North Sea, stretching between England and the Netherlands. The first field was actually found onshore - at Groningen, in the northernmost part of the Netherlands, in 1959. This was followed by the discovery in 1966 of several major gas fields off the coast of East Anglia (see Figure 8.1). Gas from these fields started to be piped onshore in 1967, beginning the process by which Britain's entire gas industry eventually converted from coal gas to natural gas.

The second phase began in 1968, with the discovery of a major oil and gas province in the middle latitudes of the North Sea, halfway between Scotland and southern Scandinavia. Developments here included the 'Cod' gas-condensate field (discovered in 1968), the huge 'Ekofisk' oil and gas complex (discovered in 1969), the equally-huge 'Forties' oil field (discovered in 1970), and, in 1974, the 'Piper' oil field. As can be seen from Figure 8.1, the oil from most of these fields was brought to Britain by pipeline, with the 'Forties' pipeline coming ashore at Cruden Bay, just north of Aberdeen. Figure 8.2 shows one of the enormous production platforms from which the oil was pumped.

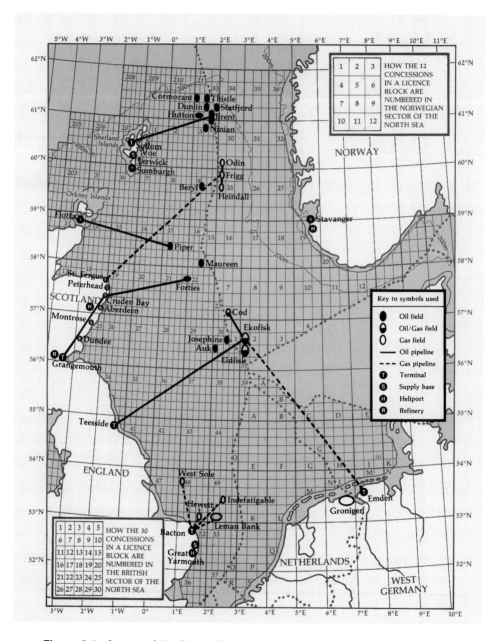

Figure 8.1 : A map of the North Sea, showing the division of mineral rights between the littoral countries and the main developments that took place between 1959 and 1980.

The third phase began in 1971, with the discovery of an even larger oil and gas province in the deep northern waters of the North Sea, between the Shetland Islands and Norway. Developments here included the 'Frigg' gas field complex (discovered in 1971), and an extensive complex of oil fields discovered even further north between 1972 and 1974. These included the huge 'Brent' and 'Ninian' fields. As can be seen from Figure

8.1, the gas from the 'Frigg' complex was brought ashore at St. Fergus, north of Peterhead, with the 'Brent' oil being landed at Sullom Voe in the Shetlands. Vast new processing plants were built at both landfalls.

**Figure 8.2 : One of the oil production platforms that were built
in the North Sea during the early 1970's**

Further oil and gas fields continued to be discovered in the North Sea at regular intervals thereafter, although none of these proved to be as large as the biggest of the early fields. In recent years, exploration and development has moved into the extremely deep waters to the west of the Shetlands, where several medium-to-small fields have now been discovered.

THE IMPACT ON ABERDEEN AND NE SCOTLAND

It has been claimed that the discovery of oil and gas in the northern half of the North Sea was 'the most important event in the entire history of Aberdeen'. Whether or not this is the case, it was certainly by far the most important development during the 20th century, turning Aberdeen into the 'oil capital of Western Europe', and revitalising the economy of the whole of the NE of Scotland. Before oil was discovered, the population of this area had been falling for over 50 years, with the decline accelerating in the period after the Second World War due to increased agricultural mechanisation. Until the mid-1960's, rural migration into Aberdeen itself had largely counterbalanced the steady emigration of its own citizens, mainly to England and the White Commonwealth, but this inward migration was now falling off. By 1970, the population of the city showed signs both of overall ageing and of absolute decline, having fallen by well over 4000 during the previous decade. The NE of Scotland as a whole was now losing approximately 4,500 people a year, and there was no sign of this rate of loss being stemmed.

All this changed with the discovery of North Sea oil. As can be seen from Figure 8.1, Aberdeen was ideally situated to act as a base for operations in the middle latitudes of the North Sea, and, when operations moved further north, was also well placed to service these, both by sea and by air. Oil-related developments in and around Aberdeen took a number of forms.

Firstly, several major operating companies, including Shell, British Petroleum, Mobil, Conoco, BNOC (later Britoil), Texaco and Schlumberger, set up their exploration and production headquarters in Aberdeen - facilities that became larger and larger as the scope of their operations increased. Shell's vast complex at Altens, for example, eventually employed over 2000 people, as did BP's equally-extensive headquarters at Dyce.

Secondly, large numbers of service companies set up operations in and around Aberdeen, mainly in the new industrial estates that were established round its periphery. Between 1960 and 1970, only one new manufacturing firm had been attracted to the area; between 1971 and 1974, no fewer than 460 new firms appeared in the city. These provided virtually all the support that the major operators required, including technical services of all types, transport, and catering. Between them, they generated many thousands of new jobs.

Figure 8.3 : An aerial view of Aberdeen Harbour, showing some of the oil-related developments that took place during the 1970's

Thirdly, Aberdeen's harbour was completely re-vitalised. At the time, the fishing industry that had for so long been its mainstay was starting to decline, partly because increasing numbers of boats were moving from Aberdeen (which was part of the National Dock Labour Scheme, with all the restrictive practices that this entailed) to Peterhead (which was not part of the Scheme). As the fishing boats moved out, the offshore-supply boats and other support vessels moved in, and the harbour became one of the busiest in the country. Silos for the storage of 'drilling mud' and similar materials also became a new part of the landscape. Figure 8.3 shows some of these developments; note the large numbers of offshore-supply boats and other support vessels moored in the main harbour basin.

Fourthly, Aberdeen's Airport at Dyce underwent major expansion. Numbers of fixed-wing flights increased steadily, with flights to London becoming particularly frequent and well-used. Also, Dyce rapidly became the World's busiest heliport, flying offshore workers to and from the many drilling rigs, production platforms and other facilities that began to appear in ever-increasing numbers in the waters to the east and north of Aberdeen (see Figure 8.4).

Fifthly, new hotels and restaurants started to be built in and around Aberdeen in order to cater for the greatly-increased trade that the burgeoning offshore oil industry generated. These became particularly busy around the time of 'Offshore Europe', the increasingly-extensive biennial trade exhibition and conference that was first held in 1973. A major Conference and Exhibition Centre was subsequently built at Balgownie in order to provide a permanent home for this.

Sixthly, large numbers of new houses started to be built in order to accommodate the ever-increasing numbers of workers that moved into the Aberdeen area, many of them highly-paid professionals. House prices, which had always been comparatively high in Aberdeen, became even higher, and (apart from a temporary slump caused by the collapse of the price of crude oil during the mid-1980's) have remained high ever since.

Figure 8.4 : A helicopter landing on a drilling rig in the North Sea

All in all, Aberdeen became one of the most prosperous cities in Britain, being largely sheltered from the various recessions that periodically affected other parts of the country by the presence of the oil industry and its related infrastructure. Nor was this prosperity limited to Aberdeen itself, with several other NE towns (notably Peterhead) also becoming heavily involved in oil-related activities, and many others becoming 'dormitory suburbs' for the main centres. Truly, the 'good times' had returned to the North East of Scotland!

THE IMPACT ON THE ACADEMIC WORK OF RGIT

Shortly after his arrival in Aberdeen as Director of RGIT, Dr. Peter Clarke realised that the rapidly-growing offshore oil industry was starting to present significant opportunities to the Institute - opportunities that it would do well to exploit before others did. One School - Mechanical Engineering - was already becoming increasingly involved with the industry, and Dr. Clarke felt that others might do likewise. By 1973, he realised that he needed someone to liaise with the 'major players' in the industry in order to identify their specific requirements, and to do this on a full-time basis. RGIT already had an Industrial Liaison Officer (Dr. Norman Mackenzie, who had been appointed by Dr. West in 1963), but he was fully committed to other work. For this reason, Dr. Clarke decided to second Dr. Eric Addinall, a recently-appointed Senior Lecturer in the School of Physics, in order to carry out this highly important task.

During the next two years, Dr. Addinall visited all the major operating companies in the NE of Scotland and many of the most important contractors, liaised with government agencies, attended conferences, meetings and launches, and generally acted as RGIT's 'roving ambassador' to the oil and gas industry. He also reported regularly to Dr. Clarke and to Heads of Schools and other staff regarding his findings. His research led to the School of Mechanical Engineering becoming even more heavily involved in oil-related work, and also helped to make a number of other Schools - including Electronic and Electrical Engineering, Physics, Chemistry, Mathematics, Navigation and Business Management Studies - aware of how they could benefit from such involvement. Possible activities included the adaptation of existing courses and development of new courses to meet the needs of the industry, oil- and gas-related research of various types, and consultancy work for all the different industrial, commercial and other organisations that were involved in oil-related activities. During the next few years, RGIT became increasingly active in each of these different areas, and, in the words of Dr. Clarke, 'gained a ten-year head-start on the "opposition"'. He himself looks back fondly on these exciting years, and regards the work that he did in promoting the development of oil-related work as 'one of his greatest achievements' as Director and Principal of RGIT.

Let us now look in some detail at how one of RGIT's Schools (Mechanical Engineering) took up the challenge of the offshore oil industry during this period. The School's involvement with the industry began in 1970, when a member of its staff, Mr.

Robert Hosie, advised one of the recently-established offshore drilling companies regarding vibration and imbalance problems being experienced with a diesel-driven alternator on their drilling ship 'Glomar III'. This led to further consultancy work, and also led to four students on the School's new 'Higher National Diploma in Engineering' obtaining six-month work placements on another of the company's ships, 'Glomar V', during the following session. These would be the first of many such student placements with the offshore oil industry.

During session 1972-73, the School became progressively more heavily involved in oil-related teaching (see Figure 8.5), and also started developing the first courses that were designed specifically for the offshore industry. These consisted of a third-year option on 'Oil Drilling Technology' for its 'HND in Engineering', and a new one-year 'Postgraduate Diploma in Offshore Engineering'. Preparation for these courses involved the acquisition of a considerable amount of new plant, laboratory equipment and resource materials. Some of this was purchased with the aid of special Scottish Education Department grants, some was provided by local oil companies, and some was designed and manufactured by the staff of the School themselves. Major items so obtained included an oil-well-control simulator (see Figure 8.6) and a number of drilling-mud-tool instruments. Both courses began operation at the start of the following session, and immediately proved extremely successful.

Figure 8.5 : Oil-related instruction being carried out in the School of Mechanical Engineering during the early 1970's

**Figure 8.6 : The oil-well-control simulator acquired by
the School of Mechanical Engineering in 1973**

During session 1974-75, the School's involvement in oil-related work continued to grow steadily. It included the development of further elective modules for its 'Postgraduate Diploma in Offshore Engineering', running a two-week specialist course on 'Drilling Technology' for Shell Exploration (UK) Ltd, and hosting a highly-successful one-day seminar on 'Aspects of Underwater Technology'. Staff also carried out an increasing amount of research and consultancy work, and attended several oil-related conferences, including the 1974 Offshore Conference and Exhibition in Houston, Texas (the world's largest event of this type). More and more of the School's students were now also carrying out projects related to the offshore oil industry. During 1974-75, these included the following:

- 'A study of well pressure control procedures and their simulation'.
- 'An experimental investigation of flow in marine risers'.
- 'A design study of equipment for training personnel in escape routines from ditched helicopters'.
- 'An investigation into the control, measurement and removal of oil slicks at sea'.

Session 1975-76 saw a number of significant developments, including the introduction of the School's first CNAA degree - a B.Sc. in 'Engineering Technology'; this was subsequently upgraded to an honours degree. Oil-related activities continued to expand during the session, during which the work on Offshore Safety and Survival that had previously been carried out in the School of Navigation was also transferred to the School (see the next section for a detailed description of how this work developed within RGIT). A new Offshore Technology Centre was also established within the School in order to co-ordinate Institute activities in this highly important area. At the end of the session, the School was re-named as the 'School of Mechanical *and Offshore* Engineering' in order to reflect the increased importance of oil-related work in its overall activities. Such work continued to increase in importance from then on, and is still carried out today.

THE ESTABLISHMENT OF RGIT's VARIOUS COMMERCIAL UNITS

In order to cater for the needs of the offshore oil and gas industry, RGIT also set up a number of specialist commercial centres and units during the 1970's and 1980's. The first of these was the Offshore Safety and Survival Unit, which had its origins in a request made to Dr. Clarke by Shell Exploration (UK) Ltd. at the end of 1972. Shell wanted to know whether the Institute could provide offshore safety and survival training for people who had to work offshore, and it was agreed that such training would be provided by the School of Navigation. With the assistance of Shell, a five-day intensive course on 'Offshore Safety and Survival' was rapidly developed, and was advertised to all companies operating drilling rigs and production platforms around the United Kingdom by the Petroleum Industry Training Board. The course was first run in February, 1973.

Initially, the training was carried out by the existing staff of the School of Navigation, but, once the viability of the course had been established and demand started to build up, a full-time Offshore Safety and Survival Instructor, Captain Ian Taylor, was taken on to run the programme. Demand for the course continued to grow, and, by the end of the year, it was being run virtually every week. Captain Taylor resigned in 1974, and was replaced by ex-Royal-Navy Lt. Joseph H. Cross. Applications for the course were now so high that a second full-time instructor had to be appointed - the first of many additional staff that would be taken on during the coming years as the demand for offshore safety and survival training continued to increase. During the 1975-76 session, the Offshore Safety and Survival Unit (as it was now known) was transferred to the School of Mechanical Engineering, since its work was becoming increasingly related to offshore technology.

Following its transfer to the School of Mechanical Engineering, the work of the Offshore Safety and Survival Unit continued to grow at a rapid rate, and its facilities were also continuously improved. These included a new custom-built Training Quay on the north bank of the River Dee, east of Victoria Bridge (see Figure 8.7). This served as a base for the Unit's growing fleet of enclosed survival craft and lifeboats, and was officially opened in October, 1977 by Mr. Frank McElhone, Undersecretary at the Scottish Office. At around the same time, the Unit was re-named as the Offshore Survival Centre, reflecting the fact that it was now carrying out research and consultancy as well as survival training. Indeed, it was rapidly gaining a national and international reputation for the highly-innovative work that it was carrying out. In January, 1978, the Centre moved to the King Street site, taking over part of the accommodation vacated by the School of Navigation when it was transferred to Aberdeen Technical College (see Chapter 7). By the end of the session, its staff complement had risen to 13, comprising a Head (Lt. Cross), eleven Instructors and a Secretary.

**Figure 8.7 : The Offshore Safety and Survival Unit's
Training Quay on the River Dee, east of Victoria Bridge**

During the next six years, the Offshore Survival Centre continued to expand, both in terms of the throughput of trainees (which rose from just over 2000 in 1977-78 to over 14,000 in 1983-84) and in terms of the scope of its work. New courses were regularly introduced, and a large number of new facilities were developed, including a state-of-the-art Drill Tank incorporating the Helicopter Underwater Escape Trainer shown in Figure 8.8. This was officially opened in July, 1980 by HRH the Prince of Wales, during an extended visit to the Offshore Survival Centre and other parts of RGIT (see Figure 8.9). Although the demand for the Centre's courses suffered a dramatic slump during the mid-1980's as a result of the collapse of the price of crude oil, it lived up to its own name, and survived! In 1989, it was merged with the Institute's Centre for Offshore Health (see below) to become an independent Company - RGIT Survival Centre Ltd. This has since undergone a number of further name changes, but continues to make a major contribution to the University's income through its profits.

The other two specialist commercial units that were set up during the 'RGIT years' in order to cater for the needs of the offshore oil industry were the Centre for Offshore Health, and Viscom. The former was established in 1982, under the direction of Professor Nelson Norman. At first, it only ran a single course - on 'Basic Life Support' - but, over the following years, its portfolio of courses and other activities expanded considerably, as did its staff complement and facilities. The Centre was originally housed in the RGIT Boathouse that had once been part of the School of Navigation, but later moved to

Kepplestone House, and then to the Merkland South building at King Street. Like the Offshore Survival Centre, it quickly established a considerable reputation at national and international level, both for its courses and for the high-quality research and consultancy work that it carried out. In 1989, it merged with the Offshore Survival Centre to become part of RGIT Survival Centre Ltd.

Figure 8.8 : The Offshore Survival Centre's Helicopter Underwater Escape Trainer (HUET) in use in its King Street Drill Tank.

Viscom was established in 1987 in order to meet the demand of Aberdeen's various helicopter companies for video-based safety briefings for oil personnel flying offshore. It soon established an international reputation in the field of aviation safety training, helping 'to improve and redefine the standards of helicopter passenger safety briefings' during the late 1980's and 1990's. Its highly-qualified technical staff now produce a regularly-updated catalogue of over 50 North Sea helicopter passenger briefings, as well as briefings for the Gulf, Danish and Norwegian sectors - all in both VHS and DVD formats. They also carry out a wide range of other work, including digital encoding and graphic design, and the production of promotional and staff-induction videos.

Figure 8.9 : The visit of HRH The Prince of Wales to the Offshore Survival Centre in July, 1980

THE BRUCE OIL MANAGEMENT GAME

Let us end this chapter on the impact of the offshore oil industry on RGIT by looking at the history of the 'Bruce Oil Management Game'. This ran successfully as a national and international competition for six successive years during the late 1970's, and attracted a great deal of favourable publicity for the Institute, both locally and nationally. It also helped to raise the profile of RGIT within the offshore oil industry at a time when it was trying to build up the various oil-related activities described earlier.

The idea for the competition came from Mr. Roger Nicholson, Assistant Managing Director of Aberdeen Journals. In November, 1973, he approached Dr. Clarke and indicated that his company would be interested in sponsoring a business-management game connected with the North Sea oil industry. He hoped that RGIT would be willing to collaborate in such a venture, and suggested that the game might be promoted and run through the medium of the Business Journal of 'The Press and Journal', the local morning paper published by Aberdeen Journals. The main aim of such an exercise would be 'to stimulate local interest in, and discussion of, the North Sea oil industry, particularly with regard to the competing (and often conflicting) interests that inevitably surround a new and rapidly-developing technology'. It was felt that this would be a particularly appropriate time to run such a game, since the next four years would see the exploration, development and production phases of the offshore oil industry running together for the first time.

RGIT was already running several courses connected with the offshore oil industry, had a traditional interest in business management, and had recently become involved in the development of a number of educational games and simulation exercises (see Chapter 11 for details). It therefore seemed highly appropriate that the Institute should collaborate with Aberdeen Journals in developing an educational competition designed to give its participants experience of the entire decision-making process associated with bringing a newly-discovered offshore oil field into full production. Dr. Clarke therefore readily agreed to Mr. Nicholson's proposal, and asked Dr. (later Professor) Norman Langton, Head of the School of Physics, and the author (who were now co-ordinating RGIT's work on educational games) to set up a joint committee with Aberdeen Journals in order to develop the game and organise the competition.

It was decided that the exercise would be known as the 'Bruce Oil Management Game' in honour of King Robert the Bruce, in view of the fact that 1974, the year when the competition would be launched, was to be celebrated as the 700th anniversary of his birth. Robert the Bruce had also been a great benefactor to the North-East of Scotland, donating to the City of Aberdeen lands that were still bringing benefit to its citizens (the Common Good Fund, which finances practically all civic entertainment in Aberdeen, derives its income from these lands). Another reason for basing the game on the hypothetical 'Bruce Field', supposedly located in an as-yet-unallocated concession to the west of the Shetlands, was that no oil company had so far used this name for one of their North Sea fields. Several years later, Hamilton Brothers (an American company) actually did, and Dr. Clarke wrote to them to congratulate them on their 'excellent choice', and pointed out the use that RGIT and Aberdeen Journals were already making of the name. He does not recollect receiving a reply!

Work on the development of the game, which took almost 12 months, was carried out in two phases. The first involved formulating the basic structure of the game, and gathering the vast amount of geographical, technical and financial information needed to make it a realistic exercise. The second involved developing the game into a form that could be handled by RGIT's mainframe computer, writing all the necessary software, and producing the associated documentation. RGIT was fortunate in having a number of enthusiastic 'computer experts' on its staff at the time, and three of these (Mr. Ronald Angus and Mr. Peter Strachan of the School of Mathematics, and Mr. Innes Hendry of the School of Mechanical Engineering) were responsible for producing the highly-sophisticated computer programs that enabled the game to be run.

The 'Bruce Oil Management Game' was launched by '*The Press and Journal*' in the autumn of 1974, with a great fanfare of publicity. Initially, it was run in two sections - an 'educational' section for teams from schools and colleges, and a 'business' section for teams from industry, commerce, local government etc. (In later runs, the 'educational' section was itself divided into a 'school' section and a 'student' section.) A total of 32 teams entered the 1974-75 competition, 17 in the 'educational' section and 15 in the 'business' section. During the following winter, these participated in five postal rounds of the game, each of which simulated two years of their 'company's' operations. This involved producing and implementing a plan to develop the 'Bruce Field', bring their oil ashore by pipeline or tanker, and sell the oil either as 'crude' or as refined products. At the start of each round, they had to submit their plans for the next two years on a specially-designed decision sheet, receiving detailed feedback on their progress from the game controllers at RGIT before the start of the following round. The object of the game was simple : to make the largest possible profit by the end of the competition.

At the end of the fifth postal round, the leading three teams in each section of the competition were invited to participate in a 'live' final round in Aberdeen. This involved being handed their updated 'company statements' and being given an hour to complete their final 'decision sheets', which were then immediately processed by the RGIT computer team. The winners of the two sections of the competition were then announced in front of an invited audience of distinguished guests, which included three local Members of Parliament. The Guest of Honour on this occasion was Mr. George Williams, Chairman of the UK Offshore Operators Association, who addressed the audience and presented the prizes to the winners in each section. The winners of the 'business' section (from Seaforth Maritime, a local contracting company) received a granite trophy and an all-expenses-paid visit to Moscow (the author remember this well, because he was asked to accompany them!). The winners of the 'educational' section (from Robert Gordon's College) also received a trophy, together with a cheque for their school and book tokens for themselves.

Because of the great success of the 1974-75 competition, it was decided to run the 'Bruce Oil Management Game' during the following winter. In the event, it was run for a further five years, during which time interest in the competition grew steadily greater. Throughout these years, the organising committee managed to update and modify the game model so as to produce new and exciting challenges that not only kept apace with, but, in some respects, also anticipated real-life developments. The years from 1974 to 1980 were exciting ones for the North Sea oil industry, and were also exciting ones for the people who ran the 'Bruce Oil Management Game' and for the teams who took part.

The number of teams participating in the competition increased steadily throughout the six years in which it was run, rising to over 130 in the Mark VI game. Several teams played the game more than once; indeed, one of the members of the winning 'business' team in the final game had taken part every year, determined to win in the end! Over the years, the 'live final' became an important social and professional occasion for many people, since the distinguished Guest of Honour invariably gave a speech on some topical aspect of the North Sea oil industry. The organisers were extremely lucky in being able to obtain some of the most important figures in the British offshore industry as Guests of Honour, the full list being given below:

1975:   Mr. George Williams (Director General of UKOOA)

1976:   The Right Honourable John Smith, MP (Minister of State in the
         Department of Energy and future Leader of the Labour Party
         - see Figure 8.10)

1977:   Lord Kearton (Chairman of the British National Oil Corporation)

1978:   The Right Honourable Christopher Tugenhadt (EEC Commissioner
         for the UK)

1979:   Sir Denis Rooke (Chairman of the British Gas Corporation)

1980:   Dr. J.H. Burgoyne (Chairman of the Government Committee of
         Enquiry into Offshore Safety and Survival)

The competition also attracted a steadily-increasing number of sponsors over its six-year life, Aberdeen Journals and RGIT later being joined by the Institute of Petroleum, Times Newspapers and British Caledonian Airways.

**Figure 8.10 : The Rt. Hon. John Smith, MP (second from right),
Minister of State at the Department of Energy, making the presentation to
'Seaforth Maritime A',winners of the 'business' section of the 1975-76 'Bruce Oil
Management Game'**

As well as its use as the basis of the six open competitions held between 1974 and 1980, the 'Bruce Oil Management Game' was run regularly within RGIT itself - as an educational exercise for postgraduate students of offshore engineering, business-management students, and several other groups. It was used in this capacity until the end of the 1980's, and was also made available to outside bodies as a self-contained commercial package.

Figure 8.11 : The board game 'North Sea' that was produced jointly by RGIT and Shell UK at the time of 'Offshore Europe 75'

One unexpected spin-off from work on the 'Bruce Oil Management Game' came in 1974, when Mr. T.J. Kenny of Shell UK Exploration and Production Ltd. approached RGIT requesting assistance with the development of a family board game based on the North Sea oil industry, since Shell wished to produce such a game for publicity purposes. Mr. Kenny subsequently retained the author and Dr. Eric Addinall (who were in fact already working on an oil-based board game) as consultants in order to carry out the work. The resulting game, 'North Sea', was produced by John Waddington Ltd., and was launched jointly by Shell and RGIT during the second 'Offshore Europe' conference and exhibition, in the autumn of 1975. It was also put on open sale to the general public in the Aberdeen area, and aroused a great deal of interest. The author and Dr. Addinall had visions of being able to retire to the Bahamas on the strength of their royalties, but, in the event, Shell only produced 6000 copies, so it was not to be!

Chapter 9 : The growth of social and management-related teaching

The steady growth in social and management-related teaching within RGIT and RGU since 1965 has been one of the institution's greatest success stories. In this chapter, we will see how this work originated in Robert Gordon's Technical College in the years following the end of the Second World War, and how it developed during the next twenty years. We will then show how it led to the establishment of a number of new Schools that ran social and management-related courses of different types, and, eventually, to the establishment of the Faculty of Management.

As we saw in Chapter 4, management was first taught within Robert Gordon's Technical College in 1945, when courses in 'Business Administration' were run for returning ex-servicemen. These courses continued until 1946, and, out of them, the College developed a three-year, part-time British Institute of Management course in 'Management Studies'. Further part-time courses followed, including a highly-popular evening course in 'Human Relations in Industry' that was run in the early 1950's, and a slightly-less-popular 'Intermediate Certificate in Management Studies' that was run throughout most of the 1950's, but was eventually phased out due to lack of support.

Until now, all management courses had been the responsibility of the College's Arts and Crafts Committee, and had been taught by *ad-hoc* lecturers. In 1960, however, it was decided to establish a separate Business Management Studies Committee, and to advertise for a full-time member of staff, with a qualification in commerce and/or economics, in order to teach Business Administration. It is not known whether this post was actually advertised at the time, but no appointment was made until early in 1962, when no fewer than three full-time lecturers were appointed in order to teach Management Studies, Work Study and the 'new' subject of Liberal Studies. A 'Department of Business Management Studies' was established in September of the same year, but this had no Head and no dedicated accommodation, with management-related teaching being carried out in any accommodation that was available, including the Students' Union in Rubislaw Terrace! An Acting Head was in fact appointed in 1963, when Mr Alexander Cormack, the College's organiser of part-time courses, was made Lecturer-in-Charge of the Department of Business Management Studies in addition to all his other duties.

By now, enrolments in the various courses run by the embryonic Department had risen to 139, and the Scottish Education Department had also given their approval to offer the prestigious 'Diploma in Management Studies' course, which had its first intake in September 1963. Indeed, the workload was now so high that it was decided to move the Department of Business Management Studies, along with the School of Navigation, into the King Street premises that had recently been vacated by the School of Domestic

Science (see Chapter 5). Once these had undergone suitable refurbishment, the moves took place in 1964.

In January 1965, the newly-appointed Technical College Director, Dr. Gerald Bulmer, presented a report to the Governors in which he recommended that a full-time Head of the Department of Business Management Studies should be appointed, and that the Department should also seek SED approval to run a three-year 'Diploma in Commerce' on a full-time basis. Dr. Bulmer also raised the question of the teaching of Liberal Studies, and its place in the overall work of the College. The Governors agreed to implement his two recommendations, and SED agreement was obtained almost immediately, enabling the 'Diploma in Commerce' to start up in September 1965. Interviews were also held for the post of Head of Department, with Mr. (later Dr.) Joseph Batty being appointed in October 1965.

Dr. Bulmer was also asked to make more detailed recommendations regarding the teaching of 'Liberal Studies', which was now emerging as a highly important subject in its own right - largely due to the influence of the recently-established CNAA. As a result of Dr. Bulmer's recommendations, responsibility for the teaching of Liberal Studies was transferred to the new School of Social Studies when this was established in 1968.

THE ESTABLISHMENT AND DEVELOPMENT OF THE BUSINESS SCHOOL

In his excellent account of the history of the Business School, Dr. Douglas Gourlay identifies 1965 as the true 'year of foundation' of the School, although the Department of Business Management Studies was not actually called a 'School' until 1968 (see Chapter 7). His reasons are that 'it had, for the first time, its own premises, a three-year, full-time undergraduate course in addition to its short and part-time management courses, and an established Head of Department to guide its fortunes'. This Dr. Batty did with considerable foresight and vigour, his first task being to plan for his Department 'a future which was not confined to the 'Diploma in Commerce', to servicing courses in other Departments, and to providing classes in Management and Business Studies on a part-time day and/or evening basis'. His success in this regard may be judged by the list of new courses that the Department was offering on its own behalf by the start of session 1966-67 - quite apart from the increased service work that it was now carrying out:

Management Courses
- Diploma in Management Studies (3 years part-time; day)
- Certificate in Business Administration (2 years part-time; day/evening)
- City and Guilds Certificate in Work Study (2 years part-time; day/evening)
- Certificate of Institute of Work Study Practitioners (block release)
- Certificate of Institute of Work Managers (2 years part-time; day/evening)
- Graduateship of Institute of Personnel Management (full-time)
- B.Sc. (Economics) for External Degree of University of London.

Commercial Courses
- Associateship of Institute of Bankers (Scotland)
- Associateship of Certified and Cost Accountants
- Associateship of Chartered Institute of Secretaries
- Membership of Institute of Hospital Administrators
- Seven further courses for other professional bodies

Extramural and Short Courses
- Courses on eight different topics

With the exception of the B.Sc.(Econ.) and the 'seven further commercial courses', all of these attracted sufficient applicants for them to be run during 1966-67, along with the various courses that were continuing from the previous session. As the work of the Department expanded during the following years, its complement of full-time staff also grew steadily, rising to 13 by the time it became the School of Business Management Studies in 1968, and continuing to rise thereafter.

During the second half of the 1960's, repeated requests had been made to the SED to allow work to start on the development of a CNAA degree in 'Business Administration' or 'Business Studies', but, until 1969, these had all been turned down. The SED had given approval for Dundee College of Technology to run such a degree (which started in 1968), and were concerned that an RGIT degree 'might adversely affect recruitment to the Dundee course'. By 1969, however, the SED had decided to rationalise the provision of management education in the region, with all part-time courses (with the exception of the 'Diploma in Management Studies') being transferred to local-authority colleges from September, 1970, thus allowing Central Institutions such as RGIT to concentrate on degree and diploma work. As a result of this new policy, the School was now actively encouraged to submit a proposal for a CNAA degree in 'Business Studies', and the Governors immediately agreed that this should be done.

Figure 9.1 : A class in the School of Business Management Studies

Responsibility for co-ordinating the CNAA submission fell to Mr. (later Professor) Ralph Hart, who replaced Dr. Batty as Head of School at the start of 1970. Dr. Gourlay recalls that this work was 'a learning process for the staff', none of whom had previously been involved in an exercise of this type. In the event, a revised second submission was requested; this proved successful, and the first CNAA degree students matriculated in September 1972. The 'BA in Business Studies', which was subsequently upgraded to an honours degree, 'has been one of the success stories of the Business School', with a very high proportion of its graduates obtaining posts in industry, commerce and the public services. One feature of the degree that has always appealed to potential employers has been the experience of 'real work' that the students gain during their third-year 'sandwich' placement. Indeed, many students end up working for their placement employer.

The work of the School continued to develop and expand throughout the 1970's. In 1975, the School became the first educational establishment in the United Kingdom to run a CNAA postgraduate course that gained full exemption from the examinations of the Institute of Personnel Management. In 1976, similar professional exemption was gained for the 'Diploma in Management Studies', which led to a significant increase in the number of organisations seeking to enhance their management development programmes through the use of the part-time version of this course. In addition, the School was carrying out an increasingly large amount of service teaching in areas such as economics, law, and general management - mainly in degree courses being run by other Schools. Finally, the School was taking full advantage of the opportunities presented by the growth of the offshore oil industry, running specialist short courses, carrying out consultancy, and becoming increasingly heavily involved in oil-industry-related research.

Figure 9.2: the new accommodation for the School of Business Management Studies that was provided at Hilton in 1980

Since moving to the King Street site in 1964, the Department/School of Business Management Studies had gradually taken over more and more of the accommodation in the main building. For a time, it shared this with the School of Librarianship, but, from 1975 onwards, it was the sole occupant. By the late 1970's, however, the continued expansion of the School meant that the accommodation at King Street was becoming progressively more cramped. As we saw in Chapter 7, the problem was eventually resolved in 1980, when the School was able to move into a large vacant block on the Aberdeen College of Education site at Hilton (see Figure 9.2). The School was to remain there until 1998, when it moved into the splendid new building that had been constructed for the Faculty of Management at Garthdee (see Chapters 14 and 15). Two years after the move to Hilton, it was decided to shorten its name to the 'Business School'.

The Business School continued to expand and diversify during the 1980's, and, by the time Professor Hart retired in 1991, had consolidated its place within RGIT as 'an extremely successful unit with potential for even further expansion'. The School was now offering an even wider range of courses, including a highly-innovative 'BA in European Business Administration with Languages,' and a part-time 'Master of Business Administration' that was run jointly with Aberdeen University (it would later run its own independent MBA). Other new courses were being developed, and more would be developed during the 1990's, under the new Head of School, Mr. David Sagar. One of his very first acts was to register the name 'Aberdeen Business School', thus enabling the School's name to be changed to this in 1994 - a not inconsiderable marketing coup on the part of the new Robert Gordon University! Mr. Sagar also set up a Business Research Unit and an Offshore Management Centre within the School, which is now the second largest in the University, after the School of Nursing and Midwifery. It has certainly come a very long way since 1962!

THE TEACHING OF LIBRARIANSHIP AND RELATED SUBJECTS

In 1946, the Scottish College of Commerce in Glasgow started to run a course in Librarianship, and, for a long time, this was the only place in the country where the subject could be studied. During the mid-1960's, the College became part of Strathclyde University and its Librarianship course was incorporated in the University's General B.A. degree. Demand for fully-trained librarians was now increasing throughout Scotland, however, and it was realised that a second teaching centre was required. The Scottish Education Department agreed that this should be located in RGIT, and, as a result, the School of Librarianship was established in 1967, with Mr. James M. Orr as its Head. It was envisaged that the School would initially run a non-degree course preparing students for the Ordinary Professional Examination of the Library Association, the UK's Professional Body for Librarians, but would eventually upgrade this to a CNAA degree. The new School was located at King Street, where it shared the main building with the Department of Business Management Studies.

Their first course, which led to the award of the Associateship of the Library

Association (ALA), started operating in 1968-69, and immediately proved successful. It involved two years of full-time study, and incorporated a mandatory four-week placement in a library during the summer break between these. Towards the end of their course, students were also required to investigate a real-life library problem as a 'Depth Study', with much of this work also being carried out in a working library environment. In 1969-70, the School also started running a one-year postgraduate 'conversion' course in Librarianship, designed for graduates in other subjects who wished to take up library work. This also proved extremely successful.

**Figure 9.3 : Students carrying out bibliographic work
in the School of Librarianship**

By the start of the 1970's, the School had grown considerably, and now employed eight academic staff. During session 1972-73, it made a significant move along the route to running its own degree course by being approved for internal examining of the Part 1 Examinations of the General Professional Course of the Library Association. Accommodation was now becoming extremely tight at King Street, however, so it was decided to move the School to a new third floor that was being built on to the west wing of the St. Andrew Street building. The move took place in April 1974, and had the added advantage of locating the School in the same building as RGIT's Central Library, thus giving the librarianship students easy access to its facilities and staff. In July of the same year, a successful submission was made to the CNAA to run a B.A. in Librarianship, but it was decided to delay the start until session 1975-76 in order to enable adequate preparations to be made. Once the new CNAA degree began operation, it gradually replaced the original General Professional Course, although the two were run in parallel for some time. A further CNAA course - a one-year, full-time 'Postgraduate Diploma in Librarianship' - was approved during the following year, and began operating in 1977-78, with an initial intake of 30 students.

Further development of the School's academic programme in Librarianship was held back for many years due to the repeated refusal of the SED to grant permission to

148

upgrade their CNAA B.A. to an honours degree; indeed, it was not until the late 1980's that this upgrading was allowed. In the meantime, the School began to develop in a different direction. During the late 1970's and early 1980's, staff started to make more and more use of computers and other aspects of 'new' information technology in their general teaching work (see Figure 9.4). Indeed, by 1984, so much of the School's work was directly related to this area that its name was changed to the School of Librarianship *and Information Studies*. The School subsequently changed the name of its degree course to a 'B.A. in Librarianship and Information Studies', and also developed articulated Postgraduate Diploma/Masters programmes in 'Librarianship and Information Studies' and in 'Information Analysis'. The teaching of various aspects of information technology was now making up an increasingly large part of its overall workload.

Figure 9.4 : Students of the School of Librarianship and Information Studies working in one of the School's IT Laboratories

During the early 1990's, the School once again broadened its teaching portfolio by developing courses in 'Publishing Studies' and in 'Communication'. In 1994, RGU's Communication and Modern Languages staff were transferred to the School from the Educational Development Unit (see next section). As a result, it underwent a further change of name - to the School of Information and Media. The School now runs a wide range of undergraduate and postgraduate courses reflecting 'the key role that the communication of information plays in government, industry, business, the media, education, healthcare and everyday life in the 21st century'. Its staff also had to make no fewer than three further moves before the end of the millennium - first to Hilton, then back to King Street, and finally, in 1998, into the new Faculty of Management building at Garthdee. They hope that their School has now found a permanent home!

THE EVOLUTION OF SOCIAL- AND LIBERAL-STUDIES TEACHING

As we saw earlier, Robert Gordon's Technical College's first full-time lecturer in 'Liberal Studies' was appointed in 1962. During the next six years, the teaching of 'General Studies' (as the subject came to be known within the Institution) spread to an increasing number of courses. This was partly due to the influence of the CNAA, which required that all their courses should help students to 'perceive their field of study in a broader perspective', and should also 'stimulate an enquiring, analytical and creative approach, encouraging independent judgement and critical self-awareness'. These requirements were embodied in their ground-breaking 'Principle 3', which had to be fully addressed by all the teams who were trying to develop CNAA degrees at the time. Indeed, it continued to have a major influence on the design of all RGIT's courses for over 25 years.

In 1968, RGIT established a new School of Social Studies at Schoolhill, and appointed Dr. John Highet as its Head. The School had a dual function - to bring all the Institute's General Studies teaching together under one provider, and to set up new courses in Social Work and Child Care. Hitherto, some Schools had employed their own General Studies lecturers, but these were all now transferred to the new School, and would henceforth provide 'service teaching' in General Studies to all the courses that required it. With the development of more and more CNAA degrees within RGIT, all requiring a substantial amount of General Studies teaching in order to comply with CNAA's 'Principle 3', this work increased steadily over the next 20 years.

Since RGIT had run no courses in Social Work or Child Care prior to 1968, it was necessary to appoint a completely new team of specialist staff in order to teach these subjects. Two courses were immediately developed. The first was a two-year, full-time course leading to the award of a Certificate in Social Work by the Council for Training in Social Work. The second was a two-year, full-time course leading to recognition as a qualified Child-Care Officer by the Central Council for Training in Child Care. One year later, a similar course leading to recognition as a qualified Probation Officer by the Scottish Probation Advisory Council was added to the portfolio. All three courses involved a mixture of theoretical study in RGIT (see Figure 9.5) and supervised placement 'in the field'. Further courses were added later, including a one-year course leading to the Certificate of Qualification in the 'Residential Care of Children and Young People' that was transferred from Aberdeen Corporation to RGIT in 1972.

During the early 1970's, the School started to develop its own CNAA degree. Initially, it was planned that this would be a 'BA in Social Studies' with options in Social Work and in Social and Public Administration, and, during session 1975-76, such a proposal was approved in principle by the Scottish Education Department. As a result of recommendations made during internal validation, the title was subsequently changed to a 'BA in Social and Public Administration' with an option in Social Work. This was approved by the CNAA, and began operation in 1978. At the start of the 1980's, however, CNAA agreed that the programme would henceforth lead to the award of separate BA degrees in 'Public Administration' and in 'Public Administration and Applied Social Studies'.

Figure 9.5 : A typical seminar being run in the School of Social Studies

In 1981, Dr. Highet retired as Head of School. He was replaced by Mr. Charles W. (Bill) Ellis, who had taught General and Social Studies in RGIT since before the School was formed. In December 1982, the School moved into the re-named Merkland Building at King Street, which had been completely refurbished after the Business School moved to Hilton in 1980. Another extremely important development took place in September 1983, when staff of the School of Health Visiting (who had also moved to King Street in 1982) became part of the School of Social Studies, operating as an identifiable unit with a Senior Lecturer in Charge. As we will see in Chapter 10, this move paved the way for a major expansion of nursing education in RGIT during the late 1980's and early 1990's.

Another important development that took place within the School of Social Studies during the 1980's was the rapid growth in the teaching of Communication Studies. This began with the appointment of a single full-time lecturer (Mr. Cameron Donaldson) in 1978, with further staff being added to what was to become the Communication Studies section of the School during the early 1980's. During this period, more and more Schools began to appreciate the importance of helping their students to develop sound oral and written communication skills, so Communication Studies units and modules started to be incorporated in an increasing number of courses. By the late 1980's Mr. Donaldson and his colleagues were carrying out service teaching for virtually every School in the Institute. During the 1990's, they would also play a major role in developing a number of new degree programmes in communication and related areas - first within the Educational Development Unit, and then within the School of Information and Media.

THE TEACHING OF INSTITUTIONAL ADMINISTRATION

As we saw in Chapter 5, the teaching of Institutional Administration began in the School of Domestic Science shortly after it transferred to Robert Gordon's Technical College in 1910. The one-year course for potential housekeepers, matrons and house mistresses that it started offering at this time was to run for many years, and would lead to the development of a whole portfolio of courses leading to awards of the Institutional Management Association. By the mid-1960's, the (now) College of Domestic Science was running a two-year 'Matron - Housekeeper's' course, a two-year Certificate course in 'Institutional Housekeeping and Catering', and a three-year Diploma course in 'Institutional Management'. At the start of the 1970's, the last of these was phased out, being replaced by a Higher National Diploma in 'Catering and Hotelkeeping'.

**Figure 9.6 : Hotel and Institutional Administration students
serving a meal to their Head of School, Mr. Armand Borisewitz, and his guests
in the Training Restaurant at Kepplestone**

We have also seen how the College of Domestic Science was split into three separate Schools in 1971, following the resignation of its Principal, Mrs. Mary Gillbe. These were the School of Home Economics (with Dr. Roderick Bennett as its Head), the School of Nutritional Science (with Dr. David Livingston as its Head) and the School of Hotel and Institutional Administration (With Miss Bathia (Beth) Henderson as Senior Lecturer in Charge). With the introduction of the new HND in 'Catering and Hotelkeeping', facilities for teaching Hotel Management were already being extended. These included the conversion of the former committee room in the Kepplestone building into a bar and reception area, and the use of the staff restaurant next door as a student training restaurant for much of the session. Later, the wall between these two rooms would be removed, and the combined bar/reception-area/training-restaurant greatly extended. For almost

30 years, this would be run as a licensed restaurant, open both to staff and to the general public (see Figure 8.6). The author has enjoyed many excellent meals there!

Miss Henderson retired in April 1975, and Mr Armand Borisewitz (see Figure 9.6) was appointed Head of the School. Under his leadership, the work of the School continued to develop, and links with the hotel and catering industry underwent considerable expansion. The School had already started running a one-year, full-time, post-experience course leading to membership of the Hotel, Catering and Institutional Management Association, and was now developing a CNAA degree in 'Hotel, Catering and Institutional Administration'. SED permission to submit the proposal to the CNAA was received during 1976-77, but it took a further six years - and numerous revisions and re-submissions - for their final approval to be received. The course eventually began operation in October 1982. It was subsequently upgraded into an honours degree in 'Hospitality Management'.

THE 1988 ACADEMIC STRUCTURE CHANGES AND THEIR CONSEQUENCES

As we saw in Chapter 7, RGIT embarked on a major review of its academic structure in 1986, and, in 1988, introduced a radically-changed Faculty and School system. This brought about a number of significant changes in the teaching of social- and management-related subjects.

Firstly, it created a completely new School - the School of Public Administration and Law. This was formed by merging the Public Administration section of the School of Social Studies with the Law section of the Business School, and transferring the staff of the latter to King Street. Dr. Joan Stringer (now Principal of Napier University) was appointed Head of the new School, which soon started developing a highly-innovative honours degree in 'Legal and Administrative Studies' to add to its existing honours degree in 'Public Administration'. It also embarked on a major expansion of its postgraduate programme. The School of Social Studies was re-named as the School of Health and Social Work, and became part of the new Faculty of Health and Food (see Chapter 10).

Secondly, it merged the Schools of Home Economics, Hotel and Institutional Administration and Nutritional Science into a new School of Food and Consumer Studies, thus effectively reversing the subdivision of the College of Domestic Science that had taken place in 1971. Dr. Richard Moody was appointed as its first Head. Under his direction, the work of the School underwent significant diversification, degrees in 'Consumer Product Management' and in 'Food Science with Management' being added to its already-extensive portfolio. The School also became part of the new Faculty of Health and Food (see Chapter 10).

Thirdly, it removed the Communication Studies section from the School of Social Studies, transferring the four staff involved to the Educational Technology Unit, which was re-named as the Educational Development Unit. The section would subsequently be expanded by the appointment of Modern Languages staff, and would eventually be divided into a Communication Section (under Mr. Cameron Donaldson) and a Modern

Languages Section (under Dr. Murray Hill). These would soon develop their own joint honours degree - in 'Communication with Modern Languages' - and run this under the auspices of the Faculty of Management. As we saw earlier in this chapter, the Communication and Modern Languages staff were later transferred to the School of Information and Media, where they remain to this day.

Fourthly, it created a new Faculty of Management, comprising the Business School, the School of Librarianship and Information Studies, and the new School of Public Administration and Law. Mr. Peter W. (Bill) McIntosh (see Figure 11.6) came to RGIT from Napier Polytechnic in order to become Dean, with executive responsibility for all aspects of the running of the Faculty, including the allocation of budgets and the overall course development strategy. Under his dynamic leadership, the Faculty of Management underwent considerable expansion during the next four years, in terms of both the range of courses offered and its total student numbers. In so doing, it made a major contribution to helping RGIT to achieve the 'critical mass' needed to attain university status, as we will see in Chapter 13.

Chapter 10 : The growth of health-related teaching

THE EVOLUTION OF THE SCHOOL OF PHARMACY

In the previous chapter, we described the phenomenal growth in social and management-related teaching that took place within RGIT and RGU from 1965 onwards. In this chapter, we will describe the similar growth that has taken place in health-related teaching - particularly since the late 1980's. For most of the twentieth century, Pharmacy and Nutritional Science were the only health-related subjects taught, but, as we will see, these were joined by Speech Therapy and Health Visiting during the 1970's, by Nursing during the 1980's, and by Occupational Therapy, Physiotherapy and Radiography during the 1990's. Let us now look at how the teaching of all these different subjects has developed during the RGIT and RGU years, starting with the oldest of them all - Pharmacy.

Figure 10.1 : One of the School of Pharmacy's general laboratories

As we saw in Chapter 2, the School of Pharmacy was originally established in Robert Gordon's College in 1889, and soon began to play a major role in the education and training of the country's Pharmacists. Until the mid-1960's, its main activity was running a non-degree course preparing students to sit the Qualifying Examination of the Pharmaceutical Society of Great Britain - the professional body that was responsible for the accreditation of Pharmacists. In 1966, however, the School made a successful application to the recently-established Council for National Academic Awards to have this course upgraded to a CNAA 'B.Sc. in Pharmacy'. In 1967, it became the first School in RGIT to start running a CNAA degree. This four-year-course had a 'pre-medical' first year that provided students with a basic grounding in chemistry, physics and biology, followed by increasingly specialised study of the different aspects of pharmacy and related subjects such as biochemistry and physiology during the three 'professional' years. It incorporated a large amount of practical work, carried out in well-equipped laboratories like the one shown in Figure 10.1.

In 1969, the School started running a new day-release Higher National Certificate course in 'Medical Laboratory Technology'. It also started making preparations for upgrading its B.Sc. in Pharmacy to an honours degree. This involved enhancing the facilities of the School so that they were capable of supporting honours-level work - by, for example, acquiring additional advanced laboratory equipment like that shown in Figure 10.2. It also involved convincing the CNAA that the staff were capable of teaching at honours level, and that this teaching would be underpinned by appropriate research - something that the CNAA regarded as essential in any School submitting an honours proposal. For this reason, high priority was subsequently given to building up the School's research profile, both in terms of the amount of research being carried out and in terms of the number of publications by staff. The upgrading was approved during 1972-73, and the new four-year honours degree was introduced at the start of the following session. Third-year students on the original unclassified degree who reached the required standard were allowed to transfer to the final year of the new course, thus enabling them to graduate with 'Honours'.

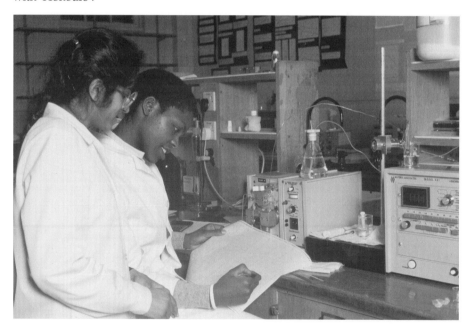

Figure 10.2 : Pharmacy students carrying out advanced experimental work

Once its Honours B.Sc. in Pharmacy became fully established, the School entered a long period of consolidation, during which it continued to build up its research activities and enhance its teaching facilities in order to keep up with the latest developments.

Although it was not able to increase its undergraduate student numbers significantly (these were effectively limited by the capacity of its laboratories), it was able to expand in other areas - particularly post-experience and postgraduate work. During the mid-1970's, for example, it started running a part-time refresher course for Pharmacists, financed by the Scottish Home and Health Department, as well as an evening postgraduate course. Later, it introduced an evening course in 'Biomedical Sciences' leading to Fellowship of the Institute of Medical Laboratory Sciences. This pattern was to continue throughout the 1980's, during which the reputation of the School continued to grow.

At the start of the 1990's, the School started running a new 'Postgraduate Diploma in Clinical Pharmacy', a course that was initially delivered by distance-learning methods. This was subsequently upgraded to an articulated P.G. Diploma/Masters programme, incorporating a major research project following on from the 'Diploma' stage. At around the same time, it introduced a unique nine-week course in 'Effective Drug Management and Rational Drug Use', developed and taught in collaboration with the World Health Organisation's Drug Action Programme. This provided invaluable training for Pharmacists and other health personnel from all parts of the world, mainly from developing countries, and won the School international acclaim.

In the latter part of the 1990's, the School became one of the first in Britain to upgrade its Honours B.Sc. in Pharmacy to an Undergraduate Masters Degree (an M. Pharm.). Even more recently, it has set up a purpose-built, state-of-the-art Pharmaceutical Care Centre, designed to help students to develop the full range of patient-oriented skills that are required by today's practitioners (see Figure 10.3). This incorporates a reception area housing 10,000 anonymised case notes, primary- and secondary-care consulting areas, a simulated community pharmacy, a dispensing laboratory, and an Internet-linked information centre. Facilities such as this help to maintain the School's proud record of producing graduates that are 'among the most employable in the UK'.

Figure 10.3 : Part of the Pharmaceutical Care Centre in the School of Pharmacy

THE DEVELOPMENT OF NUTRITION AND DIETETICS TEACHING

As was shown in Chapter 5, RGIT first started to become involved in the education of Dieticians during the 1930's, through its School of Domestic Science. Work in this area assumed progressively greater importance during the following years, leading to the development of a professional course in Dietetics. By the 1960's, this had grown into a four-year 'National Diploma in Dietetics', designed mainly for therapeutic Dieticians wishing to work in hospitals or other parts of the health service, in industry, or in commercial food-processing firms. It covered all the relevant theoretical aspects of Dietetics, as well as providing practical training in their application. It included practical placement work in a hospital or other appropriate setting, as, indeed, did all subsequent courses in Dietetics run in RGIT and RGU (see Figure 10.4).

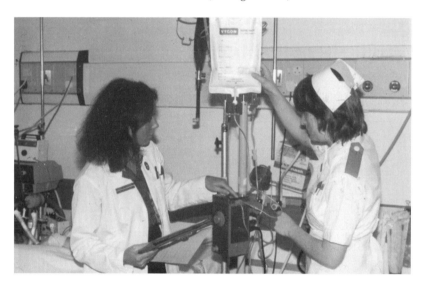

Figure 10.4 : A Dietetics student carrying out placement work in a hospital

By the late 1960's, plans were well in hand to develop a 'B.Sc. in Nutrition and Dietetics', to be run in parallel with the existing Diploma course. A successful submission was made to the CNAA in 1971, allowing the new programme to be introduced in session 1971-72. As we saw in Chapter 7, this was also the session in which the former Nutrition and Dietetics section of the School of Domestic Science was formally established as a separate School of Nutritional Science. Dr. David Livingston, who had been on the staff of the 'Do-School' for several years, was appointed Head of the new School - a post he would hold during the entire 17-year life of the School.

Once the new CNAA degree was well established, Dr. Livingston and his colleagues started making plans to upgrade it to an honours degree. It was proposed to do this by developing a one-year postgraduate 'honours extension' course, which could be taken by graduates of the School's existing degree - and also by graduates of similar courses run in other colleges. It was also hoped to develop a new four-year 'Honours B.Sc. in Food Science and Technology'. Unfortunately, neither of these planned course developments came to early fruition, and were put on hold for some time, although a number of short courses were introduced during the late 1970's. These included courses on various aspects of 'Food Hygiene' for Oil Rig Medics, and courses in 'Basic Food Hygiene' for catering workers. The long-running Diploma in Dietetics had its final intake of students in September 1979, since courses of this type were then being phased out throughout Britain.

Plans to develop the 'honours extension' to the CNAA 'B.Sc. in Nutrition and Dietetics' were revived at the start of the 1980's, and a preliminary proposal was approved in principle by the Scottish Education Department during 1981-82. During the following session, a more detailed proposal was submitted to the Scottish Education Department, but this was rejected on the grounds that it did not articulate with the courses being run by Queen Margaret College in Edinburgh and The Queen's College in Glasgow. There followed several more years of considerable frustration, during which revised proposals were passed back and forth between the various interested parties. Indeed, it was not until the latter part of the 1980's that the School's 'Honours B.Sc. in Nutrition and Dietetics' was finally approved.

By this time, the review of RGIT's academic structure that was briefly described in Chapter 7 was well underway. As we saw, one of the outcomes of this was the reversal of the tripartite sub-division of the School of Domestic Science that had taken place in 1971, with the Schools of Home Economics, Hotel and Institutional Administration and Nutritional Science being re-merged to form a new School of Food and Consumer Studies. Dr. Richard Moody was appointed as Head of the combined School, with Dr. Livingston and the other two former Heads leaving RGIT at the time of the merger.

During the next few years, the School of Food and Consumer Studies made a number of radical changes to its portfolio of courses. By 1993, these included a B.Sc. (Hons.) in 'Nutrition and Dietetics' with State Registration in Dietetics, a B.Sc./B.Sc. (Hons.) in 'Nutrition', and a B.Sc./B.Sc. (Hons.) in 'Food Science with Management'. All of these were, of course, now degrees of The Robert Gordon University rather than CNAA degrees, since RGIT had gained the power to award its own degrees when it achieved full university status in 1992. It had therefore become very much easier to start up new courses as a result of gaining such status, since prior approval from the SED was no longer required.

As we saw in Chapter 5, the Nutrition and Dietetics teaching staff were to undergo two further changes of School during the next eight years. In 1999, they were detached from the School of Food and Consumer Studies and transferred to the School of Health Sciences, in which they became a fourth Department, along with Occupational Therapy, Physiotherapy and Radiography; the remainder of the School was 're-branded' as the School of Hotel, Tourism and Retail Management, and transferred from the Faculty of Health and Social Care to the Faculty of Management. Two years later, they were moved again - joining up with the staff of the School of Applied Sciences to become the new School of Life Sciences. As far as the author is aware, they are still there - for the time being, anyway!

THE RISE AND FALL OF THE SCHOOL OF SPEECH THERAPY

Following discussions with the Scottish Education Department, Aberdeen City Authority and the College of Speech Therapists during 1971-72, it was decided to set up a new School of Speech Therapy within RGIT. This duly opened at St. Andrew Street in October, 1972, with Mrs. Anne W.M. Porteous as the Senior Lecturer-in- Charge (see Figure 10.5). The initial intake of students was 24, thus raising the number of training places for Speech Therapy students in the UK by roughly 10%. These embarked on a three-year Diploma course leading to Licentiateship of the College of Speech Therapists. In order to enable it to run this course, the new School was granted temporary registration by the College of Speech Therapists, and it was confidently expected that full recognition would be granted automatically once the course had been running for the statutory period of three years, and the first cohort of students had duly qualified. Preparations were also put in hand to upgrade the Diploma course to a CNAA 'B.Sc. in Speech Therapy', with a target starting date of October, 1976.

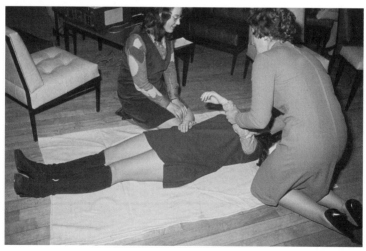

Figure 10.5 : Mrs Anne Porteous (right) carrying out a demonstration on a 'simulated patient' as part of the clinical training of Speech Therapy students.

Unfortunately, the new School ran into problems almost as soon as it started operation. It always found it difficult to recruit staff, and never succeeded in building up - and retaining - the full complement of specialists that running a professional course in Speech Therapy required. As we saw in Chapter 7, these problems were later compounded by the drastic cuts in public spending that were made as a result of the major recession that began in Britain in 1974. These made it increasingly difficult to find suitable clinical placements for the students, and also greatly reduced the job opportunities for qualified Speech Therapists. Towards the end of the 1974-75 session, the College of Speech Therapists made a visit to RGIT in order to appraise the situation. The School was subsequently advised that no new students should be enrolled in 1975-76, and that resumption of recruitment in 1976-77 would be conditional on the staffing and clinical-placement problems being resolved. This did not happen, however, largely due to the worsening national economic situation, and it was therefore decided, with great reluctance, that the School would be shut down once the existing students had completed their training. As we have seen, it ceased to operate at the end of session 1977-78. The School of Speech Therapy thus has the dubious distinction of being the only 'failed School' in the long history of The Robert Gordon University.

THE INCORPORATION OF THE SCHOOL OF HEALTH VISITING

As we saw in Chapter 7, RGIT acquired a second new School at the start of the 1972-73 session - the School of Health Visiting at Willowbank House (see Figure 7.5). Unlike the ill-fated School of Speech Therapy, this had been in existence for many years, however, as the College of Health Visiting run by Aberdeen City Authority, and also had a well-established one-year, full-time course leading to the award of the 'Certificate in Health Visiting' of the Council for the Education and Training of Health Visitors. It also had a full team of experienced staff, comprising the College Head, Miss D. Joan Lamont, two Lecturers and two Secretaries. With the transfer from the City Authority to RGIT, Miss Lamont became Senior Lecturer-in-Charge of the new School of Health Visiting, with Head of School status.

During the remainder of the 1970's, enrolments on the School's main course held up well despite the steadily-deteriorating economic climate, varying between 20 and 30. Fortunately, no major problems were experienced in finding placements for these, all of whom were already qualified nurses (Health Visiting was one of the post-registration specialisms that nurses could undertake). The School also introduced a number of new short courses during this period. These included three-week courses on 'Social Aspects of Health and Disease' and 'Community Health' run for pre-registration students at Foresterhill College, where all Aberdeen's nurses were given their basic training at the time (this would itself become part of RGU in 1996, as we will see later). Following a change in legislation, the School also started running a special six-week course in 'Obstetrics' for registered male nurses who had already trained as Health Visitors. Another important addition to its portfolio was a 13-week 'Health Education' course, run at the request of the Scottish Council for Health Education for personnel intending to work in the new Health Education Units that were set up in the mid-1970's. Miss Lamont retired in 1977, with Miss Alice M.G. Hay taking over as Senior Lecturer-in-Charge of the School.

In July 1982, the School moved from Willowbank House to RGIT's recently-renovated premises at King Street, where it had access to greatly improved facilities. These included an observation suite with a built-in intercom system and camera unit, access to RGIT's new colour television studio, and much better facilities for producing individualised-learning materials and visual aids. The School was also now in close proximity to RGIT's Offshore Survival Centre, thus providing new opportunities for the development of Offshore Health and Safety courses. In 1983, however, the School suffered a major setback, when Miss Hay had to take early retirement due to ill health. Since the School was by far the smallest in the Institute, it was decided that the prospects for the future expansion of health education would be considerably enhanced if it were to become part of a larger, more viable unit. Accordingly, the Health Visiting staff were transferred to the School of Social Studies (which was also located at King Street) at the start of the 1983-84 session. They continued to operate as an identifiable unit within the School, however, and still had a Senior Lecturer-in-Charge.

THE SUBSEQUENT EXPANSION OF NURSING EDUCATION WITHIN RGIT

As we saw in Chapter 7, it was hoped that the incorporation of the School of Health Visiting into the very-much-larger School of Social Studies would provide an environment in which health education and nursing education would be able to expand and flourish. This started to happen almost immediately, with the re-design of the long-running 'Certificate in Health Visiting' in modular form, in order to prepare the way for the possible future incorporation of a course in District Nursing. In 1984, this modular version of the course was approved by the National Board for Nursing, Midwifery and Health Visiting for Scotland. The Board also approved new courses in 'Fieldwork Teaching/Practical Work Teaching' and for 'Assessor/Supervisors of Supervised Practice' - both conducted jointly with Foresterhill College. Two years later, a joint working party was established with Foresterhill College with a view to transferring the 'Certificate in District Nursing' from Foresterhill to RGIT. This transfer was delayed by a number of logistical problems, but was eventually achieved in 1990, when a 'Diploma in District Nursing' started up in parallel with the Health Visiting course, which had itself achieved 'Diploma' status in 1987.

RGIT's on-going commitment to the expansion of nursing education was further reinforced in 1987, when a new Certificate course in 'Occupational Health Nursing' was developed and validated by the National Board. In 1990, this was also upgraded to a Diploma, with a 'conversion' course being provided for holders of the Certificate who wished to upgrade their qualification. This led to the award of a 'Diploma in Occupational Health Nursing Studies', and would be the first of several 'conversion courses' of this type. By this time, the original Health Visiting Section had been expanded into a Nursing Section within the School of Health and Social Work, following the restructuring of the School of Social Studies that took place in 1988 (see Chapter 7). During 1990-91, the Nursing Section developed a highly innovative distance-learning version of the 'Diploma in Occupational Health Nursing' with the aid of a £10,000 grant from Esso (see Chapter

11 for details). This course, which was the first of its type in the world, revolutionised the teaching of Occupational Health Nursing, and increased the number of students on the course from 30 to 120. It also provided a model for the development of other distance-learning courses, both in nursing and in other subject areas (again see Chapter 11).

By the start of the 1991-92 session, the size of the Nursing Section within the School of Health and Social Work had increased considerably. It now comprised a Co-ordinator of Health Courses (Mrs. Ann Lowis), five Lecturers and two Secretaries. Mrs. Lowis (see Figure 11.6) would later become Britain's first Professor of Occupational Health Nursing when she was awarded a Professorial title by RGU in 1994. The Section was now also running a much wider range of courses. These included Diploma courses in 'Health Visiting', 'District Nursing' and 'Occupational Health Nursing', an 'Honours BA in Nursing' (which had just started operation), and short courses for 'Practice Nurses', 'Community Practice Teachers' and 'Supervisors/Assessors of Supervised Practice'. It was therefore decided that the time was right to increase the academic status of the Section by transferring it to the recently-established Centre for Professions Allied to Medicine (see next section) as a full Department of Nursing. This transfer took place later in the session, with Mrs. Lowis becoming Director of Nursing in the new Department.

Figure 10.6 : An Occupational Health Nursing student carrying out an audiometer test on a patient as part of her clinical training

As we will see in Chapter 14, nursing education was to undergo further, even-more-dramatic expansion once RGIT acquired full university status in 1992. First, the

Nursing Department would be established as a fully-independent School of Nursing. Then, in 1996, it would be combined with the former Foresterhill College to form a new Associate Faculty of Nursing, Midwifery and Community Studies within RGU's Faculty of Health and Food. Finally, this would be re-designated as RGU's School of Nursing and Midwifery, and would become the largest School in the University, with over 2000 students. RGU's nursing staff would also have to undergo no fewer than four changes of location during the next ten years, moving to Kepplestone in 1993, then joining their new colleagues at Foresterhill in 1997, moving to Hilton in 1999, and, finally (they hope!) moving into the Faculty of Health and Social Care's new custom-built building at Garthdee in 2002.

THE INCORPORATION OF THE PROFESSIONS ALLIED TO MEDICINE

Another major expansion of RGIT's health-related activities took place in April, 1990, when Grampian Health Board's Schools of Occupational Therapy, Physiotherapy and Radiography joined the Institute. This move, which had been under negotiation for some time, was part of the general policy of transferring the educational responsibilities of the Health Boards into the higher education sector. As Professor Ian Nowell, Dean of the Faculty of Health and Food explained, the Health Boards 'were becoming increasingly aware that their primary function was the prevention of illness and the provision of health care.' Because of this, it was felt that the three Schools 'were, in some senses, being hindered in terms of their academic and educational development by being located in the Health Board', and that a transfer to RGIT 'would be appropriate for the development of both staff and courses, to the benefit of staff and the benefit of students.'

Of the three Schools, two (Occupational Therapy and Physiotherapy) were based at Woolmanhill - see Figure 10.7. The third (Radiography) was based at Foresterhill at the time of the transfer, but moved to Woolmanhill a few years later. The oldest of the three Schools was Radiography, which had been established in 1936, initially staffed by Clinical Radiographers working part-time, with its first full-time teaching staff being appointed in 1960. Its Principal was Mr. Donald Graham (see Figure 10.8), who had worked in the School since 1974. The next oldest was Physiotherapy, which had been founded in 1962; its Principal was Mrs. (later to become Dr. and then Professor) Valerie A. Maehle. The youngest was Occupational Therapy, which had been set up in 1976 by Miss Catherine Paterson, who was still its Principal at the time of the transfer. When the three Schools joined RGIT, they became Departments of the Centre for Professions Allied to Medicine within the Faculty of Health and Food. The three former Principals became Directors of their respective Departments, which retained considerable individual autonomy within the Centre.

At the time when they joined RGIT, all three Schools were running long-established three-year Diploma courses in their specialist areas. The course in 'Occupational Therapy' led to state registration by the Council for Professions Supplementary to Medicine, a

Figure 10.7 : Woolmanhill Hospital, where Grampian Health Board's Schools of Occupational Therapy and Physiotherapy were based in 1990

condition of employment for Occupational Therapists working in the National Health Service. That in 'Physiotherapy' led to membership of the Chartered Society of Physiotherapy, and was also recognised by the Council for Professions Supplementary to Medicine. The 'Radiography' course had evolved from that leading to the 'Diploma of the College of Radiographers', which was, until shortly before the transfer, the only qualification recognised for state registration in the field. All three courses consisted of an integrated mixture of academic teaching and practical work, including programmes of progressively-more-demanding clinical practice placements (see Figure 10.9).

Since one of the primary reasons for transferring the three Schools to RGIT was to provide them with the opportunity to upgrade their Diploma courses to CNAA degrees, work on the development of the necessary proposals started almost immediately. All three Departments were soon running B.Sc. degrees in their respective subjects, and, within a comparatively short time, two of these (the 'B.Sc. in Physiotherapy' and the 'B.Sc. in Occupational Therapy') were further upgraded to honours degrees. The 'B.Sc. in Radiography' followed later in the 1990's. As we saw in the last section, the three original Departments within the Centre for Professions Allied to Medicine were subsequently temporarily joined by a fourth - the Department of Nursing, which was transferred to the Centre from the School of Health and Social Work during the 1991-92 session.

During the following years, the Centre further developed its portfolio of courses, supplementing its undergraduate programmes by new integrated programmes in 'Health Promotion', 'Medical Ultrasound' and 'Health Sciences' at 'Masters' level. In 1993, it was

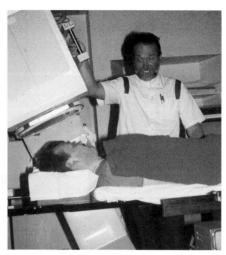

Figure 10.8 : Mr. Donald Graham, Director of the Department of Radiography in the Centre for Professions Allied to Medicine, carrying out a demonstration for students at Foresterhill Hospital

granted full School status within the new Robert Gordon University as the School of Health Sciences, with Mrs. Maehle being appointed as its Head. As a School, it continued to develop new courses and build up its research activities, while still retaining its traditional strong links with practitioners and managers in the various fields in which it operated. Within a short time, however, one of its four constituent Departments (Nursing) had grown so large that it was decided to make it a separate School (see previous section). The remaining three Departments continued to develop during the remainder of the 1990's, and, in 1999, were again temporarily joined by a fourth Department, when the Nutrition and Dietetics staff in the School of Food and Consumer Studies were transferred to the School. As we saw earlier, they were transferred out again two years later, to become part of the School of Life Sciences. In 2002, the School of Health Sciences itself underwent a move - to the new Faculty of Health and Social Care building at Garthdee (see Section 4).

Figure 10.9 : An Occupational Therapy student working with an elderly patient during one of her clinical practice placements

Chapter 11 : Changes in educational methodology

THE CHANGING FACE OF TERTIARY EDUCATION

During the 42 years between entering Aberdeen University as a student of Natural Philosophy in 1959 and retiring from The Robert Gordon University in 2001, the author has seen the face of tertiary education change almost beyond recognition. He has seen the number of universities in Britain increase almost fivefold to over 100, the percentage of school-leavers entering higher education rise from under 5% to roughly 40% (almost 50% in Scotland), and the range of courses available to these students widen to the extent that it is now possible to study virtually any subject *somewhere* in the country. He has also seen the way in which tertiary education is *delivered* undergo a number of very significant changes, and, having worked as an educational technologist and educational developer since 1973, has himself been very heavily involved in many of these changes.

In this chapter, we will take a detailed look at some of the most important of these changes in educational methodology. We will show how there has been a progressive shift away from the traditional teacher/institution-centred approach that dominated tertiary education - and, in particular, higher education - for so long. We will also see how there is now a much greater emphasis on developing transferable-process and life skills of various types, and how communication and information technology (C & IT) is playing an increasingly important role in virtually all aspects of tertiary education. Finally, we will see how college and university teachers are now expected to have a much wider range of pedagogical (or should one say andragogical?) skills than was ever the case in the past.

THE SHIFT TOWARDS A MORE STUDENT-CENTRED APPROACH

Traditionally, tertiary education has been almost entirely based on the teacher/institution-centred approach mentioned in the last section. In this, the individual student has little or no control over the nature of the instruction process, with the lecture playing a dominant role in most courses. Indeed, when the author carried out a survey of teaching methods in RGIT in 1984, he found that students spent, on average, over 30% of their contact time sitting passively in lectures - a proportion that rose to over 40% in the case of some science-based and other technical courses. It was recognised that these figures were far too high, and the author was asked to speak to all course teams in order to 'encourage' them to widen the range of the teaching/learning methods that they used. Some of them did, but, at the time, the great majority did not.

The various weaknesses of the lecture as a didactic method have long been recognised. Indeed, research carried out at Glamorgan University indicates that the traditional 'live lecture' is an extremely inefficient vehicle for bringing about effective learning, with students retaining as little as 5% of the material covered in some cases.

Other research has shown that most lectures are also far too long, since the average attention span of students is only 20 minutes or so! It is now generally agreed that self-study methods involving the use of paper-based materials, audiovisual media or computers can be much more effective in enabling lasting learning to take place - particularly if they incorporate significant amounts of student activity and self-assessment. For this reason, there has been a progressive shift towards the use of such methods during the last 10-15 years. This trend was clearly shown in a survey of innovative teaching methods that was carried out in RGU's Faculty of Management in the early 1990's, and, as we will see in Chapter 16, now appears to be accelerating throughout the University.

Let us now look at two specific examples of how staff have replaced some of the lectures in their courses with student-centred methods of different types.

Our first example is an integrated lecture/tutorial/self-study course in 'Basic Economics' that was developed by Mr. James Duncan of Aberdeen Business School in the early 1990's, as part of his School's 'Enterprise in Higher Education' programme. This was piloted in the School's 'BA in European Business Administration with Languages', and was subsequently used in five separate degree programmes. Introduction of the course enabled formal lectures in 'Basic Economics' to be reduced to one a week (previously two a week), and tutorials to be reduced to one a fortnight (previously one a week). Much of the content previously covered by lectures was now delivered via directed study of material in a standard textbook, which was made an 'essential purchase' for students. During the first part of the course, students were provided with study guides incorporating lecture summaries, but the latter were subsequently replaced by lecture guides in order to encourage the students to take progressively greater responsibility for their own learning. Although a few students did not like the new approach because it made them 'work harder', the majority were perfectly happy with the changes, and overall performance in examinations was not adversely affected. Because of its success, the approach was subsequently extended to other courses.

Our second example is an integrated 25-week course in 'Environmental Policy and Management' that Professor Alistair McCulloch of the School of Public Administration and Law developed for use in the Honours Year of the School's 'BA in Public Policy and Management' at around the same time. This was designed to make the *students themselves* responsible for delivering the bulk of the content - and also to ensure their full participation in learning activities (such as seminars) that they sometimes did their best to avoid! Following an intensive five-week introduction to the subject via lectures, videos and visiting speakers, the students spent the remainder of the session first preparing in-depth seminar papers and then presenting these in class. Each student was also provided with a full set of the seminar papers, so that the class also effectively wrote their own course 'textbook'. The students were assessed on the intrinsic quality of their papers, the quality of their presentations, their defence of their papers, and their overall contribution to the seminar programme. This method of course delivery proved extremely popular with the students involved, and served as a model for other lecturers who wished to introduce a greater degree of student participation into the later stages of honours degrees and into postgraduate courses. It is a good example of the sort of innovative thinking that became common in RGIT in the late 1980's and early 1990's, partly as a result of the 'Enterprise in Higher Education' programme.

**Figure 11.1 : A student of the former School of Chemistry
using a tape-model kit to study the molecular structure of different compounds.**

Staff have also been highly innovative in providing students with self-study materials designed to supplement and support their class teaching. Over the years, several Schools have established learning resource centres of various types, containing a wide range of paper-based, media-based and (more recently) computer-based student learning packages. One of the first to do so was the School of Chemistry during the late 1970's, whose student self-study packages included the 'tape-model' kit shown in Figure 11.1. This enabled students of organic chemistry to construct 'ball-and-spring' molecular models of different compounds, receiving instructions on how to do so and other relevant information via audiotape. Another was the School of Librarianship and Information Studies (now the School of Information and Media), which developed a series of multimedia packages on bibliographic classification and indexing during the early 1990's.. These were used both as a replacement for and as a supplement to formal classes on this topic. As we will see in Section 4, all Schools now make use of computer-based self-study packages of various types, most of them being made available to students via the University Intranet.

Another manifestation of the move towards student-centred learning is the rapid growth in distance learning that has taken place since the late 1980's. RGIT's first course of this type was the 'Diploma in Occupational Health Nursing', a one-year, post-experience, professional course that was originally developed as a conventional taught course comprising six self-contained modules that could be taken over up to three years. A market survey carried out in 1989, after the course had been running for over a year, showed that it was not fully meeting the needs of the Occupational Health Nursing community, however. The survey indicated that comparatively few working OH Nurses could manage to attend RGIT for the 27 weeks required, even when these were spread over three years. The solution was to convert the course into distance-learning format, thus reducing the attendance requirement to six weeks - one per module. The conversion was carried out by the author and Mrs. (later Professor) Ann Lowis during 1990-91, and, for the next year, the two versions of the course (taught and distance-learning) were run in parallel. The distance-learning version proved so popular, however, that virtually all the 'traditional' students asked to be transferred on to the other route; thus, the 'taught' route was rapidly phased out. As a result, virtually all the post-registration courses in Nursing that were subsequently developed were delivered by distance-learning mode, using the 'OH Diploma' as a model (see Chapter 10). Similar courses were also developed by other Schools. Initially, all such courses made use of paper-based distance-learning materials, but, as we will see in Chapters 14 and 16, delivery of courses to remote students via the Internet started to become a 'growth industry' during the late 1990's.

One of the most important and wide-ranging manifestations of the move towards a more student-centred and more flexible tertiary-education system has been the development of *Credit Accumulation and Transfer* (*CAT*). In Scotland (which is well ahead of the rest of the United Kingdom in this area), this takes the form of the SCOTCAT system in which all tertiary-education establishments now participate. This system, which was set up during the late 1980's and early 1990's, enables all tertiary-level courses and course units, and all post-school learning experiences, to be *CAT rated*, ie awarded the appropriate number of SCOTCAT points at the appropriate level. The key to the system is that such ratings are intended to be recognised by other participating institutions, so that a course unit in Institution A that attracts a certain number of points at a particular level may be recognised as being the equivalent of a similar course unit in Institution B that attracts the same number of points at the same level. This enables students to build up a 'bank' of generally-recognised credit points for all appropriate learning, to use these to contribute towards formal awards, and to move between courses - and even between institutions - in so doing. All RGU's degree and postgraduate courses are now fully CAT rated, as are most of its short courses.

THE CHANGE IN BALANCE BETWEEN CONTENT AND PROCESS

Until comparatively recently, tertiary education has generally been highly *content centred*, its main aim being to provide students with comprehensive, state-of-the art *knowledge* of the subject that they elected to study. Students were, of course, also expected to develop the various *specialist skills* associated with their subject discipline, eg laboratory skills, clinical skills or studio skills. In very few courses, however, was any systematic attempt made to help students to develop the various *transferable-process skills* that they would need in order to succeed in the outside world - things like communication skills, interpersonal and group skills, study skills and general problem-solving skills. All this has changed during the last 30 years, however, and the development of wider skills of the latter type is now regarded as one of the most important roles of tertiary education. As a result, such education has become very much more *process-centred* than was the case in the past, and now more accurately reflects B.F. Skinner's definition of 'true education' as 'what is left when the facts have been forgotten'.

Figure 11.2 : 'SODIT' - a simulated planning exercise on the impact of North Sea Oil being run in the Scott Sutherland School of Architecture during the early 1970's.

One of the first ways in which RGIT became actively involved in promoting a more process-centred approach to education was through its pioneering work on educational games and simulations. This work had its origins in the Scott Sutherland School of Architecture during the early 1970's, when Mr. Drew Mackie and his colleagues developed a number of highly-innovative simulation exercises designed for use in the teaching of planning and related areas. These included one that rejoiced in the name of 'SODIT' - the 'Scottish Oil Development Investigational Tool' (see Figure 11.2). Mr. Mackie left RGIT at the end of 1973, when the locus of the Institute's work on simulation/gaming shifted to the School of Physics and the newly-formed Educational Technology Unit. During the next twenty years, a multi-disciplinary team led by Professor Norman Langton (Head of the School of Physics) and the author developed a whole series of simulation/ games based on different aspects of science and technology, (see Chapter 12 for further details). Most of these were published by prestigious bodies such as the Institution of Electrical Engineers, the Association for Science Education, the Scottish Council for

Educational Technology, the Scottish Education Department, the United Kingdom Atomic Energy Authority and Phillips Petroleum, and several achieved widespread use throughout the world.

One of the most successful of these simulation/games was 'The Power Station Game', a role-playing simulation exercise developed on behalf of the Scottish Education Department between 1973 and 1975. This involved three teams of students drawing up plans for building different types of power station (coal-fired, oil-fired and nuclear), and then presenting the cases for building each to the 'Generating Board', who decided which scheme to adopt (see Figure 11.3). The exercise was published by the Institution of Electrical Engineers in 1975, and subsequently achieved widespread use in secondary schools, colleges, universities and training establishments, both within the UK and abroad. In RGIT, it was used mainly with science and engineering students, serving as a vehicle both for teaching them about the electricity industry and for helping them to develop a wide range of process skills, including numerical, problem-solving, decision-making, interpersonal and presentation skills. The exercise was also widely used by the IEE's Schools Liaison Service and by the Central Electricity Generating Board, who used it as a training tool for engineers and managers.

Figure 11.3 : The climax of 'The Power Station Game', in which the three teams present their cases to the 'Generating Board'

During the late 1970's and 1980's, more and more RGIT staff recognised the great potential of games, simulations and other group exercises as vehicles for developing key skills of different types, and started to make regular use of them with their students. The

Institute's Communication Studies staff proved to be particularly heavy users, since such exercises turned out to be ideal vehicles for helping students to develop their interpersonal, oral-communication and presentation skills. One particularly interesting development was the highly innovative use of group-problem-solving exercises that was made by the School of Computer and Mathematical Sciences during the late 1980's and 1990's.. These were used to develop mathematical-modelling and consultancy skills, and involved small groups of students taking on the role of 'consultants' brought in to help their 'clients' solve real-life problems, such as 'helping a dental practice to optimise its appointment system', or 'determining the most effective types of knots in different situations' (see Figure 11.4). As a result, the employment prospects of the students involved were increased significantly.

Figure 11.4 : Students of the School of Computer and Mathematical Sciences carrying out a group-problem-solving exercise on the properties of knots.

Since the early 1980's, the spread of process-centred learning throughout tertiary education has been greatly stimulated by a number of important national developments. The initial catalyst was the 1981 Government White Paper: '*A New Training Initiative : a Programme for Action*'. This recognised the need to produce a more versatile, better-trained workforce in order to enable Britain to compete successfully in the European market. The move was further stimulated by a later White Paper: '*Working Together : Education and Training*', which was published in 1986. This triggered the competence movement in tertiary education, and eventually led to the conversion of virtually all further-education courses (and most sub-degree higher-education courses) to a criterion-referenced, competence-based format. It also led to the appearance of National Vocational Qualifications (NVQ's) and General National Vocational Qualifications (GNVQ's) - and to their Scottish equivalents SVQ's and GSVQ's. As a direct result of the competence movement, higher education gradually became more and more process-centred during the late 1980's and 1990's, recognition of the importance of developing key skills and specification of programme goals in terms of clearly-defined learning outcomes eventually becoming the norm.

One specific Government initiative that had a particularly strong influence on these developments was the 'Enterprise in Higher Education' programme that was launched in 1988. This was designed to promote an 'enterprise culture', by helping the citizens of tomorrow to develop entrepreneurial, decision-making and other transferable-process skills. All Britain's higher education institutions were invited to bid for funding under the scheme. During the following three years, the Government initiated EHE projects in 56 separate universities, polytechnics and colleges, funding these to the tune of £58 million. Largely because of the initiative of Mr. Gavin Ross, the Vice Principal at the time, RGIT was one of the first ten institutions in the UK to benefit from the new scheme, receiving roughly £1 million during the next five years to finance its 'Enterprise' programme. In order to qualify for funding under this programme, all of RGIT's Schools had to produce their own 'Enterprise Plans', in which they showed how they intended to broaden their teaching methods in order to help their students develop the type of skills that the Government wanted. The programme proved to be a great success, showing that massive injection of Government funding, linked to proof of delivery, could produce results that mere 'missionary work' by educational developers like the author could never achieve on its own!

THE INCREASE IN THE USE OF COMMUNICATION AND INFORMATION TECHNOLOGY

It is difficult for the modern generation, who take computers for granted, to realise that electronic computers have been around for a comparatively short time. They were originally developed in Britain and the United States during the latter stages of the Second World War, and were used for such things as code-breaking and calculating artillery trajectories. The original 'first-generation' machines were based on thermionic valve technology, were primitive by modern standards, and were extremely expensive both to build and to run. Thus, their use was initially restricted to Government agencies, a few well-endowed universities, and large commercial and industrial organisations. This was the case until the late 1950's, when 'second-generation' computers based on the recently-invented transistor started to replace valve machines. Use of transistors enabled computers to become smaller, cheaper, faster, more powerful, and more versatile, and, as a result, they started to become much more widely used. As we saw in Chapter 7, RGIT purchased such a machine in 1966. This was run by the School of Mathematics, and, for the next eight years, its use was largely limited to facilitating the teaching of the embryonic subject of Computer Science and supporting academic research.

By the early 1970's, even more powerful and versatile 'third-generation' computers based on integrated circuits (or 'chips') started to appear. These enabled computers to be run on a 'time-sharing' basis, with many users being able to access the same central facilities simultaneously, through remote terminals. In 1976, RGIT received SED funding to purchase a machine of this type - a DEC System 20 that was installed in the Computer Services Unit at St. Andrew Street that had been responsible for the Institute's computer facilities since 1974 (see Chapter 7). The arrival of the 'DEC 20' enabled many more Schools and Departments of RGIT to start making extensive use of the computer, both to support research and administration and, for the first time, as an integral part of the teaching process, since students could now access the new machine directly. This process was accelerated by the appearance of increasingly user-friendly 'applications packages', which enabled students to do such things as study computer programming on-line, process experimental results, carry out statistical analysis of data, and work with computer simulations and computer-aided-design systems. As a result, demand for computing facilities increased rapidly during the late 1970's and early 1980's - and more and more money had to be spent regularly upgrading the Institute's computer systems.

Figure 11.5 : One of RGIT's first microcomputer laboratories

Computer development continued apace, and, during the late 1970s, 'fourth-generation' machines based on the use of microprocessors started to appear. This enabled inexpensive 'microcomputers' to be developed, and, during the early 1980's, these started to be widely used throughout the Institute. Schools could now set up their own 'computer labs' at comparatively low cost, and many of them started to do so (see Figure 11.5). They included the School of Mathematics (which later became the School of Mathematical Sciences and Computer Studies), the School of Librarianship (later to become the School of Librarianship and Information Studies), the two Engineering Schools, the various

Science Schools and the School of Architecture. During the 1980's, several of these Schools started to take over more and more responsibility for running their own computer facilities, a process that continued during most of the 1990's, when computers continued to increase in power and versatility every year. By now, all Schools were making use of computers in some way, and many were becoming more and more heavily reliant on them for the support and delivery of their teaching programmes. These developments will be described in Section 4 of the book, which will also look in detail at the way in which RGU is moving fully into the 'electronic age' by making progressively greater use of the Internet technology that was developed during the late 1990's.

Let us now look at some of the specific ways in which communication and information technology has affected the work of RGIT and RGU since the first mainframe computer was installed in 1966.

Use of the computer as a 'supercalculator'

This was the original - and, for a time, only - role of the computer, namely, as a tool for carrying out complicated and/or time-consuming calculations. Digital computers are ideally suited to this form of use, enabling calculations that would previously have taken hundreds or even thousands of man-hours to be completed in a matter of minutes or even less. Such use of the computer as a 'supercalculator' is no longer limited to people carrying out research work in colleges and universities, as was largely the case until the mid-1970's. Since then, students at all levels - from first-year undergraduates to postgraduate students - have been making progressively greater use of the computer as a tool in their day-to-day work. As a matter of routine, students now use computers to fit graphs to experimental results, to carry out statistical analysis of data, and to carry out other difficult calculations related to their work. Until comparatively recently, all such tasks had to be carried out manually, using primitive aids to calculation such as logarithmic tables, slide rules and mechanical calculators. The universal availability of electronic calculators and computers has made all of these completely obsolete, and has had an impact on education that can truly be described as 'revolutionary'.

Use of the computer as a data base

Use of the computer to store and facilitate the subsequent retrieval of information has had an equally important impact on tertiary education. Staff and students who wish to carry out a literature search in a given field, for example, no longer have to do so manually. Simply by linking up to an appropriate database, or carrying out a wider Internet search, they can obtain abstracts of virtually any paper, article or book that has ever been written on the subject - and can often also access the original sources themselves. Staff and students are now also able to build up their own personal data bases, using easily-accessible computer systems whose storage capacity is, to all intents and purposes, virtually unlimited. Needless to say, data bases are also becoming increasingly widely used for such things as storing student assessment results and other records, maintaining personnel, payroll and financial records, keeping inventories of equipment and other materials, and holding files of all types (see Chapter 16).

Use of the computer in word processing and desktop publishing

Possibly the area in which computers have had their greatest impact on tertiary education so far has been their use in word processing and desktop publishing. These technologies started to appear during the mid-1980's, and, since then, have achieved almost universal use by both staff and students. They have, for example, made it possible for lecturers to produce virtually all their own teaching-support materials, first as paper-based handouts and overhead-projector transparencies, then as 'PowerPoint' presentations for display using a data projector, and, more recently, as electronic packages that students can access directly via the University Intranet. They have also made it possible for students to produce essays, reports and other assignments in increasingly sophisticated formats. From the late 1980's onwards, students started to submit more and more of their assignments in word-processed form, and this eventually became the norm. As we will see in Chapter 16, it will probably soon become standard practice for them to submit all such assignments by e-mail - and receive feedback from staff in the same way.

Use of computers as 'simulated laboratories'

Ever since they were first invented, computers have been used to facilitate the study of models of real-life and imaginary situations of all types, enabling design features and parameters to be varied and the likely effects on the system determined. This has enabled both research workers and students to carry out a wide range of 'simulated experiments' that would otherwise be impracticable or even impossible, eg examining models of the national economy, 'running' nuclear reactors and other complicated plant, and studying the interiors of stars. It has also enabled staff and students to carry out a wide variety of computer-aided design work, something that has proved particularly useful in the teaching of subjects such as engineering, architecture and art. Over the years, computer simulations have become increasingly sophisticated, and recent developments such as multimedia and virtual reality are further enhancing their versatility and usefulness.

Use of computers as 'substitute tutors'

Computers can also be used as 'substitute tutors', and, since the late 1960's, a large amount of Government money has been invested in the development of computer-based self-study systems of ever-increasing sophistication and versatility. Such packages are particularly suitable for teaching the basic facts and principles of a subject, and for reinforcing the teaching of such facts and principles through exercises of the 'drill-and-practice' type. Until comparatively recently, however, they have not had anything like the same impact on tertiary-level teaching as the other computer applications described in this section, largely because their use has been limited to a few pioneers and enthusiasts. This was certainly the case in RGIT and RGU until the late 1990's, but, as we will see in Chapter 16, more and more staff are now starting to make serious use of tutor-mode computer-based-learning packages, eg for use in the delivery of distance-learning courses via the University's Virtual Campus.

Use of computer networks for communication purposes

Since microcomputers and personal computers started to spread throughout institutions such as RGIT during the early 1980's, they have been interlinked with one another to form networks of ever-increasing size and complexity - local area networks, institute-wide networks, metropolitan area networks, national networks such as JANET and SUPERJANET, and, finally, the World-wide Internet. These networks enable institutions to communicate with their students, enable students to communicate among themselves through 'computer conferences' and 'chat' facilities, and also enable staff and students to communicate with external individuals and organisations. They also support completely new methods of teaching such as videoconferencing, whereby groups of staff and students in different parts of the same institution or in different institutions can interact with one another almost as if they were in the same room, and on-line distance-learning systems such as those that are now being delivered via RGU's Virtual Campus. As we will see in Chapter 16, computer-mediated communication of these various types is currently changing tertiary education in ways that could not have been imagined twenty years ago.

THE INTRODUCTION OF FORMAL TRAINING FOR LECTURERS

It is one of the major anomalies of British education that there has never been any mandatory requirement for people taking up teaching posts in universities, colleges and other higher-education establishments to undertake any formal training in teaching methodology. Since the late 1980's, however, an increasing number of such establishments have started to provide such training on a voluntary basis, and a number have now made it compulsory for new, inexperienced teaching staff. As a result of the recommendations made in recent national reports such as the 1997 *Dearing Report*, however, all of Britain's universities and other higher education institutions (HEI's) are coming under increasing pressure to provide such training, and to ensure that their staff avail themselves of it. As we will now see, RGIT was the first HEI in Scotland - and, indeed, in Britain - to run a course of this type for its staff.

People who embark on teaching careers in higher education come from a wide range of backgrounds. Many come straight from university, often building on their initial undergraduate degree by undertaking specialist postgraduate work in some particular area of their chosen discipline, or a research programme taken to masters, doctoral or post-doctoral level. Others decide to move into teaching after a period of work in industry, commerce or one of the professions. Only a small minority will have received any systematic instruction in the theory and practice of tertiary education, however, and even fewer will have obtained a formal postgraduate qualification in this area.

Until comparatively recently, two main routes were open to British higher-education teaching staff who wished to obtain such a qualification. The first was to undertake a postgraduate training course in tertiary-level teaching at a college of education or university. The second was to undertake an academic course such as a Dip.Ed. or an M.Ed. The first option often proved less than satisfactory, however, because the available courses were all designed to meet the needs of *further* education rather than *higher* education, and tended to concentrate on skills training rather than on the provision of rigorous academic education. The second option was also less than ideal, since most Dip.Ed.'s and M.Ed.'s tended to concentrate on the academic and theoretical aspects of education rather than on the development of teaching skills, and were again seldom designed to meet the specific needs of higher-education teachers. What was clearly needed was a completely new type of course that:

(a) was specifically designed to meet the needs of academic staff working in the higher-education sector;

(b) provided a proper balance between the development of teaching skills and the provision of rigorous academic education.

It was in order to fill this very real gap in current training provision that, in 1987, Dr. David Kennedy took steps to develop a course of the type required. At the time, he was Chairman of the Committee of Principals and Directors of the Scottish Central Institutions, and, in this capacity, he asked the Central Institutions' Committee for Educational Development (CICED) to set up an *ad-hoc* working group in order to do so. He specified that such a course would have to be generic in nature, so that it could be used in all the CI's, and would also have to be designed in such a way that it could be fitted into the work schedules of in-post staff with the minimum of disruption. In order to give the course credibility, it would also have to lead to a recognisable postgraduate qualification such as a P.G. Certificate.

The resulting working party was chaired by the author, and also contained representatives of Dundee Institute of Technology (now Abertay University), Napier Polytechnic of Edinburgh (now Napier University), the Northern College, Paisley College of Technology (now Paisley University), Queen Margaret College, Edinburgh, the Queen's College, Glasgow and the Scottish Further Education Unit. The working group first met in March, 1988, and, during the next six months, developed what subsequently became known as the 'CICED Postgraduate Certificate in Tertiary-Level Teaching Methods'. Since the bulk of the work on the development of the course documentation had been carried out by the author, it was agreed that the new programme should be piloted in RGIT. The course was therefore formally validated in RGIT at the end of 1988 as part of the portfolio of the Faculty of Management, thus allowing it to start at the beginning of 1989, with the author as Course Leader.

The CICED P.G. Certificate was primarily designed for new, inexperienced lecturers, although it was intended that more experienced staff should also be able to benefit from it. Its overall aim was to provide course members with the basic knowledge and skills that are required to teach effectively at tertiary level. Specifically, the course was designed to enable them:

- to make effective use of *objectives* in planning their teaching;
- to select appropriate *teaching/learning methods* for achieving these objectives;
- to make effective use of the full range of teaching/learning methods appropriate to their discipline, including *mass-instruction, individualised-learning* and *group-learning* methods;
- to make effective use of all the various *presentation techniques* and *instructional media* that were then available, including computers;
- to make effective use of the full range of *student assessment* techniques that were then available;
- to make effective use of *evaluation* in course, curriculum and personal development.

In order to maximise its flexibility, it was decided to package the course in the form of eight self-contained modules, each dealing with a specific aspect of tertiary-level teaching. Each of these eight modules had its own detailed set of learning targets, expressed in the form of the behavioural objectives that were standard at the time (in later versions of the course, these were expressed in terms of learning outcomes, since these had become the new fashion). Since the course was designed to fit round the normal work schedules of course members, there were no formal classes, all the work being carried out on an open-learning, self-study basis. Each module of the course involved working through a customised self-study programme broken down into a series of activities, each designed to help the course member achieve one of the detailed behavioural objectives for the module. Once this stage of the work was completed, the course member underwent a formative-assessment tutorial with their Personal Course Tutor, and then carried out a negotiated assignment on which the summative assessment for the module was based (the course had no examinations). The first two people to be awarded the new P.G. Certificate were Mr. James Christie, a Lecturer in Computing, and Mrs. (later Professor) Ann Lowis, then a Lecturer in Nursing - see Figure 11.6. These became the first people in Britain to gain a specialist teaching qualification of this type.

Once the course had become well established within RGIT, and was seen to be running successfully, it was decided to proceed with its dissemination throughout the other Scottish Central Institutions. Two practical measures were taken in order to promote and facilitate this. The first was to hold a half-day seminar on the course in RGIT, a seminar that was open to representatives of all the CI's and other interested parties. At this seminar, the author gave a presentation on how the course had been set up and run in RGIT, and participants also had the opportunity to talk to course members and other people involved in the course. The second was to produce a package of resource materials for course organisers. This provided general guidance on how to set up and run the course, details of how the course had been validated at RGIT, a full set of the RGIT course documentation, detailed information about how the course was being run at RGIT, and feedback on the RGIT experience. The package was circulated to all Scottish CI's, and was also made available to other interested parties at a nominal charge.

Figure 11.6 : The first two people to complete the P.G. Certificate in Tertiary-Level Teaching Methods at RGIT - L to R, Bill McIntosh (Dean of the Faculty of Management), Ann Lowis, James Christie, the author.

The above dissemination proved extremely successful, with the course eventually being taken up and run by five of the largest CI's - Glasgow College of Technology, Napier Polytechnic of Edinburgh, Queen Margaret College, The Queen's College, and Paisley College. Two smaller CI's (The Scottish College of Textiles and the Scottish College of Agriculture, Aberdeen) subsequently entered into collaborative arrangements with Napier and RGIT to enable their staff to have access to the course. The CICED course also aroused a great deal of interest outside Scotland, serving as a useful model for other HEI's who were considering setting up similar training courses for their staff.

Within RGIT, the course soon became established as a key part of the Institute's overall staff development system, with staff from all Schools enrolling in ever-increasing numbers. Subsequent evaluation showed that it was proving extremely successful in achieving its various educational objectives, and was making a significant contribution to the enhancement of the overall quality of teaching. Nor was the educational benefit of the course limited to the people who had actually undertaken it, since feedback received from course members and from their Heads of Schools indicated that it also appeared to be having a beneficial 'spin-off' effect. Not only were course members improving the quality of *their own* teaching, they were also helping to increase general awareness of what constituted 'good practice' by talking to their colleagues.

Indeed, in their report on the 1995 Quality Audit of The Robert Gordon University (see Chapter 14), the Higher Education Quality Council commented extremely favourably on its contribution to the general enhancement of teaching quality throughout the University.

In 1996, RGU's version of the course was completely re-written in order to prepare it for accreditation by the Staff and Educational Development Association (SEDA), conform with new national specifications for Postgraduate Certificates, and take account of other recent developments in higher education. Its name was also changed to the 'Postgraduate Certificate in Tertiary-Level *Teaching*', since it now dealt with a much wider range of topics related to tertiary education. Two years later, a 'portfolio'-based version was developed in order to enable experienced teaching staff to obtain the P.G. Certificate without having to work through the full course, and this was run in parallel with the 'traditional' open-learning version. At the start of the new millennium, the course was accredited by the newly-established Institute for Learning and Teaching, and became the standard route to full ILT membership for new teaching staff. It was also made possible for staff to undertake both versions of the course electronically, using the new Intranet that was installed throughout RGU between 2000 and 2002 (see Chapter 16).

Chapter 12 : Research, consultancy and external collaboration

THE GROWTH OF RESEARCH WITHIN RGIT

One of the features of the 'RGIT years' was the steady growth of research, consultancy and collaboration with external bodies that took place under all three of its Directors and Principals. In this chapter, we will take a detailed look at these related sets of activities, all of which were important manifestations of the Institute's strong involvement with industry, commerce, the professions and the community at large. First, we will show how research grew from a 'cottage industry' involving only a handful of staff to a key activity carried out in every single one of its Schools on an increasingly-large scale. Then, we will look at the Institute's involvement in industrial liaison and consultancy, showing how these were often closely linked to its research activities; indeed, in some cases, they were virtually the same thing. Finally, we will examine some of the educational development work that Institute staff carried out in collaboration with outside bodies.

Until the mid-1960's, very little research was carried out in Robert Gordon's Technical College, and that which *was* done involved only a small number of staff in a few Schools. As we saw in Chapter 5, the first staff to become involved in 'serious' research were some of the Nutritionists working in the School of Domestic Science, who carried out work on the nutritional value of locally-caught fish and other foods during the First World War, and helped the Professor of Medicine at Aberdeen University to carry out ground-breaking work on the dietary needs of anaemic women during the 1930's. Two of the staff of the School of Chemistry - Dr. Mearns B. Watson (the Head) and Dr. George Youngson - also began a long and fruitful collaboration on the stereochemistry of organic compounds in the years after the Second World War, publishing many papers in this area. Apart from the supervision of student projects, the author has found little evidence of other research activity, however - at least until 1963, when the newly-appointed Industrial Liaison Officer, Dr. Norman Mackenzie, started to put staff in contact with firms with problems that they required help to solve (see next section).

With the establishment of the Council for National Academic Awards in 1964 and the subsequent development of CNAA degree courses within RGIT, it soon became apparent that research would have to be taken much more seriously from then on. The CNAA made it clear from the start that it expected teaching at degree level - and, in particular, at 'honours' level - to be informed and underpinned by appropriate research work on the part of the staff involved. Since none of the institutions that would be running the new CNAA degrees received the type of 'dual funding' that enabled the universities to carry out extensive research work as well as teaching, and were highly unlikely to receive such funding in the foreseeable future, if ever, very little financial support could be provided for such work. Indeed, in Scotland, the funding body made it clear that recurrent grants to the Central Institutions were *not* to be used to fund research.

Although this restriction was sometimes overlooked, it greatly impeded the development of research in the non-university HE sector. Nevertheless, research soon started to build up in several of RGIT's Schools, with Chemistry, Physics, Pharmacy and Electrical Engineering leading the way (these were the first Schools to develop CNAA degrees, as we saw in Chapter 7). Others soon followed, and, by the early 1970's, research had become something of a growth industry throughout a large part of the Institute.

**Figure 12.1 : One of the key research facilities in the School of Physics
- the electron microscope that it acquired during the late 1960's**

Until now, the control and direction of all research carried out in RGIT had been the responsibility of the Heads of the Schools involved. It was up to them to 'encourage' staff to carry out research if they felt that this was important, to allocated time, and to find any money needed for equipment and materials out of their annual budgets. If a School required any particularly expensive equipment (such as the electron microscope shown in Figure 12.1), a special case for its purchase had to be made to the Scottish Education Department. Such a case had to demonstrate a need for the equipment for teaching purposes. The Institute did, however, pay half the fees of any member of staff who enrolled on a research degree, meeting this out of a central staff development budget. (The author was one of the first people to benefit from this when he completed a part-time Ph.D. on gaseous electronics at Aberdeen University during the late 1960's.)

In 1972, however, RGIT established a Research and Higher Degrees Committee, and made this responsible for the overall direction and control of research within the Institute. Now, any member of staff wishing to pursue research leading to a higher degree of a university or the CNAA was required to make a formal submission to this Committee through their Head of School. Such submissions were only approved if the Committee was satisfied that the proposed project was consistent with the Institute's research policy, and that adequate time and other facilities would be made available. The Committee was allocated an annual budget by the Academic Council for the support of research within RGIT, under the general mantle of staff development, and had considerable delegated powers regarding the allocation of this to specific projects. The Committee was also made responsible for allocating funded research studentships, which the SED first started to make available to the Institute in 1973; 14 were initially provided, and were distributed among the Schools most actively involved in research at the time. More were to follow, some funded by the SED, some by other external bodies, and some by the Schools themselves.

At this point, it would be useful to describe the Government policy regarding research in the non-university higher-education sector under which institutions like RGIT had to operate. As we have seen, such institutions were not provided with 'dual funding' to pay for research; they were primarily regarded as 'teaching establishments', and were therefore only funded for this aspect of their activities, particularly in respect of the provision of staff. Any Government money that *was* provided for research (eg for funded studentships and specialised equipment) was made available on the understanding that research in the non-university sector should complement rather than compete with research in the university sector. Such research should therefore be of an 'applied' nature (as opposed to the 'pure' research carried out in the universities), and should be related to - and justified by - 'its contribution to the essential teaching purpose of the institution'. Also, the greater part of the necessary finance (apart from any 'pump-priming' money provided by the Government) 'should come from outside bodies', eg from the Research Councils, research establishments and private firms.

One School that was particularly successful in building up its research profile, and attracting external funding for its work, during the 1970's was the School of Electronic and Electrical Engineering. Early work included research on microwave signalling of the type shown in Figure 12.2. In 1972, the School received a £10,000 grant from the (then) Science Research Council (SRC) to help support the work on stochastic computing that was being carried out by a team led by Dr. (later Professor) Philip Mars. During the coming years, Dr. Mars and his colleagues established a considerable national and international reputation in this field. In 1977, they received further funding totalling almost £35,000 from the SRC to support work on digital stochastic computing and its application to on-line control and simulation. Through this work, valuable links were formed with a number of outside bodies, including the Universities of Yale and Illinois, the Massachusetts Institute of Technology, and Bell Telephone Laboratories, New Jersey. Other research teams that received funding during this period included the Solid State

Electronics Group, which received over £13,000 from the SRC and private industry, and the Computer Aided Design Group, which received over £27,000 from the same sources. In 1981, the Science and Engineering Research Council (SERC) awarded £98,000 to a new joint Offshore Machine Condition Monitoring Group formed with the Department of Engineering at Aberdeen University. Between 1972 and 1981, staff of the School published well over 100 papers on their work.

Figure 12.2 : Radio communication research being carried out in the School of Electronic and Electrical Engineering during the early 1970's

By the start of the 1980's, 12 of the Institute's 15 Schools were actively involved in research, as evidenced by submitting reports for inclusion in RGIT's annual Research Review. By now, there were 36 research students in post - 18 on SED studentships, 10 on SRC studentships, 2 funded by the SERC, and 6 funded by other bodies, mainly overseas government departments. In addition, 14 members of staff were working on postgraduate research degree programmes - 10 for Ph.D.'s and 4 for 'Masters' degrees. Overall activity continued to build up during the next few years, with the Research Committee (as the Research and Higher Degrees Committee had been re-named) making a particular effort to persuade those Schools which did not have a tradition of research to become active in this area. The Research Committee also carried out a survey designed (*inter alia*) to determine the importance of research in underpinning teaching. This clearly showed that research and other scholarly activities helped in the preparation of up-to-date course syllabuses, provided a platform for the development of new courses, made high-technology equipment available for teaching, and made an important contribution to personal staff development and the maintenance of professional credibility. In short, it confirmed the official Institute view that research was now an essential area of activity that warranted increased support from central funds. This was subsequently provided in a number of ways, eg by increasing the funding for research-related staff development.

**Figure 12.3 : Research work on computer interfacing being carried out in the
School of Physics during the mid-1980's**

By the time of the 1988 Institutional Inspection by the SED, research activity had undergone a further significant increase, with all Schools now being involved in some way - albeit some still very much more than others. The Institute was now allocating roughly 1.2% of its non-staff-related recurrent grant to the support of research activity, including the funding of studentships. Indeed, of the 68 research students now in place, roughly half were funded in this way. Schools had also been encouraged to generate a further sum, equivalent to roughly 3% of their recurrent grant, through industrial grants and consultancy, and many were well on the way to achieving this. In addition, over 150 members of the Institute's academic staff (roughly 50% of the total) were now actively involved in research at some level. The Inspectors noted that this was 'a satisfactory level of commitment' which might 'be expected to develop further'. The Inspectors did, however, identify a number of areas in which more could be done, eg in strengthening the links between the Research Committee and the Faculties, and in encouraging Schools where research activity was still at a low level, or had decreased in recent years, to increase their involvement. It suggested that 'the stimulation of group research work' might be of help to such Schools.

As we saw in Chapter 7, Dr. Kennedy and his colleagues made a number of radical changes to RGIT's organisational structure and operational systems during the late 1980's, partly in response to suggestions made by the CNAA following their staged quinquennial visits in 1983, 1984 and 1985. The last of these visits had dealt with the Institute's staff development and research policies, and had shown that significantly greater resources needed to be committed to both these highly-important areas if RGIT was to attain the

187

CNAA-accredited status that it was now actively seeking. Considerable progress had in fact been made in both areas by the time of the 1988 Institutional Inspection, and further progress was made in response to the report on the visit. The introduction of the new Faculty structure, with its 'Executive Deans', played a key role in this regard, enabling the central planning and cross-faculty integration of research and consultancy work to be greatly improved. Research also received a massive boost through the allocation of a sum equivalent to roughly 7% of the Institute's total payroll cost to the support of staff development. Most of this money was at the disposal of the four Deans, and a very large proportion was used to support research within their Faculties. In practice, this meant that an average sum of roughly £1000 a year was available from central funds to support each academic member of staff, quite apart from any additional funding that was raised from external sources.

Figure 12.4 : Research on mathematical modelling being carried out in the School of Computer and Mathematical Sciences during the late 1980's

Largely as a result of these various measures, research underwent a considerable further expansion during the late 1980's and early 1990's, with all of the Institute's Schools and other Teaching Departments becoming fully involved for the first time. Each School now had to plan its research in a much more systematic way than had been required in the past, and had to ensure that its plan fitted in with that of its Faculty and with that of the Institute as a whole. Schools also had to produce detailed annual reports on their research activities, showing to what extent their objectives had been met. The upshot of all this effort proved highly satisfactory, with RGIT being granted CNAA-accredited status in respect of its undergraduate and taught-postgraduate courses in 1989, and similar accreditation in respect of its postgraduate research degrees in 1991 - shortly before it attained full university status. After 1992, the new Robert Gordon University entered a completely new world regarding its research activities, as we will see in Chapter 14.

INDUSTRIAL LIAISON AND CONSULTANCY

As we saw in Chapter 8, the Governors of what was then Robert Gordon's Technical College first set up an Industrial Liaison Centre in 1963, appointing Dr. Norman Mackenzie as its full-time Industrial Liaison Officer. The Centre had two main roles - to promote the use of the Technical College's resources by industry in the North of Scotland on a consultancy basis, and, in addition, to provide a 'sign-post' service, putting firms with problems which the Technical College was not equipped to handle in touch with the most appropriate source of help available. In 1967, the Department of Trade and Industry started to contribute towards the upkeep of the Centre, and continued to do so until 1973.

During the first ten years of its existence, the Industrial Liaison Centre played an increasingly important role in helping the Technical College and Institute of Technology to build up their consultancy work. Such work was regarded as an important complement to their growing research activities, and the two were very often closely connected. Staff were actively encouraged to become involved in such consultancy 'within reasonable limits', since it was regarded as one of the best ways of learning about 'real-life' industrial problems - thus helping staff to devise meaningful student projects, which were then being introduced into more and more courses. Providing assistance to industry and commerce was also regarded as an important part of the institution's overall role, since it helped it to integrate with the industrial and commercial community that it had been set up to serve. By the late 1960's, recorded enquiries handled by the Centre were averaging over 300 a year, and, by 1973, 16 of RGIT's 17 Schools were carrying out consultancy on a regular basis. A brief summary of their involvement in this work is given below.

School of Architecture : Consultation on a variety of architectural problems, both within the UK and abroad, eg, the design of new buildings, restoration of historical buildings and the use of new materials.

School of Art : Provision of help and advice on problems of design, typography and display, as well as producing specially-commissioned works of art.

School of Business Management Studies : Provision of all types of management and business advice to industrial firms, agricultural organisations, banks, local authorities and government bodies.

School of Chemistry : Provision of a wide range of specialised analytical services to local industrial firms, and to the police.

School of Electronic and Electrical Engineering : Helping local industrial firms and large national organisations to solve problems in areas such as instrument calibration, motor selection, use of automatic equipment for fishing and farming, and

189

telecommunications.

School of Health Visiting : Provision of advice on health-related matters to Health Departments, professional bodies and government agencies.

School of Home Economics : Provision of advice on various aspects of food preparation and display for local industrial firms and public bodies.

School of Hotel and Institutional Administration : Provision of advice on the design of training leaflets to Food Marketing Boards.

School of Librarianship : Provision of advice to industrial, commercial and educational organisations on the setting up of specialist libraries.

School of Mathematics : Use of computer methods to help industrial firms and local-government bodies to solve a wide range of problems.

School of Mechanical Engineering : Helping local industrial firms (including those in the rapidly-expanding oil industry) to solve design problems, select materials, carry out control tests, balance generators, solve vibration problems, and so on; carrying out consultancy for the National Engineering Laboratory.

School of Nutritional Science : Carrying out a wide variety of work on nutrition and dietetics for the food industry and for bodies such as the Herring Industry Board.

School of Pharmacy : Solving problems related to such things as particle size measurement and counting in industrial fluids, pollution in liquids, contamination and bacterial action in food products, and testing of medicinal and cosmetic products.

School of Physics : Carrying out noise measurements and analysis of industrial noise, and providing subsequent advice on noise control; advising architects on matters relating to acoustics; materials testing, X-ray analysis and microscopic work.

School of Social Studies : Provision of advice on social problems to Directors of Social Work, Training Officers and official bodies.

School of Speech Therapy : Provision of speech consultancy in connection with the work of the Medical Rehabilitation Service.

In 1973, the 'sign-post' service work of the Industrial Liaison Centre was transferred to a newly-established Small Firms Information Centre in Glasgow, and funding from the Department of Trade and Industry for the Centre was withdrawn as a result of a change in Government policy. It was therefore decided to re-name the Centre as the Liaison Service, and to widen the range of the Liaison Officer's duties to include general public-relations work. He still continued to provide a link between local industry and Institute staff, however, and his workload in this important area was by no means diminished. Indeed, consultancy work relating to the offshore oil industry built up steadily during the ensuing years. The School of Mechanical Engineering (soon to be re-named as the School of Mechanical and Offshore Engineering) became particularly heavily involved in such work (see Figure 12.5). Later, the two new commercial units (the Offshore Survival Centre and the Centre for Offshore Health) also became heavily involved in such consultancy work, both establishing considerable reputations at national and international level as a result (see Chapter 8).

Figure 12.5 : Consultancy work on fluid flow in pipes being carried out in the School of Mechanical and Offshore Engineering during the mid-1970's

The Institute's consultancy work continued to expand and diversify during the late 1970's and early 1980's, although its oil-related work fell back during the mid-1980's because of the downsizing of the local oil industry that followed the totally-unexpected collapse in the price of crude oil. Another factor that adversely affected consultancy during this period was the increasing pressure on institutions such as RGIT to improve their student/staff ratios (SSR's). This caused staff to claim that they were now having to carry out the bulk of their consultancy work outside their contracted hours, and to request additional remuneration in respect of same. New formulae designed to ensure that the Institute, the Schools and the staff involved all received appropriate financial benefit from consultancy were introduced in 1986-87, but consultancy income continued to drop for some time thereafter. Indeed, in the report on the 1988 Institutional Inspection, specific mention was made of the need to expand RGIT's consultancy work and increase the net income therefrom. Steps were taken to help ensure that this did indeed happen, and the overall situation gradually improved during the early 1990's. As we will see in Chapter 14, the subsequent establishment of Univation as a commercial company through which consultancy and other full-cost work could be channelled eventually brought about an even more substantial increase in RGU's income from such activities.

COLLABORATIVE EDUCATIONAL DEVELOPMENT WORK

In addition to its mainstream research and consultancy activities, RGIT became heavily involved in a wide range of highly-innovative educational development projects during the 1970's, 1980's and early 1990's, many of which involved collaboration with outside bodies. Let us now end this chapter by looking at some of the most important of these.

As we saw in Chapter 11, RGIT became involved in educational gaming and simulation during the early 1970's, through the ground-breaking work carried out by Mr. Drew Mackie and his colleagues in the Scott Sutherland School of Architecture. We also saw how the locus of such work moved to the School of Physics and the newly-established Educational Technology Unit in 1973, after Mr. Mackie had left the Institute. During the remainder of the 1970's, this led to the development of a large number of new educational games, including the highly-successful 'Power Station Game' that was developed for the Scottish Education Department in collaboration with Grampian Education Authority and H.M. Inspectorate, and was published by the Institution of Electrical Engineers in 1975. This initiated a highly productive long-term collaboration between RGIT and the IEE in the development of educational games, several of which were heavily used by the IEE's Schools Liaison Service. In the late 1970s, several of these games were adapted for use in the new 'Science in Society' course that the Association for Science Education was developing for use in secondary schools throughout the UK, and played a significant role in ensuring the success of this course. During the early 1980's, a further suite of educational games designed for use in teaching Foundation and General Level Science in Scottish secondary schools was developed with the aid of a £4000 grant from the Scottish Economic Planning Department.

RGIT also became involved in the planning and running of a number of major competitions based on educational games during the 1970's. The first of these was the 'Bruce Oil Management Game', which was developed in collaboration with 'The Press and Journal', Aberdeen's local morning paper, and run as a national and international competition for six successive years between 1974-75 and 1979-80 (see Chapter 8). The second was 'Hydropower 77', a competition for secondary schools based on the design of a hydroelectric pumped-storage scheme that was run in collaboration with the North of Scotland Hydro-Electric Board over the winter of 1976-77. The third was 'Project Scotia', a similar competition based on the design of a UHF television broadcasting network that was developed in collaboration with the IEE, the BBC and the Independent Broadcasting Authority, and was run throughout Britain over the winter of 1978-79. Figure 12.6 shows Dr. Peter Clarke, RGIT's Principal at the time, participating in the judging of the 'live final' of this competition at the IEE's London headquarters in September, 1979, along with IEE President Sir James Redmond and Mr. Tom Robson, Director of Engineering at the IBA.

During the first half of the 1980's, staff of the School of Physics and ETU also collaborated with Phillips Petroleum in three major projects. The first was the development of 'Ile de Performance', a simulated design exercise on alternative energy that was run as a competition during the 1980 Annual Conference of their Petroleum Products Group in Guernsey. The second was the development of 'Ekofisk — One of a Kind', a multiple-media package of resource materials on the offshore oil industry designed for use in schools, and made available through Phillips' Public Affairs Department in London. The third was 'Licensed to Drill!', a further multiple-media package for schools and colleges incorporating computer exercises that was based on the economics of North Sea oil; this was again made available through Phillips' Public Affairs Department, and was publicised via a programme of launches held throughout Scotland in the mid-1980's.

Figure 12.6 : the three judges at the 'Project Scotia' London final examining Aberdeen Grammar School's model of Scotia (extreme right: Sir James Redmond; second right: Dr. Peter Clarke; extreme left: Mr. Tom Robson)

Mention has been made in Chapter 4 of the long-running collaboration with the United Kingdom Atomic Energy Authority's Fast Reactor Development Establishment at Dounreay that began in the 1950's. During the late 1970's, RGIT staff helped to develop a series of tape-slide programmes on Dounreay for use in public-relations and school-liaison work, and subsequently collaborated with their Fast Reactor Training Centre in several major projects. These included developing 'The Nuclear Debate', a suite of educational games and simulation exercises designed for use in schools and colleges that was published by the Scottish Council for Educational Technology in 1983. Later in the 1980's, RGIT staff helped the UKAEA to develop an interactive database on the use of energy and electricity in Britain - designed to demonstrate the key role that nuclear power was expected to play in providing the latter. Figure 12.7 shows Dr. David Kennedy,

RGIT's Principal, watching a demonstration of the package at its Aberdeen launch in 1989.

Figure 12.7 : Dr. David Kennedy, RGIT Principal (extreme right) at the 1989 Aberdeen Launch of the UKAEA's Interactive Database on Energy and Electricity Usage.

RGIT was also heavily involved in two major curriculum-development projects that were run in primary schools throughout Grampian Region during the mid-1980's and early 1990's. Both were sponsored by Goodfellow Associates, a firm of Offshore Oil Consultants. The first of these projects was run over the winter of 1986-87 as part of RGIT's 'Industry Year' programme, and involved helping the pupils to tackle real-life problems based on different aspects of industry. The project had its climax in a spectacular 'Show Day' held in the Institute's Kepplestone premises in May 1987 (see Figure 12.8). The second was the 1990-91 'Grampian Primary Industry Project', which involved teams of pupils studying the 'business' side of industry through the medium of simulation/ gaming. This also ended with a major 'Show Day', held in Grampian Region's Summerhill Education Centre in June 1991. As a follow up to this project, RGIT helped Grampian Education Authority to develop a 'do-it-yourself' pack for primary and secondary teachers on the design and use of classroom games and simulations. This was distributed to all Grampian Region's schools during the mid-1990's.

The collaborative educational-development work described in this section involved staff from several Schools and Departments of RGIT, including the Schools of Architecture, Business Management Studies, Electronic and Electrical Engineering, Mathematics, Mechanical and Offshore Engineering, and Physics, the Computer Services Unit, the

Centre for Enterprise and the Educational Technology Unit (which later became the Educational Development Unit); members of the Senior Management Team also made significant contributions. The work not only played an important role in helping the Institute to become involved with the industrial and educational community and providing it with excellent publicity, but also generated a large number of publications - well over 150 between 1970 and 1992. In addition, it resulted in Institute staff being invited to give talks, make conference contributions and run workshops all over the World.

Figure 12.8 : Local MP Alick Buchanan-Smith talking to pupils at the 'Show Day' that formed the climax of RGIT's 1986-87 'Industry Year' Project involving primary schools throughout Grampian Region.

Chapter 13 : The achievement of university status

THE CHALLENGES FACING RGIT IN THE MID-1980'S

In Chapter 7, we saw that RGIT entered something of a crisis period during the mid-1980's, being confronted by a number of serious challenges that also constituted opportunities for future development and growth. In this chapter, we will take a closer look at these challenges and opportunities, and show how Dr. Kennedy and his colleagues met them head-on, thus preparing the ground for the eventual attainment of full university status in 1992.

The first major challenge that the Institute would have to meet was the inescapable fact that the number of 18-year-old school leavers would decrease by roughly 25% over the next ten years or so according to demographic projections. This meant that the number of traditional entrants to higher education would fall off dramatically, thus increasing the competition for 'good' students, and putting the viability of small Schools at increasing risk. Clearly, RGIT would have to take steps to ensure that its student numbers held up by introducing new courses and generally widening its recruitment base - something that would involve integrated planning of the type that the highly-devolved academic structure that had been put in place in 1979 was singularly ill-equipped to provide. Although the increased democracy that had been introduced under this scheme had seemed a good idea at the time, it was becoming widely realised that the current Faculty and School structure was (to quote Dr. Kennedy) 'totally inappropriate for the task in hand'. The need for more effective central planning would become even greater during the late 1980's, when RGIT would have to play its part in the massive expansion of higher education heralded in the 1987 White Paper: *'Higher Education : Meeting the Challenge'*. This envisaged the percentage of school leavers entering higher education more than doubling by the end of the millennium.

The second major challenge with which the Institute was confronted was the steadily-deteriorating financial situation in which it found itself from the mid-1980's onwards. This was partly due to the fact that the Scottish Education Department was no longer taking financial account of the many thousands of part-time trainees that passed through the Offshore Survival Centre every year when calculating the overall student numbers on which RGIT's academic staff establishment was based. Thus, RGIT found that it not only had far too many academic staff for its conventional student base to sustain, but also had far too many of these in highly-expensive promoted posts. The same was true of its technical-support staff structure, which was also highly 'top heavy' due to the promotions that had been made during the 1970's and early 1980's. As Dr. Clarke explained to the author, RGIT had found itself with very little choice over this; had its technicians *not* been upgraded, they would have deserted RGIT *en masse* to go and work in the burgeoning oil industry - which was paying very high salaries at the time. The Institute's long-term financial prospects were made even worse by the 'Switch to Technology' initiative that the Government had introduced in 1985. Initially, this had provided money for more staff and equipment, but many of the new staff had been appointed to promoted posts in order to attract suitable people from industry, and, once the 'Switch' funding ran out, would all have to be paid for out of normal revenue. Since the 'Switch' programme had failed to attract the greatly-increased numbers of science and engineering students that had been hoped for, this was likely to prove difficult.

The Institute's third major challenge was the new 'Accreditation' scheme that the Council for National Academic Awards introduced during the mid-1980's, following on from the 'Partnership in Validation' procedures that had been in operation since 1979. The latter had made it possible for institutions such as RGIT to take a much more pro-active role in developing the course validation and review procedures that they operated in collaboration with the CNAA. The scheme had proved so successful that the CNAA now proposed to allow the more mature institutions that conferred awards under the Council's Charter to take on even greater responsibilities for the validation and review of these. It was envisaged that such institutions would be able to move towards full CNAA-accredited status, under which they would become 'fully responsible, under the CNAA Charter and Statutes, for maintaining the standard of courses leading to CNAA awards'. Accredited institutions would have authority to approve new courses and modify existing courses, and would be granted such accreditation 'on recognition of an institution's ability to set up and run satisfactory procedures for the initial validation and subsequent periodic review of all its taught courses leading to CNAA awards'. In other words, such accredited institutions would effectively become independent 'universities' in all but name. It was clearly vital to the future of RGIT that it should make every effort to attain such accredited status as soon as possible. It was also clear that much remained to be done before this could happen, as had been spelled out in detail in the reports on the three CNAA visits that had taken place between 1983 and 1985. There was some ground to be made up, since the Institute had not responded to the 'Partnership in Validation' initiative as fully as it might have done during the late 1970's and early 1980's.

Ensuring the Institute's long-term viability

As we saw in Chapter 7, one of the first things that was done in order to ensure the long-term viability of RGIT was the instigation of a wide-ranging review of the Institute's academic structure. This was carried out by a Working Party of the Academic Council that was set up in July, 1986, under the convenorship of Mr. (later Professor) Seaton Baxter, Head of the School of Surveying. The Working Party (of which the author was a member) met eleven times before the end of December 1986, when it was due to present its findings and recommendations. These were subsequently discussed and modified by the Academic Council, and eventually led to radical revisions being made to RGIT's Faculty and School structure in 1988 (see Chapter 7 for details). One of the most important of these revisions was the return to a four-Faculty system in which the Deans were appointed, and also had extensive executive powers, thus enabling them to work with their Heads of Schools in a strategic way that had simply not been possible since 1979. Another was the implementation of a new 'large School' policy, designed to produce fully-viable teaching units that would all have the resources to expand and diversify their course portfolios. The main manifestations of this policy were the merging of the Schools of Chemistry and Physics to form a new School of Applied Sciences, and the re-merging of the Schools of Home Economics, Hotel and Institutional Administration and Nutritional Science to form a new School of Food and Consumer Studies - a change that was implemented not without considerable controversy. As Dr. Kennedy explained to the Governors at the time, senior- and middle-level management had hitherto 'dealt mainly with the management of academic processes'. Now, however, 'significantly different demands would be made of them as the Institute's income-generating activities developed'. Academic Council therefore 'considered a stronger Faculty structure, combined with stronger Faculty management, essential in order to sustain the Institute's activities'. Future developments would fully vindicate this policy.

At the same time as it introduced its revised academic structure, RGIT established a new, enlarged Senior Management Team, comprising the Principal, Vice Principal, and Institute Secretary together with the four Deans/Assistant Principals. In addition to their executive duties in respect of their Faculties, the latter were each given Institute-wide remits, covering Resources, Personnel, External Relations and Academic Affairs. Subsequent developments such as the new financial arrangements that were introduced by the Scottish Education Department in April 1989 led Dr. Kennedy to carry out an even more radical review of RGIT's management and administrative structure in 1990. This involved dividing the Institute into twelve separate (albeit interdependent) management areas, each under one of the members of the Senior Management Team, which now included the recently-appointed Director of Finance; the four Deans/Assistant Principals each managed their Faculty plus one other area, with the Institute Secretary and the Director of Finance each managing two of the remaining areas. Overall responsibility for the direction and control of the twelve management areas was divided between the Principal and Vice Principal, as shown below:

Principal	Vice Principal
Commercial Services	Faculty of Design
Customer Services	Faculty of Health and Food
External Affairs	Faculty of Management
Finance	Faculty of Science and Technology
Human Resources	Academic Affairs
Information and Systems	Physical Resources

In order to free the members of the Senior Management Team from the demands of operational management and facilitate the effective implementation of the new structure, a number of new managerial posts were also created. The revised system was fully in place by the start of the 1990-91 session, and subsequently proved to be extremely effective.

As we have seen, RGIT was also faced with the problem of improving its financial position during the latter part of the 1980's. It did this by taking measures to reduce its overall staffing costs, to increase its external income in various ways, and - most important of all - to increase its mainstream income from 'funded students'. Let us now look at each of these in turn.

Reducing overall staff costs

This involved implementing revised staffing policies designed to enable the Institute to comply with the SED's new financial arrangements. On the academic side, they included the introduction of a new '80/20' policy, whereby 20% of the academic staff complement would henceforth be on part-time or temporary contracts in order to increase operational flexibility, and, at the same time, enhance vocational connections with the world of work. They also included reducing the number of promoted posts to roughly 30% of the overall establishment, and replacing senior lecturers at or near the top of their salary scale by new, younger lecturers appointed at the lower end of the scale (the so-called 'new blood' policy). Such an adjustment was necessary in order to reduce overall staffing costs. On the technical-support side, they included the introduction of a revised grading structure for faculty-based technicians, designed to reduce overall costs to more manageable proportions. In order to help achieve all of these changes, all academic and technical staff over the age of 50 were advised that enhanced early retirement would be available for a limited period; as a result, 10 senior lecturers and 11 technicians were granted premature retirement by the Governors in 1990. The Institute took further measures to reduce its overall staffing costs by 'contracting out' its catering and refectory services at the start of the 1990's.

Increasing external income

This was achieved through a wide range of measures, one of the most important of which was the introduction of a policy of actively recruiting full-cost-fee-paying overseas students. Until the mid-1980's, only a few Schools - notably Pharmacy, Architecture and Surveying - had enrolled such students in significant numbers. Starting in 1986, however, the Institute began sending staff on overseas recruitment visits, with a view to attracting international students to the full range of its courses. This policy proved extremely successful, and overseas students eventually became one of the institution's most important sources of external income. It also brought about a number of extremely worthwhile educational benefits, by, for example, creating a more diverse student body with a wider 'cultural mix'. As we saw in Chapter 12, RGIT also took active steps to increase its income from consultancy and externally-funded research during the late

1980's. Following the 1988 academic restructuring, all Schools were expected to become increasingly active in these areas, and, during the following years, income from such sources started to meet a significant part of several of their budgets. Schools were also encouraged to increase their income from short courses and full-cost postgraduate courses, and several Schools again began to do so. All these activities would continue to build up in later years.

Figure 13.1 : A reception being held for new overseas students

Increasing funded-student income

But the area in which RGIT achieved by far its greatest success in increasing its income stream during the late 1980's and early 1990's was through the recruitment of ever-greater numbers of 'funded students', ie students enrolling on undergraduate courses of various types. As soon as he took up office, Dr. Kennedy started urging Schools to develop new courses, and this process was subsequently greatly facilitated by the academic restructuring that took place in 1988. As a result, the Institute's portfolio of award-bearing courses more than doubled in size between 1985 and 1991, and continued to expand steadily thereafter. Once these new courses started to come on stream, the Institute's total FTE figure (the number of full-time students to which its overall student population was equivalent) also started to rise. This had remained fairly static at just over 3000 for several years, but started to increase dramatically in 1988-89, passing the 'magic figure' of 4000 during 1990-1991, and continuing to rise throughout the remainder of the 1990's.

This was achieved despite the fall in the total number of 18-year-old school leavers that had taken place since the mid-1980's, and was partly due to the introduction of new, attractive courses, and partly due to the implementation of a highly-successful 'wider-access' policy. The institution was now recruiting students from a much wider age range than it had ever done before, and was also admitting them on the basis of their likely ability to do well in their chosen course rather than on their paper qualifications alone. It was also attracting them from a much greater 'catchment area'.

The various measures described in this section went a long way towards ensuring the institution's future viability, and also enabled it to live with the so-called annual 'efficiency savings' that were imposed on the entire higher-education sector by Central Government funding agencies throughout the late 1980's and for most of the 1990's. They did, however, also have a down side, since they placed a great deal of pressure on all staff, due to the ensuing extra workload. Given the radical nature of some of the changes, and the speed at which they had to be introduced, it was also almost inevitable that some individuals and groups of staff found it hard to cope, or felt that they had been unfairly treated. As a result, there was a period when RGIT and RGU had poor industrial relations with some of the staff trade unions. Unfortunately, these led to a number of high-profile disputes, which were extremely upsetting for all concerned - and did little good for the institution's public image. Many of Britain's other higher education institutions had to cope with similar problems.

ACHIEVING AND RETAINING CNAA-ACCREDITED STATUS

Because of the importance of attaining CNAA-accredited status as soon as possible, RGIT embarked on discussions with the CNAA Council in the summer of 1985. In the following summer, the new 'Accreditation' policy was announced. These discussions continued throughout the 1985-86 and 1986-87 sessions, being co-ordinated at the RGIT end by the new Vice Principal, Gavin Ross (see Figure 13.2); he made himself thoroughly familiar with the CNAA and its procedures, serving as the Scottish Secretary of State's representative on the Council of the CNAA from 1986 until its disbanding in 1992. The discussions led to a draft agreement between RGIT and the CNAA being implemented in session 1986-87, when 'as if' arrangements were put into operation for most validation and review visits, with a formal agreement coming into force in time for implementation during 1987-88. This embodied the following three principles:

- A commitment to the concept of external peer review in respect of both *quality assurance* (the validation and periodic review of courses) and *quality control* (the on-going process of course monitoring and evaluation).
- Fulfilment of this commitment by ensuring that all visiting parties, both for new course validations and for School progress reviews, had a majority of members external to the Institute, and also had an external Chair; it was ensured that these external members constituted a balanced mix of academics and practitioners.
- Incorporation of the various quality-assurance and quality-control procedures

as an integral part of the workings of the Academic Council and its Standing Committees, in order to imbue an ethos of concern for quality and standards as widely as possible throughout the academic community.

Figure 13.2 : Mr. Gavin Ross, Vice Principal during the period when RGIT achieved CNAA-accredited status

By the end of 1988, RGIT had gained considerable experience of operating under the new agreements, and had developed quality-assurance and quality-control systems that were both rigorous and robust, and which fully complied with the requirements of the CNAA. It had also gone a long way towards implementing the various recommendations regarding staff development and research that had been made by the CNAA in the 1980's. It was therefore decided to apply to the CNAA for institutional accreditation in respect of all its taught courses, both at undergraduate and at postgraduate level. Such a submission was duly made in February 1989, with the accreditation visit taking place in June of that year. This proved extremely successful, and RGIT became an accredited institution of the CNAA in respect of its taught courses on September 1, 1989. Two years later, it received similar accreditation in respect of its research degrees. These were highly important, indeed, essential, milestones on the route to acquiring full university status.

In order to ensure that the quality-assurance and quality-control procedures were fully implemented and complied with by all Schools and course teams, RGIT produced a comprehensive Quality Handbook giving full details of what was involved. It was one of the first - if not *the* first - of the UK's higher education institutions to do this, and the resulting Handbook (which was published at the start of 1990) attracted widespread interest among the UK-wide academic community. Indeed, it served as a model that many other institutions would subsequently copy. The main body of the Handbook explained RGIT's accredited status with the CNAA, described its quality-assurance and quality-control procedures, and spelt out the roles of all the various committees, departments and individuals that were involved in these processes, including external examiners. It also contained 13 appendices that described the various quality procedures and processes in even greater detail, with easy-to-follow process flow charts and standard proformas and templates for use in their implementation. Copies of this Handbook were provided for all academic staff. The original Quality Handbook has since been revised and updated at regular intervals, and still continues to play a key role in the institution's academic quality procedures. The latest version is available on-line, thus making it much easier for staff to make use of its various proformas and templates when preparing the documentation for validation and review events and for on-going course appraisal.

When the Institute was granted CNAA-accredited status for taught courses in 1989, it was expected that the CNAA would make a return visit in 1995-96 or thereabout to determine whether the arrangement should continue. In order to ensure that it did so, RGIT would be required to demonstrate that its quality-assurance and quality-control systems had fully satisfied the standards that had been set, and had properly met all CNAA requirements for accredited institutions. Having been heavily involved in the work of the CNAA as a Member of Council, Gavin Ross was fully aware of the searching nature of the questions that were likely to be asked of the institution at such a re-accreditation event. These would stem from the basic question asked by Mr. Malcolm Frazer, the (then) Chief Executive of the CNAA, of all institutions seeking CNAA accreditation:

> 'Is this a **self-critical** academic community, and does that ethos run **widely** and **deeply** throughout the institution?'

Providing a satisfactory answer to this question, together with supporting evidence, would be the key to demonstrating the presence of academic quality in RGIT. The Institute therefore took immediate steps to help to ensure that this could be done.

The method agreed by the Academic Council was to set up an Internal Quality Audit Team (later re-named as the Internal *Academic* Quality Audit Team). This would monitor the Institute's quality-assurance and quality-control systems by carrying out wide-ranging internal audits of their efficiency and effectiveness, and would also carry out any other quality-related tasks felt necessary. Such a team would effectively act as a 'meta-quality-control' system, thus serving both as a monitor of overall quality and as a catalyst for the on-going improvement of such quality. It was also decided that responsibility for co-ordinating the Team should rest with the Educational Development Unit, since this had an Institute-wide brief for promoting and supporting academic development work of all types. It was also 'neutral' in course-related matters, since it did not itself (at the time) offer any course leading to a CNAA award. The Team was chaired by the author in his capacity as Director of the EDU, and included other EDU staff, representatives of the Registry (which was responsible for the management and co-ordination of RGIT's quality programme), plus representatives from each of the four Faculties.

The Internal Quality Audit Team was formally established at the start of the 1990-91 academic session, and, during the next four years, carried out a wide range of quality audits and other tasks. These included:

- A comprehensive audit of RGIT's quality-control procedures during 1990-91; this resulted in radical revisions being made to these procedures.
- A comprehensive audit of RGIT's quality-assurance procedures during 1991-92; this also resulted in a number of changes being made.
- Development of a scheme for the evaluation of teaching quality at the point of delivery during 1992-93; the resulting scheme, which was based on critical self-appraisal by staff, was fully implemented throughout RGU starting in 1994-95.
- An audit of RGU's central staff development, staff development and career review, and staff promotion procedures in 1993-94.
- An audit of the interaction between the Academic Council and its Standing Committees (also in 1993-94).
- An audit of the interaction between Faculties and their constituent Schools and Sub-committees, and of the roles of other Committees (also in 1993-94).
- An audit of RGU's promotional materials and students' perceptions thereof (also in 1993-94).
- An audit of the effectiveness of the operation of RGU's School Committees (in 1994-95).

Although the original function of the Internal Quality Audit Team (helping RGIT to prepare for the CNAA re-accreditation visit that was expected in 1995-96) apparently became irrelevant once the Institute attained full university status in 1992, RGU was soon faced with the prospect of preparing for an institutional visit by the new Higher Education Quality Council (HEQC). This took place in 1995, and covered roughly the same areas as would have been looked at during the aborted CNAA visit. The various audits and other work that had been carried out by the Team were therefore just as useful as they would have been during a CNAA re-accreditation visit, and played a significant role in ensuring that the HEQC visit was a success (see Chapter 14). Following the 1995 visit, responsibility for co-ordinating the work of the Internal Academic Quality Audit Team was taken over by RGU's Academic Affairs Department; the Team is still active today.

THE SUCCESSFUL CAMPAIGN FOR A UNIVERSITY TITLE

Before examining the events that culminated in RGIT being awarded a university title and degree-awarding powers in 1992, let us take a brief look at the history of Britain's university system. Prior to the 1990's, this had gone through four distinct phases of development and expansion. The first involved the founding of the two 'ancient' English universities (Oxford and Cambridge) in the 12th and 13th centuries. The second phase saw the establishment of the four original Scottish universities (St. Andrews, Glasgow, Aberdeen and Edinburgh) during the 15th and 16th centuries. The third phase involved the establishment of the 'civic' universities - Durham, London, Birmingham, Manchester, Liverpool, and so on - during the 19th and early 20th centuries, eventually increasing the total number of British universities to 23. The fourth phase was the 'Robbins' expansion that took place during the 1960's (see Chapter 7), which saw the Colleges of Advanced Technology gaining university status and several completely new universities (such as Stirling and Keele) being established; this increased the total number of universities in Britain to 44, and also led to the foundation of most of the polytechnics. The subsequent fifth phase of development, which was initiated in 1991, would eventually increase the number of universities in Britain to well over 100.

Until the appearance of the White Paper : *'Higher Education - A New Framework'* in May 1991, the Government had given no indication whatsoever (at least in public) that it intended to initiate by far the largest expansion that the British university system had ever known. Indeed, it had steadfastly refused to countenance any requests by institutions in the non-university higher-education sector that they be allowed to call themselves 'universities'. Dr. Kennedy had commented on this fact - and the harm that it was doing to institutions such as RGIT in terms of their perception in the world at large - at the time of the publication of the 1987 White Paper. What caused the Government to change its mind has been the subject of a great deal of speculation, but the author will resist the temptation to add to this here. Nor will he comment on the fact that two of the largest non-university higher education institutions in Scotland had added the word 'Polytechnic' to their titles between 1988 and 1991, although they were clearly not 'Polytechnics' in the sense that the term was used elsewhere in the UK.

The 1991 White Paper hit the higher-education sector like a bombshell, and made the following main proposals:

- The removal of the 'binary line' between the universities and 'public sector' higher education institutions such as the English and Welsh Polytechnics and the Scottish Central Institutions.
- The establishment in England, Scotland and Wales of new Higher Education Funding Councils that would be responsible for funding *all* higher education institutions in their respective countries for both teaching and research, and the linking of such funding to the assessment of quality.
- The winding up of the CNAA, and allowing certain CNAA-accredited institutions (including all the Polytechnics) to award their own degrees and choose whether or not to call themselves universities, but requiring other HEI's to have their courses validated by an institution of their choice with degree-awarding powers.

Apart from stating that all 'Polytechnics' would be awarded full university status automatically, the White Paper did not specify the criteria that other institutions would have to meet in order to attain such status. It announced that these would be developed 'in due course', and that the Government had 'an open mind' on what they should be; they would, however, be 'flexible', it was promised.

At the time, Scotland had five large polytechnic-type Central Institutions - Dundee Institute of Technology, Glasgow Polytechnic, Napier Polytechnic of Edinburgh, Paisley College and RGIT. On making inquiries to the Scottish Office regarding the implications of the White Paper, Dr. Kennedy was informed that only two of these - Glasgow and Napier - would automatically be entitled to call themselves universities, since they had the name 'Polytechnic' in their titles, and would therefore be treated in the same way as the English and Welsh Polytechnics. The position of the other three institutions was far from clear, however, and would only become known once the criteria for the award of full university status had been decided by the Government. This was clearly an absurdity, not least because the two self-styled 'Polytechnics' had only become Central Institutions comparatively recently.

In July, 1991, RGIT's Governors confirmed their faith in the future of the Institute as 'an important and autonomous higher education institution with a clear sense of its own identity and purpose', firmly stating that RGIT 'should continue to make its distinctive contribution to education and training in the North East by:

i.) Achieving degree-awarding powers and university status;

ii.) Opposing any proposals for merger with the University of Aberdeen'.

Such a merger was again being discussed as a possible way forward, and had strong support in some quarters. Indeed, if RGIT had *not* succeeded in attaining full university status, it might well have been the only way in which it could continue to award degrees, since the CNAA route would no longer be available after 1992. However, both the Governors and the staff of RGIT regarded the attainment of degree-awarding powers and a university title as absolutely essential for the future of the institution, and were confident that more than enough had been achieved during the previous few years to warrant the award of these. It was therefore decided to mount a vigorous campaign designed to make both the Government and the general public aware of RGIT's case for being allowed to call itself a university, with all the status and powers that this entailed.

The campaign document was drawn up by Dr. Kennedy, and presented an extremely powerful and well-argued case. First, it showed that RGIT was already effectively a 'university' in everything but name, since it was fully accredited by the CNAA in respect of both its taught courses and its research degrees, offered a wide and distinctive range of courses that compared favourably with that of any other institution in the country, had impressive links with industry, commerce, professional bodies and the community at large, had a high and rapidly-increasing FTE, was highly efficient in terms of its unit costs, and was in every sense a 'quality' institution. It also showed that RGIT compared favourably with Glasgow Polytechnic and Napier Polytechnic of Edinburgh in all the criteria that were likely to be used to determine an institution's suitability for the award of university status, including the number of degree and postgraduate awards from taught courses, and the number of research degrees awarded. Thus, if these two institutions were to be allowed to call themselves universities because of their 'Polytechnic' titles, natural justice demanded that RGIT should be accorded the same recognition and treatment.

RGIT's Campaign for University Status was launched at a press conference held on 18th July, 1991 - see Figure 13.3. The campaign document was widely circulated to opinion-leaders and decision-makers throughout the local and national community, inviting them to support the campaign by writing directly to the Secretary of State for Scotland. The resulting support for the Institute's case from employers, public bodies (including the CNAA), private bodies, the press, individuals and local politicians of all parties was overwhelming, several hundred letters being received by the Secretary of State.

Figure 13.3 : RGIT Principal Dr. David Kennedy (centre) and Institute Governors Mr. Iain Souter (left) and Councillor John Porter at the Launch of the Campaign for University Status held on 18th July, 1991.

In due course, the criteria for the granting of full degree-awarding powers and university title to Scottish higher education institutions were announced by the Government. These specified that institutions seeking such powers and title should have full CNAA accreditation in respect of both teaching and research, have a total FTE of at least 4000, and have an FTE of 300 or more in at least six of the Funding Areas to be operated by the new Scottish Higher Education Funding Council. On October 31, 1991, soon after the publication of these criteria, Scottish Secretary of State, Mr. Ian Lang, announced that university status for RGIT was 'virtually guaranteed'. So it subsequently proved, since the Institute clearly met all three of the Government's criteria.

**Figure 13.4 : The Academic Council of the new Robert Gordon University
processing to Aberdeen's Town and County Hall on 12th June, 1992.**

At their meeting on 18th March, 1992, RGIT's Governors formally agreed to ask
the Privy Council to grant the Institute full degree-awarding powers, together with the
title of 'The Robert Gordon University'. Such powers and title were duly granted by the
Privy Council on 12th June, 1992, under the terms of the 'Further and Higher Education
(Scotland) Act 1992'. On the same day, the elevation of RGIT to full university status was
celebrated at an official luncheon hosted in the Town and County Hall, Aberdeen, to
which the new Robert Gordon University's Academic Council processed in full academic
dress (see Figure 13.4). All those present were presented with a commemorative gold
medallion, which is now one of the author's proudest possessions.

Section 4

The Robert Gordon University

(1992 to date)

Chapter 14 : Review of RGU's first ten years

CONTINUING DEVELOPMENT UNDER DR. DAVID KENNEDY (1992-1997)

As we saw in Chapter 13, RGIT became The Robert Gordon University on 12th June 1992, when the Privy Council approved its request to change its name and acquire the right to award its own degrees. This was done under the terms of the 'Further and Higher Education (Scotland) Act 1992', the primary legislation that brought about the restructuring of Scotland's tertiary-education system and established the new Scottish Higher Education Funding Council (SHEFC). As can be seen in Figure 14.1, the change of name took immediate effect, although further legislation was required in order to finalise the transition. This took the form of 'The Robert Gordon University (Scotland) Order of Council 1993', which dealt in detail with the nature and functions of the new University, the constitution and powers of its Governing Body, and the roles and responsibilities of its Principal and Academic Council. This secondary legislation came into force on 19th May, 1993, and, among other things, enabled the new University to proceed with the appointment and installation of its first Chancellor.

Figure 14.1 : The name above the door to RGU's main administration building at Schoolhill being changed in June, 1992.

All British universities have a Chancellor as their titular head, and, although the position is a largely symbolic one, the Chancellor does have one key role to play - the conferring of degrees and other awards at the University's graduation ceremonies. In the event of the Chancellor being unable to be present in person, the power to confer degrees is delegated to the Vice-Chancellor, which is the second official title of all Scottish University Principals; in England, they use this as their actual title. Under the terms of the 1993 Order of Council, the Governors of the new Robert Gordon University were empowered to appoint such a Chancellor, and were extremely fortunate in that one of Britain's leading industrialists - Sir Bob Reid - agreed to take on the role. Sir Bob was born in Fife and educated at St. Andrews University. He joined the Shell International Petroleum Company in 1956, spending most of his career with them working overseas in Brunei, Nigeria, Thailand and Australia. He became a Director in 1984, and went on to become Chairman and Chief Executive of Shell UK. In 1990, he became Chairman of British Railways, and was knighted in the same year.

Figure 14.2 : Sir Bob Reid, first Chancellor of The Robert Gordon University

The installation of Sir Bob Reid as Chancellor of The Robert Gordon University took place at a splendid ceremony held in Aberdeen's Music Hall on Saturday 26th June, 1993. This began with the presentation to the University of a Ceremonial Mace, as an extremely generous gift from the City of Aberdeen. This was designed and made by one of the Jewellery lecturers at Gray's School of Art, Mr Gordon Burnett. Sir Bob Reid was then awarded the Honorary Degree of Doctor of Business Administration before being formally installed as Chancellor. In presenting Sir Bob for his degree, RGU's Vice Principal, Gavin Ross, observed, in the introduction to his oration, that while most boys had to be content with a model train set, Sir Bob now had the real thing to play with! Following the installation, Aberdeen's 'new' University was presented with a commemorative gift by Professor J. Maxwell Irvine, Principal and Vice-Chancellor of Aberdeen's 'old' University. Four further Honorary Degrees were then conferred by the new Chancellor - his first official duty for the University. A celebratory luncheon was subsequently held in the MacRobert Hall, and was thoroughly enjoyed by all. It was a day that the author will always remember with great pleasure and pride.

Figure 14.3 : Sir Bob Reid conferring an honorary degree at one of RGU's graduation ceremonies.

At their meeting on 18th March, 1992, the Governors had not only considered the name of the new University; they had also affirmed its overall statement of purpose, or 'mission statement'. This took the following form:

'The purpose of The Robert Gordon University is to produce versatile and resourceful practitioners, who are relevantly qualified for their chosen professions and vocations within an educational environment that fosters innovation, enterprise, and an enthusiasm for excellence.'

The University would do this by providing:

- high-quality education leading to awards that are widely recognised by employers (in the UK, Europe, and abroad) as being relevant to the employment and career development of employees, and by employees and the self-employed as being relevant to their own career development;
- a caring and responsive environment for study, for recreation, and for the physical and intellectual well-being of students;
- worthwhile and satisfying careers for staff with opportunities for personal development and career advancement;
- services, including research and consultancy, to support private firms and public endeavours both local and national;
- assistance in promoting local enterprise and culture.

This confirmed that the new University would continue the institution's long tradition of providing *vocational* higher education that was fully recognised by relevant professional bodies, and was informed by appropriate research and scholarship. The Governors also confirmed that RGU would continue to run sub-degree-level courses leading to the awards of other bodies such as the Scottish Vocational Educational Council (SCOTVEC). Indeed, Dr. Kennedy and his colleagues regarded this as a highly important aspect of its overall role.

One important consequence of the 1992 Act was that *all* Scottish Higher Education Institutions were now funded through the new Scottish Higher Education Funding Council (SHEFC). Prior to 1989, RGIT had been financed on a 'deficit funding' basis, with the Scottish Office determining each year's budget on the basis of what it had taken to run the institution during the previous year, plus an element to take account of inflation. In 1989, however, it had changed to a 'unit cost' funding system, with the budget being directly linked to the number of enrolled students. Institutions such as RGIT had also been given much greater responsibility for managing their own budgets than they had previously been allowed. From 1992 onwards, however, all HEI's became totally responsible for their own finances, and could no longer rely on being 'bailed out' by the Government if they got into difficulties. Indeed, some in academe believed that the Government would not be too unhappy to see one or two institutions go to the wall *'pour encourager les autres'*, as Voltaire would no doubt have put it.

Matters were made worse by the progressively-more-stringent 'efficiency savings' (reductions in the amount of funding received per student) that were being imposed year after year. These meant that institutions such as RGU *had* to expand in order to make income meet expenditure without shedding staff. It also became more and more important to meet student recruitment targets in all subject areas, since failure to do so could result in severe financial penalties - including permanent loss of funded student places. As we saw in Chapter 13, RGIT had made expansion of its various income-generating activities a high priority during the late 1980's and early 1990's, and these were now making a very significant contribution to the institution's annual income. Increasing income from activities such as running full-cost courses, carrying out consultancy, and attracting external funding for research continued to be a high priority after 1992, as did the recruitment of overseas students. Indeed, by 1997, income from such students would rise to roughly £3 million a year - almost one tenth of the University's total grant and fee income. The operations of RGIT Ltd. also continued to make a major contribution to the University's external income.

One immediate consequence of the establishment of SHEFC was that institutions such as RGU gained access to possible Government funding of their research activities for the very first time. As we saw in Chapter 12, the Scottish Central Institutions were regarded by the Scottish Office as *teaching* establishments, and were only funded for this aspect of their work, whereas the universities were funded for both teaching and research. Now, however, RGU could compete directly with the pre-1992 universities for research funding through the periodic Research Assessment Exercise (RAE), which allocated such funding on the basis of the research ratings that an institution gained in different subject areas and the number of people who were actively involved in each of these areas. All the post-1992 universities were, however, at a considerable disadvantage in the RAE. Not only were they competing against well-established research teams in the older universities, but, in accordance with their stated missions, were also mainly carrying out 'applied' research; this was not rated highly by the assessment panels, which were dominated by 'pure' research practitioners drawn mainly from the pre-1992 universities.

The 1992 RAE, the first in which RGU participated, employed a simple 5-point rating scale, where '5' represented research of internationally-recognised quality. Having had no previous experience of preparing for such exercises, and comparatively few active researchers, the University did not expect to come out particularly well. It was assessed in 12 different subject areas, receiving 4 '1's, 7 '2's and only a single '3' - in 'Art and Design'. In this RAE, all subject areas that gained a grading of 2 or over were awarded on-going funding, and the University subsequently received roughly £300,000 a year as a result. It was gratifying to note that this was the highest funding received by any of the post-1992 Scottish universities. The largest funding allocation went to the 'Art and Design' team led by Dr. (later Professor) Carole Gray, which was able to undergo considerable expansion as a result (see Figure 14.4).

Figure 14.4 : Research being carried out in Gray's School of Art during the mid-1990's.

During the following years, the University invested a large amount of time and effort in building up its research activities in those areas in which it felt it could do well in the next RAE - scheduled for 1996. By then, however, the 'rules of the game' had undergone a number of significant changes, with teams now being required to gain a '3' rating or above in order to receive funding. Moreover, the '3' category was subdivided into '3a ' and '3b', with the former attracting significantly higher funding. The University was assessed in 13 different subject areas, receiving 2 '1's, 5 '2's, 4 '3b's and 2 '3a's - in 'Art and Design' and 'Library and Information Management'. As a result, the total annual funding rose to almost £1 million, most of which went to the two most successful research groups. This represented a real breakthrough on the research front, and the University confidently expected to do even better in the next RAE, which was due to take place in 2001.

Another important feature of the new higher education environment in which RGU had to operate after 1992 was the growth of the 'academic quality industry'. In the case of the Scottish universities, this was controlled by the Scottish Higher Education Funding Council (SHEFC) and by a completely new body - the Higher Education Quality Council (HEQC) - which had a UK-wide remit. The former was responsible for carrying out a rolling programme of 'quality assessments' in respect of specific cognate subject areas, awarding a summative classification of 'excellent', 'highly satisfactory', satisfactory' or 'unsatisfactory' as a result. During the following five years, RGU underwent quality assessments in respect of virtually all the subject areas covered by its portfolio of courses, receiving 2 'excellent' ratings (in 'Chemistry' and in 'Dietetics and Nutrition'), 9 'highly satisfactory' ratings, and 9 'satisfactory' ratings. All these quality assessments made extremely heavy demands of the staff involved, and, although they undoubtedly made *some* contribution to raising the quality of delivery of courses, there was a widespread feeling that this could have been equally well achieved through RGU's own highly effective internal quality-assurance and quality-control procedures. The author tends to agree with this view, and is pleased to note there has been a considerable move towards such an approach in the second round of subject-based quality assessments that is currently taking place.

The Higher Education Quality Council was made responsible for carrying out periodic 'quality audits' in all Britain's universities. These were conducted on a university-wide basis, and were concerned with the overall quality of the university's operations and procedures - and, in particular, with its quality-assurance and quality-control procedures. RGU had its first HEQC Quality Audit in April 1995, an event that effectively replaced the 'return visit' by the CNAA that had been scheduled for around that time (see Chapter 13). It involved producing comprehensive documentation dealing with the various areas to be covered by the audit, and then undergoing an intensive three-day visit by the HEQC audit team. The outcomes of the audit were extremely satisfactory, with the University being commended for its 'robust and well-developed quality-assurance system', and also (*inter alia*) for its work-placement arrangements, its student-support systems, its management of research students, its staff-induction procedures and the activities of its Educational Development Unit in promoting 'good teaching'. The audit team also identified a number of areas in which the University's systems could be further improved, suggesting, for example, that its formal quality-assurance systems could be even more closely integrated with its ongoing monitoring and review processes. All such suggestions were subsequently taken on board in the course of a major revision of the University's quality systems that was carried out during 1996-97. This was co-ordinated by Professor John Harper, the Assistant Principal who was now responsible for Academic Affairs.

As we saw in Chapter 10, nursing education became one of the major growth areas in RGIT during the late 1980's and early 1990's. In 1992, the rapidly-expanding Nursing Section in the School of Health and Social Work was transferred to the recently-established Centre for Professions Allied to Medicine as a full Department of Nursing. In 1993, it was moved out again, to become a fully-independent School of Nursing, based in RGU's new Kepplestone Annexe (see below). The School continued to concentrate on post-registration nursing education, since basic nursing education was then carried out at Foresterhill College, which had been established on the site of Aberdeen's main hospital complex in 1967 (see Figure 14.5). Under the dynamic leadership of Professor Ann Lowis, this work continued to expand throughout the mid-1990's, with most of the School's courses being delivered by the distance-learning methods that she and her colleagues had pioneered earlier (see Chapter 11).

Figure 14.5 : Foresterhill College of Nursing and Midwifery

In 1996, after several years of discussion and negotiation, Foresterhill College became part of The Robert Gordon University, joining forces with RGU's existing School of Nursing to form a new Associate Faculty of Nursing, Midwifery and Community Studies within the Faculty of Health and Food. Mr.Thomas Moore, Principal of Foresterhill College, became Associate Dean, with Professor Lowis becoming Director of Post-Registration Nursing. The amalgamation was consistent with a nation-wide initiative to integrate the academic and professional education of nurses into the higher-education sector, and came about as a result of RGU winning the contract to deliver all pre-registration nursing and midwifery education in the North-East of Scotland. As an immediate consequence, RGU's FTE increased by over 700, although all the pre-registration nursing and midwifery students that transferred to the University continued to be taught at the Foresterhill site. In 1997, most post-registration work was also transferred to Foresterhill, with the staff that had previously been based at Kepplestone moving into the Annexe at Foresterhill Campus that had been occupied by the Department of Radiography within the School of Health Sciences prior to its transfer to Woolmanhill.

Let us now look at some of the other significant developments that took place during the last five years of Dr. Kennedy's highly eventful Principalship.

On the buildings front, work on the expansion of the University's student accommodation continued apace, with the completion of the remaining blocks of self-catering flats at Woolmanhill. The University also took over full responsibility for these, by 'buying out' of the leasing arrangement with the property developer with which it had originally worked. This was made possible by the new financial freedom under which the institution now operated, and, although it cost a considerable amount of money at the time, proved to be a reasonably good long-term investment on the part of the University. With the aid of a generous grant from a charitable trust, the University also built two residential blocks at Garthdee, adjoining the Scott Sutherland School of Architecture. Although modern in ethos, their design was informed by the 'tower houses' that are found throughout the NE of Scotland, and won a number of architectural awards. One of the towers, which can be clearly seen from the South Deeside road, is shown in Figure 14.6.

The University also took steps to resolve the increasing pressure on teaching accommodation by erecting two short-life 'system-built' complexes. The first of these was Kepplestone Annexe, which, although no thing of great architectural beauty, was big enough to hold two entire Schools (Applied Social Studies and Nursing) plus four Departments (the Educational Development Unit, Univation, Viscom and Physical Resources). The second was a similar annexe that was built to the south of the existing Gray's School of Art building at Garthdee. This short-term solution to the School's chronic accommodation problems was dictated by economic considerations, given that the University was also committed to the construction of its new Faculty of Management building at Garthdee, on a site to the east of its existing campus. The planning and construction of this magnificent building, which was designed by Sir Norman Foster, will be described in detail in Chapter 15.

On the academic front, the University made two very significant changes to the way in which its courses were designed and delivered. The first was to adopt a 'course unitisation' policy, whereby the great majority of its taught courses were built around standard 10-credit units, each involving roughly 100 hours of notional student effort. The University also developed a standard 'Course Unit Descriptor' for the specification of the objectives, content, teaching methodology and assessment procedures for each of these units, and was thus able to build up a data base containing detailed descriptions of all the course units delivered throughout RGU. This made it much easier to develop new courses, since many of the units needed for these could now be lifted 'off the shelf'. The University also changed from the traditional three-term academic year to a two-semester

**Figure 14.6 : One of the 'Garthdee towers'
that were built during the early 1990's**

year similar to that used in the USA. This brought about a number of immediate benefits, including simplification of the University's assessment arrangements, and the earlier release of students onto the job market.

RGU also greatly expanded its overseas activities during the first half of the 1990's. By the time it became a University, it was already heavily involved in a number of European initiatives, including the 'Erasmus' programme, which promoted the establishment of collaborative links with higher-education institutions throughout the European Union. During the following years, RGU became more and more heavily involved in programmes of this type, all of which were co-ordinated through its new European Office. The University also continued to expand its foreign language teaching, in order to improve the skills of its graduates in this highly important area. It eventually established a Centre for Modern Languages within the School of Information and Media, under Dr. Murray Hill. Its facilities included several state-of-the-art language laboratories (see Figure 14.7). During this period, the University also established collaborative links with educational establishments in many other parts of the world, including Russia, India, China, Malaysia, Thailand, Australia, New Zealand, Brazil and the USA.

Figure 14.7 : Teaching being carried out in one of RGU's language laboratories

One of the highlights of the early RGU years was the visit of Baroness Thatcher, who delivered the University's 1993 Leadership Lecture in the MacRobert Hall (see Figure 14.8). This programme of annual public lectures had been initiated in 1990, and was sponsored by Hamilton Oil Company Ltd. and supported by the Institute of Management. Other speakers included business 'trouble-shooter' Sir John Harvey Jones, leadership Professor John Adair, General Sir Michael Rose, polar explorer Robert Swan, Scottish rugby captain Gavin Hastings and the model and charity worker Heather Mills. The University also initiated an on-going programme of Professorial Lectures during the mid-1990's, some of these being given by 'established' professors, and some taking the form of inaugural lectures given by people recently awarded the title. (The author is pleased to report that the University was now starting to award such titles to women as well as to men, the first recipient being Dr. Joyce Lishman, Head of the School of Applied Social Studies, in 1993.) These and other similar public events continued to raise RGU's profile among the local community.

In April, 1997, RGU's Vice Principal, Gavin Ross, took early retirement. Four months later, Dr. Kennedy followed him, having reached the mandatory retirement age of 65. Both men could look back on their 12 years of office with considerable satisfaction, and a very real sense of achievement. As we saw in Chapters 7 and 13, they and their colleagues had been faced with some of the greatest problems and challenges that the institution had ever faced. They had also had to deal with a number of extremely bitter industrial disputes, one of which - a redundancy case involving a long-serving senior lecturer - had left everyone involved permanently scarred. They had, however, overseen the greatest and most rapid expansion that the institution had ever experienced, set its finances on an extremely sound footing, established robust and effective academic and management structures, and steered RGIT safely through to full university status. When Dr. Kennedy's successor, Professor William Stevely, took up office on 1 September, 1997, he found himself in charge of a mature University with almost 7000 full-time students, with an excellent reputation among the local industrial and commercial community, and with one of the best graduate employment records in the UK. He had every reason to be grateful for what Dr. Kennedy, Mr. Ross and their colleagues had achieved since 1985; this had certainly made his own task very much easier!

Figure 14.8 : Baroness Thatcher delivering her Leadership Lecture in the MacRobert Hall on 23rd October, 1993

PROFESSOR WILLIAM STEVELY AND THE 'NEW VISION' (1997 ONWARDS)

William Stevely (see Figure 14.9) is an Ayrshireman who was educated at Ardrossan Academy and Glasgow University, from which he graduated with an Honours BSc. in Chemistry in 1965. He then obtained a D.Phil. at St. Catherine's College, Oxford, before returning to Glasgow University as an Assistant Lecturer in Biochemistry in 1968. He was subsequently promoted to Lecturer and Senior Lecturer, establishing a considerable reputation both as a teacher and as a researcher on the biochemistry and molecular biology of the herpes viruses. In 1988, he moved to Paisley College of Technology as Professor and Head of the Biology Department. Like RGIT, Paisley was awarded full university status in 1992. In the same year, Professor Stevely became its Vice Principal - a post that he held until he moved to RGU as Principal and Vice-Chancellor.

Figure 14.9 : Professor William Stevely, Principal and Vice-Chancellor of RGU since 1997

Shortly after his arrival in Aberdeen, Professor Stevely proposed a 'new vision' for The Robert Gordon University:

'To be widely recognised as the premier vocational university in the UK'.

He also proposed a revised mission statement:

'To provide high-quality, practice-based higher education and training programmes, research and consultancy services'.

Following a period of discussion by the Academic Council and Governors, both were adopted.

In pursuance of this vision and mission, Professor Stevely and his colleagues decided that it would be necessary for the University to complete the move towards full modularisation of its course portfolio that it had begun earlier in the 1990's, when it had adopted partial 'course unitisation' and changed to a two-semester academic year. Having come from a University that had been operating a full-blown modular system for several years, Professor Stevely had been able to see the very tangible benefits that could accrue from such a system. These included greater efficiency in terms of course delivery and assessment, and much greater flexibility in respect of new course design. He and his colleagues also decided that RGU should now follow the national trend by changing to a common course architecture based on 15-credit modules - the size now recommended under the Scottish Credit Accumulation and Transfer (SCOTCAT) Scheme in which RGU had been a full participant since its inception. Other than in exceptional circumstances, all such modules would also be delivered over a single semester rather than spread over an entire academic year, as had sometimes previously been the case. This meant that a full year of study comprising 120 credits, each credit representing roughly 10 hours of notional student effort, would now normally involve undertaking eight standard 15-credit modules - four in Semester 1 and four in Semester 2.

While carrying out this radical repackaging of its course portfolio, it was decided that the University should address two further major issues that were likely to affect all UK higher education institutions over the following few years. The first was the recommendation in the 1997 *'Dearing Report'* that all course teams should henceforth produce detailed programme specifications, identifying the different types of skills that students were expected to develop in the course of their studies. The second was the increasing move towards the benchmarking of levels of student achievement at the different stages of a course, as set out in the 1997 *'Partington Report'* and other policy documents. In order to help course teams to do so, the University produced a ground-breaking set of *generic level learning outcome templates*, covering the four stages of the Scottish Honours Degree and also work at 'Masters' level. These made it very much easier to write student learning outcomes at the appropriate level for each stage of a course, and also made it easier to match teaching and assessment methods to these outcomes. The templates produced by RGU attracted a great deal of interest outside the University, and served as a model for the subsequent development of national templates by the new Quality Assurance Agency that replaced the Higher Education Quality Council in the aftermath of the 'Dearing Report' (see below).

Work on the conversion of RGU's portfolio of undergraduate courses to the new common course architecture began in the spring of 1998, and was completed by the start of the 1999-2000 academic session. The work was carried out on a 'rolling' basis, with each School being set a deadline by which its new course documentation had to be ready for internal validation. This was a truly massive task, involving the running of staff-development workshops for all Schools to show their staff how to carry out the work, the re-writing of the course documentation for all of the University's undergraduate degree programmes, and the subsequent vetting and internal validation of this documentation. Although there was some grumbling on the part of staff because of the amount of work involved, most of them could see the advantages that would accrue as a result. When the work was completed, RGU probably had the best course documentation in the UK, as well as being several years 'ahead of the field' in terms of course and curriculum development. The conversion process was subsequently extended to the University's taught postgraduate programmes, with equally satisfactory results.

Because of the success of the above common course architecture programme, the University subsequently decided to develop a criterion-referenced *common grading scheme*, with a view to ensuring that academic standards would be 'more transparent, consistent, equitable and assured' across all subjects and disciplines. This involved changing from traditional percentage marks to assessment based on grades, with each piece of assessed work being assigned a grade on a six-point scale ranging from 1 (fail) to 6 (excellent). Following a successful pilot in Stage 1 of all undergraduate courses during session 2000-2001, it was agreed that the new scheme would be implemented in Stages 2, 3 and 4 on a phased basis, over the following three sessions. It was seen to be a logical extension of the common course architecture scheme, and was intended to achieve 'enhanced assurance of output standards in terms of their consistency and explicitness'. As with common course architecture, staff were provided with comprehensive training on how to implement the new scheme.

As we saw in the previous section, RGU carried out a major review of its academic quality systems as a result of the recommendations made in the report on the 1995 HEQC Quality Audit. This review also covered the University's academic committee structure, and, after considerable discussion, was implemented at the start of the 1997-98 session. One of the major changes introduced as a result of the review was the establishment of a new Planning Executive Group (PEG), comprised of the Principal and other appropriate members of the Strategic Management Team (as the Senior Management Team had been re-named some years previously). PEG's main function was to enhance the efficiency and effectiveness of the procedures for approving new course developments, changes to existing courses, and collaborative arrangements of all types. In fulfilling its remit, PEG was intended to work in close collaboration with the University's Planning committee. In 2001, the latter became a joint committee of Academic Council and the Board of Governors, and was re-named as the Strategic Planning Committee.

Professor Stevely also made a number of changes to the way in which the University was managed once he took up office. As we saw in Chapters 7 and 13, Dr. Kennedy had divided the institution into twelve separate (albeit strongly interdependent) management areas, with overall responsibility for the direction and control of these being split between himself and the Vice Principal. This system had served the University well, but Professor Stevely felt that it was now time to introduce a 'flatter' management structure, with all members of the Strategic Management Team reporting directly to himself. He therefore decided not to appoint a replacement for Mr. Ross, who, as we have seen, had retired in April, 1997. The Vice Principal's portfolio of responsibilities was divided among the four Assistant Principals/Deans. Four years later, following the early retirement of one of the Assistant Principals/Deans and the amalgamation of two of the University's Faculties, the remaining three were re-designated as Vice Principals/Deans in order 'to better reflect their level of responsibility and authority'.

Other significant developments during the early years of Professor Stevely's Principalship included the conversion of the Associate Faculty of Nursing, Midwifery and Community Studies into a School of Nursing and Midwifery, as part of the Faculty of Health and Food, at the start of the 1998-99 session. Since the Associate Dean, Thomas Moore had left the University, the post of Head of School was advertised. Dr. Sally Lawton, a Senior Lecturer in the School, was subsequently appointed, but had to demit office shortly afterwards due to ill health; she was eventually replaced by Mrs. Jennie

Parry. The new School was now the largest in the University, with almost 2000 students enrolled on its various full-time and part-time courses, many of which continued to be delivered by distance-learning methods.

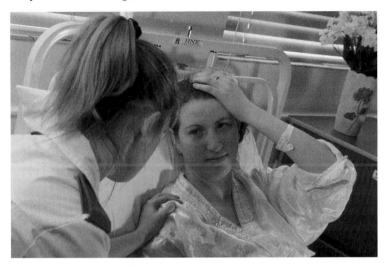

Figure 14.10 : A nursing student on ward-based work placement

1998 also saw the long-awaited move of the Faculty of Management into its new 'super-building' at Garthdee (see Chapter 15 for more detailed information). This was officially opened by Sir Ian Wood, Chairman of Scottish Enterprise, on April 7, 1999. At around this time, work also began on the detailed planning of a second new 'super-building' at Garthdee, immediately adjacent to the Faculty of Management (again see Chapter 15 for details). This was to house most of the Faculty of Health and Food, which was re-named as the Faculty of Health and Social Care later in 1999, when the Kepplestone-based School of Food and Consumer Studies was 're-branded' as the School of Hotel, Tourism and Retail Management and became part of the Faculty of Management. As we saw in Chapter 10, the Nutrition and Dietetics staff of the School were initially transferred to the School of Health Sciences, but subsequently became part of the new School of Life Sciences during the major reorganisation of the University's academic structure that took place in the summer of 2001 (see below).

A number of important developments also took place on the IT front from the late 1990's onwards, developments that would eventually lead RGU fully into the 'electronic age', and completely transform the way in which teaching/learning was delivered and supported. The first was the establishment, in September 1998, of the Centre for Open and Distance Learning, and the subsequent development of a 'Virtual Campus' that enabled distance-learning courses to be delivered electronically, via the Internet. The second was the appointment of the University's first Director of Information Technology, Mr. Andrew McCreath, in 1999, and the subsequent complete reorganisation of RGU's IT services and systems. The third was the development of the Faculty of Management

Intranet during session 2000-01, a state-of-the-art computer network that provided staff and students with an unprecedented range of electronic support facilities, and would later be extended to other Faculties. The fourth was the progressive change to an electronic business environment throughout the University. All these developments will be described in detail in Chapter 16, the final chapter of the book.

RGU's commercial activities and externally-funded research also went from strength to strength during the latter part of the 1990's. As we saw in Section 3, Dr. Clarke and Dr. Kennedy had set up a number of full-cost commercial units and departments from the 1970's onwards, including the Offshore Survival Centre and the Centre for Offshore Health (which merged in 1989 to form an independent Company that later became RGIT Ltd.), Viscom, and Univation. These were later joined by other commercial units, including the Offshore Management Centre in Aberdeen Business School, and 50K Design, which is based in Gray's School of Art and provides a wide range of design services to external clients. The University has also set up a Centre for Entrepreneurship, with a view to 'embedding entrepreneurship into the curriculum', and a Research Commercialisation Unit, which helps research teams to convert their ideas into money-making schemes. One important recent development has been the merger of RGIT Ltd. with Montrose Scota Training International to form RGIT Montrose Ltd. (see Figure 14.11). This is now one of the world's leading players in offshore health and safety, and continues to make a very significant contribution to the University's external income, through its profits.

Figure 14.11 : The Altens Headquarters of RGIT Montrose Ltd.

The steady expansion of Univation since Mrs. Vivien MacKinlay became its Managing director in 1993 has been one of RGU's great success stories. Univation now has an annual turnover of over £3 million, providing customised educational and training programmes for industrial and commercial clients in many different parts of the world, including the UK, Libya, Nigeria, Kuwait, Iran, Kazakhstan, Russia, China, Vietnam and Venezuela. One of its most important projects in recent years has been the development of the Shell Intensive Training Programme, a specialised postgraduate programme designed to train petroleum engineers, petroleum geologists and IT specialists to work in Nigeria's thriving oil industry. This has involved setting up and running what is in effect a 'mini university' in one of Shell's industrial compounds in Warri, an 'oil town' in the Niger Delta. The programme has recently been validated by the University as a suite of three linked 'Masters' degrees.

The University has also been extremely successful in attracting external research funding in recent years. Major awards since 1999 have included the following:

- £76,667 awarded to the Scott Sutherland School of Architecture by the Macaulay Land Use Research Institute (MLURI) and Scottish Enterprise in order to develop a computer-based tool to aid the design of 'people-friendly, economically-viable town centres';
- £70,000 awarded to the School of Applied Sciences by the Scottish Environmental Protection Agency and the Scottish Office in order to develop a groundwater monitoring network throughout Scotland in collaboration with MLURI..
- £70,000 awarded to the School of Public Administration and Law under EU Research Framework Programme V to help fund two major international conferences;
- £155,000 awarded by SHEFC to fund a collaborative project involving RGU, Aberdeen University and Aberdeen College on the development of the C&IT skills of the staff at the three institutions;
- £300,000 awarded to Gray's School of Art under the Humanities Research scheme in order 'to examine the factors that make visual art both creative and sustainable within a specific geographic region';
- £700,000 awarded to the Centre for Environmental Engineering and the Environmental Biotechnology Research Group by the European Commission for 'an eco-friendly project to develop a system for removing deadly toxins from water';
- £1 million awarded to the School of Mechanical and Offshore Engineering by the European Union in order to develop economic systems for generating electricity from tidal energy;
- £1.5 million awarded by the Scottish Higher Education Funding Council in order to fund two major projects involving the Schools of Applied Sciences and Computer and Mathematical Sciences (carrying out implant research, and designing intelligent web-based computer systems);
- Over £1 million of awards made to support 15 projects run under the Teaching

Company Scheme, which is designed to keep academic staff in touch with industrial practice and foster mutually-beneficial technology transfer between academic institutions and SME's;

• Outstanding success in both rounds of the 'Proof of Concepts' competition, which is aimed at identifying potential spin-out developments; RGU is currently receiving support for six projects, to an overall value of roughly £1 million.

Figure 14.12 : Environmental monitoring work being carried out by staff of RGU's Centre for Environmental Engineering

As we saw earlier, RGU did rather well in the 1996 Research Assessment Exercise, raising the total amount of annual funding that it received to roughly £1 million. It expected to do even better in the next RAE, scheduled for 2001, and again invested a great deal of time, effort and resources in order to increase its ratings in the areas in which it was active. The work was co-ordinated by Professor Frank McIntosh, Chairman of RGU's Research Committee. The University eventually made submissions in 15 subject areas, receiving 3 '2's, 7 '3b's and 5 '3a's - in 'Computer Science', 'Metallurgy and Materials', 'Law', Politics and International Studies', and 'Art and Design'. By now, however, direct funding was only being awarded for ratings of '3a' and above, and, even in the case of the '3a's, only went to these that had *increased* their rating from the previous RAE. Thus, 'Art and Design' received no direct funding, since they had gained a '3a' in 1996. The total annual funding received by RGU as a result of the 2001 RAE was roughly £1.2 million - a 20% increase compared with 1996. Overall, the results were extremely disappointing, however, with RGU falling behind some of the other 'new' Scottish universities for the first time.

As was pointed out earlier, post-1992 universities such as RGU were always going to find it difficult to secure significant funding through the RAE system, because most of their research is of an 'applied' nature, as opposed to the 'pure' research that is favoured by the assessment panels. Two disturbing trends have also emerged from the three RAE's that have been completed since RGIT attained full university status in 1992. Firstly, threshold standards for the different grades appear to have been raised over the years, making it more and more difficult to attain high ratings under the scheme. Secondly, more and more of the total funding available under the scheme has been concentrated at the higher end of the scale in successive RAE's. Thus, despite increasing its average overall rating significantly between 1992 and 2001, RGU has actually seen the number of subject areas receiving direct funding *fall* steadily - from 8 in 1992 to 6 in 1996, and to only 4 in 2001. At the risk of sounding cynical, the author is tempted to say that the development of the RAE over the last 10 years has been a perfect illustration of the 'Matthew Principle':

'For unto every one that hath shall be given, and he shall have abundance; but from him that hath not shall be taken away even that which he hath.'
                                              - Matthew; Chapter 25; Verse 29.

Following the publication of the 'Dearing Report' on the future of British higher education in 1997, a number of important developments took place on the 'academic quality' scene. The first was the formation of the Institute for Learning and Teaching (ILT) - a completely new 'professional body' for higher education teachers and learning support staff that was also given the job of accrediting training courses for such staff. Professor Stevely served on the 'Shadow Council' for the new body, and played a significant part in bringing it into operation. RGU became one of the first institutions in the country to have its own training course for teaching staff - the 'Postgraduate Certificate in Tertiary-Level Teaching' - accredited by the ILT (see Chapter 10). All new teaching staff are now expected to join the ILT, either by undertaking the PGCTLT or by submitting a portfolio of their work as tertiary-level teachers.

Another important development was the conversion of the Higher Education Quality Council into the Quality Assurance Agency (QAA), and the transfer to the new body of responsibility for carrying out subject-based quality assessments as well as institute-wide quality audits. The QAA also became responsible for producing policy documents on the future structure and mode of operation of higher education, including a wide-ranging Code of Practice with which all institutions were expected to comply - and produce evidence of so doing. As we saw in the previous section, RGU had undergone a highly-successful quality audit by the HEQC in 1995, and was scheduled for a second audit roughly six years later. This duly took place in April 2001, when a QAA audit team spent five days holding meetings with various groups of staff and studying the documentation that had been lodged in the audit 'base room'. The subsequent report, which was published in January 2002, was once again extremely positive, concluding that there could be 'general confidence in the University's ability properly to discharge its responsibility for the academic standards of the degrees awarded in its name and for the quality of the programmes of study that lead to those awards'. The University was also commended (*inter alia*) on the changes that it had made to its quality systems in response to the report on the 1995 audit. A number of areas requiring 'further consideration' were also identified, including the need to establish robust quality procedures in respect of the operation of its new 'Virtual Campus'.

RGU also carried out yet another major review of its academic structure in the summer of 2001, coinciding with the early retirement of Professor Frank McIntosh, Dean of the Faculty of Science and Technology. For some time, this particular Faculty had been having problems relating to the recruitment and subsequent retention of students, in common with its counterparts in most other British universities. It was also realised that there was a need to re-align the teaching of science within the University in order to concentrate on areas of strength, and to create new teaching units that would facilitate the inter-disciplinary developments that were seen as such an important part of RGU's future. With these considerations in mind, it was decided to merge the Faculty of Design with the Faculty of Science and Technology, to merge the two Engineering Schools, to re-merge the Scott Sutherland School of Architecture and the School of Construction, Property and Surveying, and to create a new School of Life Sciences. The overall structure that was produced as a result of the review is shown below:

Faculty of Design and Technology (Dean : Professor Jim Penman)
- Gray's School of Art
- School of Computing (previously the School of Computer and Mathematical Sciences)
- School of Engineering (formed by the amalgamation of the School of Electronic and Electrical Engineering and the School of Mechanical and Offshore Engineering)
- The Scott Sutherland School (formed by re-merging the Scott Sutherland School of Architecture and the School of Construction, Property and Surveying)
- School of Graduate Studies
- Centre for Interdisciplinary Studies

Faculty of Health and Social Care (Dean : Professor John Harper)
- School of Applied Social Studies
- School of Health Sciences
- School of Life Sciences (previously the School of Applied Sciences, but now including the Nutrition and Dietetics sections from the School of Health Sciences)
- School of Nursing and Midwifery
- School of Pharmacy

Faculty of Management (Dean : Professor Bill McIntosh)
- Aberdeen Business School
- School of Hotel, Tourism and Retail Management
- School of Information and Media
- School of Public Administration and Law

As we saw earlier, the three remaining Assistant Principals/Deans were re-designated as Vice Principals/Deans in order to reflect their greater responsibilities; they were allocated the following University-wide portfolios:

Professor Penman : Strategic Planning, Research and Commercialisation.
Professor Harper : Academic Quality and Enhancement.
Professor McIntosh : Academic Development.

An Associate Dean was also appointed to each Faculty, to work with the Dean and Heads of School to deliver each Faculty's strategy and improve inter- and intra-Faculty communication.

Another highly significant event took place in September 2001, with the launch of RGU's 'Energy University' initiative at the 'Offshore Europe' exhibition and conference at the Bridge of Don. Through this, the University announced its intention 'to capitalise on its huge expertise in oil and gas and its growing reputation in alternative energy'. Approximately 40% of RGU's business was by now directly related to the energy sector, in which the University had established a world-wide reputation in education, research, telemedicine, offshore management, emergency response, and survival training. The aim of the new initiative was 'to pull together all the University's expertise in energy under one brand', and thus 'make industry aware of the wide range of services and depth of knowledge that it can offer'. The initiative is being co-ordinated by Univation, RGU's main 'commercial arm'.

Figure 14.13 shows Professor William Stevely, Principal of RGU, and Professor Duncan Rice, Principal of the University of Aberdeen, deep in conversation on the RGU

Figure 14.13 : RGU Principal Professor William Stevely (left) and Aberdeen University Principal Professor Duncan Rice at 'Offshore Europe 2001'

stand at 'Offshore Europe 2001'. This turned out to be a highly significant photograph, since it subsequently emerged that the two Universities had for some time been exploring the possibility of more extensive collaboration. They had worked closely together in a number of disciplines over the years, and, building on this spirit of co-operation, RGU's Board of Governors and the Aberdeen University Court had agreed 'that there could be scope for further collaboration'; they had therefore instructed the two organisations 'to investigate possible models that could be of mutual benefit'.

In a written message to all RGU staff on 22nd February 2002, Professor Stevely stressed that the discussions were not cost-driven, since both Universities were financially strong and currently in surplus. The primary aim was 'to examine opportunities where partnership could further enhance the academic record and achievements of the two Universities, and strengthen the City's role as a centre of excellence in higher education'. At the time of writing (April 2002), a report is being prepared for discussion within both Universities, suggesting ways in which they might benefit from greater partnership. This report is due to be published later in the summer, and the author awaits its contents - and the outcome of the subsequent discussions - with interest. Watch this space!

Note: Since this chapter was completed, the above-mentioned report has been published, and its recommendations approved by RGU's Board of Governors and the Aberdeen University Court - see the 'Postscript' that follows Chapter 16 for more detailed information.

Chapter 15 : New buildings for a new University

THE DEVELOPMENT OF RGU'S ESTATES STRATEGY

In this chapter, we will look at the development of RGU's estates strategy, and show how this led to the decision to transfer most of the University's teaching work to Garthdee. We will discuss the reasoning behind this decision, and take a detailed look at the two major building projects that enabled the bulk of the transfer to take place over the period 1998-2002. As we will see, these have provided the University with two state-of-the-art teaching buildings that are ideally suited to take RGU fully into the electronic age.

As we saw in Sections 1 - 3, the institution that was eventually to become The Robert Gordon University started out on a single campus - Schoolhill - but gradually spread to other parts of Aberdeen as its activities diversified and its student numbers grew. In 1910, it became a two-campus institution, when the former School of Domestic Economy at King Street became part of the new Robert Gordon's Technical College. In 1955, it became a three-campus institution, when Tom Scott Sutherland presented the Governors of Robert Gordon's Colleges with his entire Garthdee estate, in order to enable them to build a new School of Architecture for the Technical College. Eight years later, it became a four-campus institution, when the School of Domestic Science moved to its new building at Kepplestone. During the RGIT years, it also acquired premises at St. Andrew Street and leased accommodation at Hilton, Woolmanhill and Foresterhill, so, by the time it became a University in 1992, it was operating on no fewer than eight different sites, separated by distances of up to four miles.

The many disadvantages of multi-site operation had become increasingly apparent as the number of campuses grew. These included high running costs, time wasted through inter-site travel, communications and logistical problems, the difficulty of fostering cohesive academic links, the fragmenting of the staff and student community, and the need to provide proper library facilities on all sites. The problem was compounded by the fact that only one of the University's four Faculties - Design - operated on a single campus, with one - Health and Food - being spread over four different sites! Towards the end of the 1980's, RGIT's Vice Principal, Gavin Ross, himself an architect and town planner, and Professor Robin Webster, Head of the Scott Sutherland School of Architecture, had prepared a strategy paper for the Scottish Education Department on the possible future development of the institution's estates policy. This had presented a strong case for reducing the number of sites on which the institution operated, and had identified an expanded Garthdee campus as a suitable site on which future activities might be concentrated. Preliminary discussions then took place with Aberdeen City Council regarding the acquisition of land at Garthdee, adjacent to the existing campus, on which these developments might take place, and also with the local Planning Authority. These prepared the way for what was to follow during the 1990's.

Once RGIT became a University and thus assumed full responsibility for the development of its future estates strategy, a highly-detailed appraisal of the various options available to it on the estates front was carried out, with the aid of two Edinburgh-based firms of consultants - Architects and Engineers, RMJM Scotland Ltd., and Chartered Quantity Surveyors, Kean Kennedy. This was done with the following three key objectives in mind:

- To make progress towards the realisation of the long-term strategic aim of concentrating the University's operations on a smaller number of sites;
- To re-locate the rapidly-expanding Faculty of Management (which was by then partly based in accommodation on short-term lease at Hilton, partly based at King Street, partly based at Blackfriars Street, and partly based at Kepplestone) as an 'immediate priority';
- To consolidate the School of Health Sciences (then based in accommodation on short-term lease at Woolmanhill and Foresterhill) on a single University-owned site in the 'medium term'.

In all, eleven different possible strategies were initially considered, but these were later reduced to the following five:

1. A 'do-minimum' three-campus strategy in which the Faculty of Science and Technology plus the School of Pharmacy would remain at Schoolhill/St. Andrew Street, the Faculty of Health and Food (apart from the School of Pharmacy) would be based at Kepplestone, and the Faculty of Management would join the Faculty of Design at Garthdee.

2. A more ambitious three-campus strategy in which only the Faculty of Science and Technology would remain at Schoolhill/St. Andrew Street, with the whole of the Faculty of Health and Food being based at Kepplestone, and the Faculty of Management again joining the Faculty of Design at Garthdee.

3. A two-campus strategy in which only the Faculty of Science and Technology would remain at Schoolhill/St. Andrew Street, with the Faculty of Management and then the whole of the Faculty of Health and Food moving to Garthdee to join the Faculty of Design.

4. A one-campus strategy in which the Faculty of Management, then the whole of the Faculty of Health and Food, and then the whole of the Faculty of Science and Technology would move to Garthdee to join the Faculty of Design.

5. A one-campus strategy in which the entire University would be re-located on an (unspecified) greenfield site in or around Aberdeen.

Apart from the 'do-minimum' strategy, which assumed that the University would make no effort to increase student numbers beyond its existing commitments, all strategies were based on a projected growth in student numbers to between 8,000 and 10,000 FTE over the following ten years. In the event, these projections turned out to be remarkably accurate, although they were felt to be 'wildly optimistic' by many people, both in the Scottish Education Department and within the University itself.

The various options were subjected to rigorous evaluation and comparative appraisal, both by non-financial benefit analysis based on the use of questionnaires, and by economic assessment based on Treasury Green Book and SHEFC guidelines. It was eventually decided that phased re-location of all the University's mainstream operations to Garthdee would be the most desirable option, but that this could not be implemented within the ten-year period originally envisaged because of its high capital cost; implementation over a period of twenty years, would, however, probably be a realistic proposition. The University therefore decided to adopt an Estates Management Strategy based on this. One of the factors that made this particular strategy so attractive was the fact that, on the basis of the earlier study described above, RGU had already obtained an option to acquire all the necessary land at Garthdee, which was owned by Aberdeen City. This stretched all the way from RGU's existing Garthdee campus to the site of the former 'Richards' mill, to the west of the Bridge of Dee. This strip of land, on a south-facing slope overlooking the River Dee, must be one of the most attractive available to any British university.

When the new Estates Strategy was agreed in 1994, it was envisaged that it would be implemented in the following stages:

- Construction of a new Faculty of Management building, incorporating a new Central Library that would cater for the Faculties of Management and Design, at Garthdee, immediately to the east of the Scott Sutherland School of Architecture (as we will see in the next section, partial funding for this project had already been promised by SHEFC); vacation of the premises at Hilton and King Street then occupied by the three Schools of this Faculty, and disposal of the latter.
- Relocation of the School of Health Sciences in a new building at Garthdee, thus enabling the premises at Woolmanhill and Foresterhill then occupied by the School to be relinquished.
- Relocation of the other Schools of the Faculty of Health and Food to Garthdee, thus making additional accommodation available for the Faculty of Science and Technology at Schoolhill, and enabling the main Kepplestone building to be disposed of before an expensive mid-life refurbishment had to be carried out.
- Relocation of the various Schools of the Faculty of Science and Technology to Garthdee, provided that this was still considered to be in the best interests of the University; this would not happen until well into the new millennium, however.

Plans were also made to provide playing fields and other sporting and recreational facilities at Garthdee once those at Kepplestone were lost, and also to provide additional student residences.

As we will see, the main strategic aims for the first ten years of this plan - reduction of the number of sites on which the University operated, relocation of the Faculty of Management to Garthdee, and relocation of the Faculty of Health and Food to Garthdee - have been fully achieved within the timescale envisaged. The tactical details of the plan did have to be changed in a number of ways in the light of subsequent developments, however, as we will see in the next two sections.

The move of the Faculty of Management to Garthdee

As we saw in the previous section, the idea of moving the Faculty of Management into a new, state-of-the-art building at Garthdee had its genesis in the late 1980's, as part of the strategy paper on the possible future development of RGIT's estates policy that was prepared for the SED. By 1990, the Institute was in a position to submit a request for 100% capital funding for the new building, and, a year later, this was approved by the Department, enabling a request for outline planning consent to be submitted to the local authority.

When RGIT gained full university status in 1992, however, the SED ceased to be responsible for its funding, and the newly-established Scottish Higher Education Funding Council was not prepared to meet the full cost of the project, offering only 50%. This made it necessary to secure other sources of funding, and it was not until 1993 that RGU was able to commission Sir Norman Foster to design the new building, and submit for detailed planning consent. Further complications arose regarding the acquisition of the land from Aberdeen City and the details of the planning application, which aroused considerable opposition from local residents. As a result of these externally-imposed delays, it was not until almost four years later that planning consent was eventually obtained.

Figure 15.1 : An aerial view of the Faculty of Management building

By now, the cost of the project had risen to £19.5 million - £5 million more than the estimate that had been incorporated in the 1994 Estates Strategy. This increase was due to a combination of inflation, the imposition of new planning conditions, and some technical problems relating to the geography of the site. Nevertheless, the University was able to find the necessary money because of its strong overall financial position, enabling building work to start early in 1997. Tribute should be given to the (then) Estates Director, Barry Ostle, and his staff in Physical Resources, for, by dint of herculean efforts on the part of everyone involved as well as the various contractors, work was completed in the summer of 1998. This enabled the three Schools then in the Faculty of Management (Aberdeen Business School, Information and Media, and Public Administration and Law) to move into their magnificent new home just in time for the start of the 1998-99 session.

Figure 15.1 shows an aerial view of the new building and its splendid setting overlooking the River Dee. Immediately behind it is Kaim House, which was later acquired by the University, and beyond this are the Scott Sutherland School and Gray's School of Art. Just as the latter was rightly described as 'the best mid-20th-century building in Aberdeen', so the new Faculty of Management can equally justly be claimed to be the finest late-20th-century building. It has certainly been widely recognised as such, and has gained design awards from prestigious bodies such as the Royal Institute of British Architects. The enlightened and far-sighted policy of the Governing Body, established in the late 1980's, of appointing architects of world standing for major new building projects, was now bearing fruit in terms of the recognition this brought to the University. Figure 15.2 shows how the building looks from ground level, with its six-storey stepped box structure enclosed by Norman Foster's dramatic curved roof, which follows the slope of the ground down to the river.

Figure 15.2 : The Faculty of Management building seen from the ground

Inside, the building is equally impressive, one of its finest features being the four-storey-high atrium that separates the staff accommodation on the north side from the teaching accommodation and library complex on the south side (see Figure 15.3). Nigel Dancey, Norman Foster's Project Director, prefers the term 'street' to describe this 'social hub' of the building. As he explains, 'We wanted to create informal meeting areas that would encourage interaction between students and staff'. Dancey's intentions for the 'internal street' have been borne out by subsequent experience, since, for most of the day, it 'throngs with students and staff moving between classes, taking a bite to eat in the adjacent refectories, socialising with colleagues, or conferring briefly over work'. It has also established itself as the University's main venue for social events, such as receptions following professorial lectures and other public presentations. It is certainly a magnificent setting for such occasions.

**Figure 15.3 : The atrium that forms the 'social hub'
of the Faculty of Management building**

Passing through the glass screen that forms the southern wall of the atrium, you enter the Georgina Scott Sutherland Library, as the Garthdee Library is now named in honour of Tom Scott Sutherland's widow. Here, the atmosphere is completely different, with the dark slate flooring of the atrium being replaced by thick carpeting, and the buzz of conversation giving way to the respectful hush of academe. Straight ahead is a wide, free-standing staircase, that slopes back toward the atrium, and connects the Library's four floors. As Martin Spring observes in his excellent article in 'Building Review': 'It takes a moment for the scale of the library hall to sink in. All four levels have rows of desks on either side - 630 study places in total. Such a multitude of desks would look oppressive in conventional low-ceilinged rooms, but here they are effortlessly absorbed by the hall, thanks to its scale, open terracing, lofty ceiling and ample daylight'. Figure 15.4 shows part of the upper area of the library, looking towards the west.

Particular thought was given to the design of the teaching spaces that occupy most of the two lowest floors of the new building, as well as the areas supported by pillars to the south of the atrium (see Figure 15.3). In addition to three large tiered lecture theatres, the biggest of which seats 300 people, it contains a balanced mix of smaller classrooms, seminar rooms and IT laboratories, designed to support all the different modes of teaching and learning that take place in a modern university. Computer work stations are particularly plentiful, since most of the learning resources that have been produced by staff are available online, thus enabling students to gain access to them at any time. All lecture theatres and other classrooms are fitted with the latest electronic teaching aids, as well as being connected to the Internet and to the Faculty's own internal Intranet. One of the main lecture theatres is shown in Figure 15.5. Note the roof-mounted data projector, and the lecturer's control console in the lower right hand corner; things have certainly come a long way from the 'chalk and talk' that the author remembers from his own time at university!

**Figure 15.4 : Part of the new Georgina Scott Sutherland Library
in the Faculty of Management building.**

241

Accommodation for most of the academic staff who work in the new building is provided in three floors at the northern end of the block, overlooking the car parks. The great majority are housed in large, semi-open-plan offices, where they have their own personal work stations and storage facilities for books, documents etc. While every effort was made to provide a working environment that was both flexible and in keeping with the latest thinking regarding educational architecture, it has to be pointed out that the accommodation has not proved popular with many of the staff involved. It would appear that most academics prefer to work in much smaller offices, a view with which the author has considerable sympathy. Such traditional arrangements are seldom practicable in large, modern buildings like the two that have been built at Garthdee, however.

**Figure 15.5 : One of the main lecture theatres
in the Faculty of Management building**

The new Faculty of Management building was officially opened on April 3, 1999 by Sir Ian Wood, Chairman of Scottish Enterprise, who unveiled a granite plaque to mark the occasion (see Figure 15.6). In addition, Councillor Margaret Smith, who later became Lord Provost of Aberdeen City, planted a commemorative tree in the grounds of the building. The event was attended by over 300 guests, including local dignitaries, representatives from business, industry and the local community, supporters of the University, and members of RGU's own staff. In his address, Sir Ian pointed out that 'the Knowledge Revolution has taken over from the Industrial Revolution', and that 'we are living in an entirely new world of information technology, vastly enhanced communications, and globalisation - a world that will change our lives'. He went on to observe that the new building 'is exactly the right kind of environment for study for the new world', being the 'complete antithesis of the traditional image of a university', with an atmosphere that is 'busy, high-tech and business-like'. In his opinion, 'this new 21st century campus provides a quality environment consistent with the legacy of Robert Gordon himself'.

Figure 15.6 : Sir Ian Wood, Chairman of Scottish Enterprise, opening the new Faculty of Management building on April 7, 1999

THE MOVE OF THE FACULTY OF HEALTH AND SOCIAL CARE TO GARTHDEE.

In view of the various developments that had taken place since its original Estates Strategy was agreed in 1994, the University took a further look at the Strategy in 1997, and made a number of changes as a result. For example, it now had to cater for all the nursing and midwifery staff and students in Foresterhill College that had joined the University in 1996, raising its FTE by over 700 at a stroke. It was also becoming much more difficult to make accurate projections of future student (and therefore staff) numbers, because of the many largely-uncontrollable factors that now affected these. The progressive adoption of more student-centred learning strategies throughout the University was also having a significant affect on space-per-student projections. The University did, however, confirm its main strategic objective of lowering the number of sites on which it operated, aiming to reduce this 'to between 2 and 4 within the next 10 years'. It also confirmed its intention to move more of its teaching activities to Garthdee as soon as circumstances allowed.

Once the moves of the Faculty of Management and Central Library to Garthdee had been satisfactorily completed in the summer of 1998, Assistant Principal Bill McIntosh and his staff in the Physical Resources Department turned their attention to the next phase of the strategic plan - provision of new accommodation for the Faculty of Health and Food. They eventually came up with a highly-ambitious plan that would involve moving four of the Faculty's five Schools into a second new 'super-building' at Garthdee, immediately adjacent to the Faculty of Management building. Figure 15.7 shows an artist's impression of how the new building, which was being designed by Architects, Halliday Fraser Munro, would look. Most of the money needed for its construction would be provided by selling the entire Kepplestone campus to Safeway, who planned to build an underground supermarket on the site, together with a high-quality housing estate and an extensive 'nature trail'.

Figure 15.7 : An artist's impression of the new Faculty of Health and Food building that it was planned to build at Garthdee.

After considering the matter for some time, Aberdeen City Council eventually granted planning permission for both projects, but approval for the construction of a supermarket at Kepplestone was subsequently rescinded by the Scottish Executive, thus greatly reducing the effective sale value of the Kepplestone site. By this time, however, work on the construction of RGU's new building at Garthdee was well in hand, and the four Schools involved were committed to moving into it in the summer of 2002. The project therefore went ahead as planned, with alternative sources of funding being found to make up for the likely shortfall caused by the collapse of the Safeway project. It says much for the financial strength of The Robert Gordon University and the quality of its senior management that this was able to be done, since the total cost of the building was over £21 million. Not many of Britain's post-1992 Universities could have funded a major project of this size.

When the new Faculty of Health and Food building was being planned back in 1998, it was envisaged that four of the Faculty's five schools (Applied Social Studies,

Food and Consumer Studies, Health Sciences, and Nursing and Midwifery) would move into it. The other School in the Faculty - Pharmacy - would remain at Schoolhill, since its highly-specialised laboratory requirements would make relocation extremely expensive; it might be moved at some later date, however. By the time work started on the new building in 2001, however, one of the Schools in the Faculty (Food and Consumer Studies) had been 'rebranded' as the School of Hotel, Tourism and Retail Management, and had become part of the Faculty of Management. The name of the Faculty of Health and Food had also been changed to the Faculty of Health and Social Care. Thus, the new 'Faculty of Health and Social Care' building would now actually contain only three Schools from that Faculty, and one from the Faculty of Management.

Figure 15.8 shows the new building as it looked at the start of April 2002, when it was nearing completion. As can be seen, it is very similar to the Faculty of Management building, again consisting of a stepped box enclosed by a curved roof that follows the slope of the ground down to the River Dee. It is, however, slightly larger (13,500 sq.m. compared with 12,500 sq.m. in the earlier building), and has one more floor (seven compared with six). It again has an extensive atrium, but in this case it runs from north to south, separating the staff accommodation that occupies much of the eastern part of the building from the teaching accommodation that occupies most of the western part. As in the case of the Faculty of Management building, the bottom two floors consist almost entirely of teaching facilities, which include two large tiered lecture theatres and a mix of smaller classrooms, seminar rooms, IT laboratories and specialist laboratories. It is designed to accommodate 260 staff and 2,950 students - considerably more than the Faculty of Management building was originally intended to hold.

**Figure 15.8 : The new Faculty of Health and Social Care
building at Garthdee under construction.**

At the time of writing (April, 2002), work on the new building is slightly behind schedule, but it is confidently expected that it will become fully operational in time for the start of the 2002-03 academic year. Both staff and students are looking forward to moving into the new building, which will have just as great an impact on the work of the University and its image in the outside world as the Faculty of Management block next door. Like the latter, it will be ideally suited to taking the Faculty of Health and Social Care fully into the 'electronic age'.

POSSIBLE FUTURE DEVELOPMENTS ON THE ESTATES FRONT

Once the new Faculty of Health and Social Care building at Garthdee has been brought into service and the planned sales of the Kepplestone and King Street campuses have been completed, the University intends to carry out a further review of its Estates Strategy. This will be largely driven by academic considerations, particularly projections of student numbers, but will also probably be strongly influenced by the discussions that are taking place with the University of Aberdeen regarding a possible future merger (see the 'Postscript' that follows Chapter 16). The University is, however, also having second thoughts about its stated long-term aim of eventually moving all its operations to Garthdee, partly because of additional planning restrictions that have been imposed on the further development of the Garthdee campus. It thus seems likely that RGU will eventually become a two-campus institution, with all its work being concentrated at Garthdee and at Schoolhill/St. Andrew Street. All this could change in the light of the discussions with Aberdeen University, however.

Figure 15.9 : One of the student activities that will be catered for in the new Sports Centre at Garthdee.

In the meantime, RGU has a number of further developments at Garthdee in the pipeline. These include the construction of a new Sports Centre for the University, on a site between the Faculty of Management building and the Faculty of Health and Social Care building. Planning permission for this exciting new development, for which the Architects are Thomson, Craig and Donald, has already been obtained. It will include a large Sports Hall suitable for basketball and indoor football, three smaller Halls, a Fitness Area, a Fitness Assessment Room, and a Sports Injury Clinic, as well as a Social Area and extensive changing and shower facilities. Completion of this Centre will greatly enhance the facilities available to RGU's many highly-active student sporting societies (see Figure 15.9).

The University also has provisional plans to build a number of new student accommodation blocks at Garthdee. Some of these will be built on vacant ground between the existing Garthdee buildings, with others being built further to the east. All will command a glorious view of the River Dee. At the moment, the University only has two student accommodation blocks at Garthdee - the two 'towers' that were built next to the Scott Sutherland School of Architecture during the early 1990's. Building the additional blocks that are currently envisaged will do a great deal to increase the vitality of the Garthdee campus, turning it into a genuine residential university campus as opposed to one to which students only come to study. The author looks forward to seeing what happens on this front during the next few years. Whatever happens, they will almost certainly be very exciting ones for the University.

Chapter 16 : Moving the University into the 'electronic age'

THE DEVELOPMENT OF RGU'S IT STRATEGY SINCE 1997

As we saw in Chapter 14, a number of extremely important developments took place on the information technology (IT) front from the late 1990's onwards, developments that would eventually lead RGU fully into the 'electronic age' so vividly described by Sir Ian Wood when he opened the Faculty of Management building in April, 1999. In this final chapter of the book, we will look in detail at these developments. First, we will show how RGU's overall IT strategy evolved from 1997 onwards, and how this eventually led to the appointment of a Director of Information Technology and to the complete reorganisation of the University's IT systems and services. Then we will look at three of the most important manifestations of the University's increasingly-IT-based approach to its operations - the development of its exciting new 'Virtual Campus', the development of its internal 'Intranet' system, and the progressive move towards an 'electronic business environment'. Finally, we will try to predict where all these various developments are likely to lead the University as it moves further and further into the third millennium.

Before he demitted office in1997, Dr. David Kennedy had brought RGU's four main Educational Service Departments - the Library, Computer Services Unit, Educational Development Unit and Graphics and Printing Department - together under one organisational 'umbrella' - the Directorate of Information. The four Departments had always worked closely together, and, for several years, had co-ordinated their activities through an informal Educational Services Forum, chaired by the Heads of the Departments involved on a rotating basis. Mrs. Elaine Dunphy, Chief Librarian, was now appointed Acting Director of Information, and was given the task of bringing about further integration of the services provided by the four Departments. She was also charged with solving some of the problems that had arisen in connection with the University's graphics and printing services and IT systems, since these were having an adverse effect on RGU's mainstream operations.

During the next two years, considerable progress was made in most of the areas that came under the auspices of the new Directorate of Information. The University's learning support services, for example, became much better integrated than had been the case in the past, and a major review of its graphics and printing services led to a number of significant improvements being made. Progress was also made in improving the University's IT systems, on which an increasingly large proportion of its non-staff-related budget was now being spent. By 1999, however, it had become clear that information technology was becoming so important for RGU's future development that it needed to be put under the overall control of a high-level IT specialist, with a place on the Strategic Management Team. It was therefore decided to appoint the University's first Director of Information Technology, a post to which Mr Andrew McCreath (see Figure 16.1) was subsequently appointed. He came to RGU from the industrial sector, and had all the knowledge, skills and experience needed to ensure that the University developed the 'state-of-the-art' IT systems that it would need in order to move fully into the new electronic age. Since the new Directorate of Information Technology had effectively taken over a major part of the portfolio of the Directorate of Information, the latter was disbanded, with Mrs. Dunphy returning to her post as Chief Librarian. In this capacity, she would continue to play a key role in the development of the University's learning support infrastructure.

**Figure 16.1 : Mr Andrew McCreath, RGU's first
Director of Information Technology**

In its overall Strategic Plan, RGU had identified six key areas in which information technology would play a vital role in future years:

1. **Multimedia technologies**, which would increasingly be used as the primary delivery vehicle for teaching and learning activities, progressively taking over from more traditional methods.

2. **Virtual learning spaces**, which would combine the use of multimedia technologies with modern communication and networking technologies to provide a 'Virtual Campus' and an internal 'Intranet', as parts of a widely-accessible and flexible learning environment.

3. **Global reach**, which would use the Virtual Campus and its associated infrastructure and support mechanisms to allow academics to teach a truly global audience, and afford this audience access to the University's teaching and learning resources.

4. **Entry**, where the University would build a 'Virtual Shop Window' to provide comprehensive online information on its prospectus, environment and facilities, and

would enable students to enrol and matriculate electronically.

5. **Communication**, where the latest technologies would be used to ensure that all relevant information passed effectively and efficiently to the right people at the right time.

6. **Administration**, where the latest technologies would be used to enhance the efficiency of all the University's operations, both in the provision of administrative and support services and in the preparation and maintenance of teaching/learning materials.

In order to enable all this to happen, RGU's new Director of Information Technology developed a revised IT strategy that addressed the following issues:

- **IT delivery**, which was recognised as being increasingly critical to the University's core business, with system failure and inadequacies having a progressively greater impact; the aim would therefore be to provide high-quality IT services that were robust, flexible, and focussed on RGU's core requirements.

- **Staff development**, which would become more and more important in order to enhance the IT awareness and skills of users, and help develop a modern and progressive 'IT culture'.

- **Infrastructure**, where the various initiatives envisaged were putting increasing pressure on the current underlying structure (particularly the network) in terms of its reliability, resilience, capacity, reach and consistency; the aim would be to identify the critical characteristics required of the IT infrastructure, and ensure that these were in place.

- **Access**, which was becoming an increasingly important factor as teaching/learning strategies become progressively more IT-centred; this would be addressed by enhancing on-campus access facilities and opening up remote and mobile access systems, taking full account of the special needs of disabled students.

- **A common approach**, whereby agreed standards and a unified approach to IT across the University would be used to achieve consistency of methodology and access, and remove technological barriers to progress.

A comprehensive action plan was also put in place in order to achieve these various aims. Initially, this involved the following:

- Restructuring of the existing Information Technology and Network Services (ITNS) and Business Information Systems (BIS) Departments to form a single Department with a strong service delivery culture; this would work closely with other IT groups around the University.

- Improvements to the underlying infrastructure, to provide a credible foundation for achieving cultural change throughout the University; principally, this would involve the deployment of a more up-to-date e-mail system, the provision of remote-access facilities, and performance improvements on critical parts of the network.

- Collaboration with the Faculties and with all non-academic Departments to implement a programme designed to achieve deep and wide-ranging cultural change in the approach to, and use of, information technology throughout the University.

• Collaboration with the new Centre for Open and Distance Learning (see next section) to achieve successful rollout of the planned 'Virtual Campus' and Faculty of Management 'Intranet', and to put in place good on-going support for these.

• Consolidation of the recent implementation of the University's Management Information Systems to ensure that they were delivering their planned benefits, and, in particular, to ensure that they were being used effectively, and not simply alongside manual and other traditional sources of the same information.

All the various elements of this action plan were subsequently implemented, with the establishment of the new integrated IT Services Department being completed by the Summer of 2000. This was relocated in refurbished office space at St. Andrew Street. A new computer room was also commissioned at St. Andrew Street, thus enabling all the University's critical centrally-managed servers to be housed in a purpose-built, secure environment. Over 2500 PC's were now linked to the University's various networks, with over half being directly available to students through its various IT labs. The various changes have already made a very significant contribution to the University's strategic development. Let us now look at some of the main IT-related projects that have benefited as a result.

THE DEVELOPMENT OF RGU's 'VIRTUAL CAMPUS'

When he came to RGU in 1997, Professor Stevely was aware of the pioneering work that it had carried out in the development of distance-learning courses since the early 1990's. He now wanted to add a new dimension to this work by setting up a 'Virtual Campus' that would enable the University to deliver such courses to students in any part of the world, via the Internet. Paisley University, where he had previously been the Vice Principal, had been operating such a system for several years, and had built up a considerable amount of highly-profitable overseas business as a result. Professor Stevely wanted RGU to do the same. He therefore asked the University's Educational Development Trust to make funds available to establish a Centre for Open and Distance Learning (CODL). This would have the following mission:

'To develop a learning community, where attention to flexibility, quality and support will make RGU the University of choice for life-long learning (in key areas) irrespective of where an individual lives and works'

The new Centre came into being in September 1998, with the appointment of its first Director, Dr. Ian Heywood. Its primary objective was to set up a Virtual Campus that would enable fully-interactive distance learning to be delivered via the Internet, regardless of the geographical location of the students involved. This would allow the University to convert existing courses to electronic format, develop completely new e-learning courses, and provide a wide range of continuing professional development (CPD) opportunities to business people, professionals and other working people of all types. These would be able to study at their place of work, at home, while travelling on business, or wherever there was convenient access to the Internet. It was recognised that there was an increasing need for online courses of this type.

During the following months, Ian Heywood and Assistant Principal Bill McIntosh made an extensive tour of leading IT centres in the USA in search of the best platform on which to build RGU's new Virtual Campus. Their trip took them to Harvard, to Massachusetts Institute of Technology, to Microsoft's headquarters in Seattle (where they were very well received despite it being virtually a 'cold call'), to various organisations in and around San Francisco, and, finally, to the Environmental Systems Research Institute (ESRI) in San Bernardino, with whom they eventually entered into a collaborative agreement. ESRI had been delivering a wide range of training courses through their own highly-sophisticated Virtual Campus for some time, and were willing to allow the University to adapt their system for its own use. This enabled RGU to get its Virtual Campus up and running very much more quickly - and at a much lower cost - than would have been the case if it had had to 'start from scratch'. One year later, CODL had a full complement of staff in place, and was ready to begin operations. Its Virtual Campus was launched in October 1999, at the World Open Learning Conference and Exhibition in Birmingham.

RGU's new Virtual Campus was designed to be used as a vehicle for the following activities:

> • enabling students in all parts of the world to access course materials;
> • facilitating communication between the University, tutors and students, allowing in-depth student support, the provision of feedback, and the support of group-based work and tutorials;
> • enabling students to access course 'classrooms', discussions and assessments;
> • enabling students to publish their own Web pages;
> • allowing students to organise links to relevant Web sites in their own 'student offices'.

Specific facilities available within the Campus included the following:

> • A comprehensive e-mail system that enabled students, staff and other participants to communicate with one another both on a private one-to-one basis and on a wider basis, either asynchronously or synchronously.
> • A wide range of discussion lists, bulletin boards, forums and chat areas, covering the specific courses, course units and aspects thereof and other areas or topics likely to be of interest to individual students or student groups.
> • The facility for participants to form ad-hoc community groups, which could take the form of study groups to support a particular course or course unit, planning groups for projects, or simply social groups comprising people with a common interest.
> • The facility for each participant to set up a personal Campus site ('My office'),

which could be used to provide information about themselves, the courses they were undertaking, the people they were currently connected to via the Campus network, and so on.

• The facility for each participant to set their own 'ground rules' for participation in campus activities, by deciding (for example) what information about them other participants could have access to, whether other participants could e-mail them directly, whether they wished to receive the bi-monthly Campus Newsletter, and so on.

• Personal student account facilities that enabled students to enrol on courses or course units, obtain passwords to restricted sites, pay course fees, and so on.

The underlying aim was to foster an ethos of group belonging, help establish relationships among the participants, facilitate exchange of ideas, opinions and personal experiences, and hence develop a shared experience from which everyone could benefit. It was realised that the computer-conferencing and other facilities made available through the Virtual Campus could not *by themselves* create such a learning community; rather, they made the formation of such a community possible - by facilitating interaction in situations where geography, working life or social commitments made conventional, face-to-face interaction difficult or impossible.

New users can access the Virtual Campus at http://campus.rgu.com, and, as can be seen from Figure 16.2, can immediately open a free account that gives them access to the course catalogue, 'taster' modules, and a wide range of other facilities. This includes information about the staff who run the Campus - see Figure 16.3 for the page on the current CODL Director, Judith Smith, which is similar to the Web pages that participants can open up on themselves.

The initial suite of courses to be put up on the Virtual Campus included the e-Business' Programme described in Figure 16.4, as well as courses in 'Oil and Gas Engineering', 'Publishing Studies' and 'Nursing Studies'. As can be seen from Figure 16.2, many more programmes have since been added, with a total of 15 currently being listed. By the time of writing (April, 2002), over 5000 students had registered on the Campus, drawn both from within RGU and from over 100 countries in all parts of the world. Feedback from participants has been excellent, with the following comment from one of the students on the 'e-business' programme being typical:

'I felt I knew a lot about e-business but quickly appreciated how little I really knew. I have already found elements of the course beneficial in my day-to-day employment. I feel the course gives me a comprehensive picture of e-business. The innovative use of on-line discussion groups helps keep me focussed on the course and where I am in relation to my peers'.

Figure 16.2 : The Web home page for RGU's Virtual Campus (April 2002)

∞ virtual
campus
at The
Robert Gordon
University

A little info about me...

Judith Smith

Centre for Open & Distance Learning, RGU

Location: United Kingdom

Industry: Higher Education

Time Zone: United Kingdom

Visit my homepage!

My professional interests centre around online learning and the electronic communication of information. As Director of the Centre for Open and Distance Learning I am involved in promoting access to learning using online environments to support both the educational experience and the virtual "student" experience. I have an interest in KM and the ways in which organisations gather and disseminate learning.

Where to find me on Campus

I am a member of these Community Groups:

- eLearning communities helping students learn
- Faculty of Management Online Learning Support
- Esf Projects 2000
- Knowledge Management
- e-Business Taster Course
- Virtual Campus Authors Group
- Centre for Open Distance Learning
- CTLA Committee on teaching Learning Assessment

Or you could find me surfing these sites

I visit these sites frequently:

- The Robert Gordon University
- The Centre for Open and Distance Learning
- Business, Technology & Knowledge Management Forum
- Centre for Knowledge Management, RGU
- Digital Commerce Centre
- KM Case Studies

Figure 16.3 : The Web page on the CODL Director, Judith Smith (April 2002)

Welcome to the
e-Business Programme

THE
ROBERT GORDON
UNIVERSITY
ABERDEEN

At the beginning of June 2002, the Aberdeen Business School is running the next exciting new programme in e-Business.

You can study full courses leading to Certificate, Diploma and MSc qualifications or you can study individual modules on a CPD (Continuing Professional Development) basis.

Basic course details are given below. In addition, much more information can be obtained by clicking on the following links.

- *A comprehensive set of Frequently Asked Questions*
- *Testimonials from students around the world*
- *Descriptors for each of the Modules*
- *The main Application Form*
- *A Module Information Sheet to assist in completing the Application Form*

You can apply by printing off and completing the Application Form and the returning it to us as directed.

Figure 16.4 : The start of the Web entry on the 'e-Business' Programme that is available through RGU's Virtual Campus (April 2002)

As a result of the establishment and development of its Virtual Campus, RGU has become one of the leaders in the field, and is well on the way to becoming a major global provider of higher education. To quote Professor Bill McIntosh, who has overall responsibility for the programme: 'This is not a marginal activity - this is mainstream'.

THE DEVELOPMENT OF RGU's IN-HOUSE 'INTRANET' ('iNET')

As we saw in the previous chapter, RGU's Faculty of Management moved into a new 'super-building' on the University's Garthdee Campus in the summer of 1998. This incorporated all the latest digital equipment for the delivery and support of courses, since it had been agreed that the Faculty would pioneer a move towards much greater use of electronic delivery throughout RGU; Figure 16.5 shows one of the many IT laboratories in the new building. In order to facilitate such a change, it was decided to set up a highly-sophisticated Faculty Intranet, which would provide staff and students with a far wider range of tools and services than the University's existing network. This would subsequently serve as a model for RGU's other Faculties, whose staff would also be able to benefit from the experience of Management staff in running such a network.

An 'intranet' is a computer network that uses the technologies that have been developed for the Internet and World Wide Web to provide people working within an organisation with a wide range of shared communication and information technology (C&IT) facilities. In terms of its overall design and operational software, the new Faculty of Management Intranet was based on the same systems that had been used to set up the University's Virtual Campus. It differed from the Virtual Campus in terms of the main use to which it was to be put, however. The latter had been primarily designed to enable *new students* in all parts of the world to access the University's courses, and was thus effectively a vehicle for the delivery and support of distance learning. The former was primarily intended to provide the Faculty's own *existing students* with online access to course modules and support materials, which had previously only been available via more conventional routes such as live lectures and paper-based handouts. It was thus designed to serve an *internal* rather than an *external* client base.

The Faculty of Management Intranet was developed by a Faculty Working Group under the Direction of the Dean, Professor Bill McIntosh (the driving force behind its introduction), the Development Manager being Mr Les Tarr. It incorporated the following three basic elements in its overall structure:

- A *learning support mechanism*, designed to support conventional teaching and facilitate more effective learning by providing students with a much wider range of electronic facilities than had been available hitherto.
- A *corporate communication system* for students and staff, operating at corporate level (eg announcements; event calendar), at group level (eg threaded discussions on specific topics), and at one-to-one level (eg e-mail links between staff and students).
- A *working simulation* of the latest techniques and practices that operated in the corporate world, thus enabling students of the Faculty to prepare for entry to that world by obtaining first-hand experience of how it worked.

Figure 16.5 : One of the IT Laboratories in the new Faculty of Management building at Garthdee

Specific facilities that were made available via the Intranet included the following:

- Online access to particular teaching units, sections of course modules, and entire modules as and when it was appropriate for students to gain such access.
- 'Virtual office' facilities similar to those made available via the Virtual Campus, with different people being given access to different facilities as and when appropriate.
- Online access to Library facilities and services, and, in particular, to digitised materials.
- A campus-wide online information source and communications forum, available to all staff and students.
- Facilities for individuals or groups to communicate with one another on particular issues.

We have seen that the overall purpose of RGU's Faculty of Management Intranet was to provide a vehicle for the electronic support of courses run by the Faculty for its own internal students - not for the support of distance-learning students, as was the case with the University's Virtual Campus. As with the latter, however, it did provide support for students within a 'virtual environment', and also provided a wide range of support facilities for the staff responsible for delivering the Faculty's courses. Such staff were not, however, being asked to load up free-standing distance-learning materials, as was the case with the Virtual Campus, but to use the technologies and tools available via the Web to support their existing teaching methods. This was a key difference between the philosophies that underlay the use of the two networks.

Since first becoming available at the start of Session 2000-01, the Faculty of Management Intranet has proved extremely successful, and has achieved widespread use by both students and staff, despite some initial scepticism that such a revolutionary change in the approach to teaching/learning could be made to work. It also won the prestigious 2001 UCISA Web Award for Managed Learning Environments. The system has now been re-named as 'iNET', and is in the process of being rolled out to the entire University. This rollout began at the start of session 2001-02, when iNET's facilities were made available to students and staff of the Faculty of Design and Technology. It will be completed at the start of session 2002-03, when they will also be made available to the Faculty of Health and Social Care, once the Faculty's new building at Garthdee becomes operational. When this happens, all RGU's students and staff will have access to one of the finest electronic learning-support systems in the country - and, indeed, in the world. The system can be accessed at http://inet.rgu.com. At the time of writing (April, 2002), it has almost 9,000 regular users.

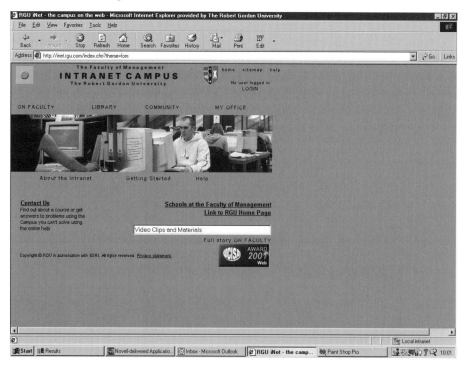

Figure 16.6 : Part of the Web home page for the Faculty of Management Intranet Campus (April 2002)

THE MOVE TOWARDS AN ELECTRONIC BUSINESS ENVIRONMENT

Since the latter part of the 1990's, RGU has been converting more and more of its internal systems into electronic format. This process was accelerated by the appointment of Andrew McCreath as Director of Information Technology in 1999, and by the arrival of the University's new Secretary, Dr. Adrian Graves, the following summer. (The previous Secretary, Mr. David Caldwell, had left RGU at the end of 1999, to take up the post of Director of the Committee of Scottish Higher Education Principals in Edinburgh). Dr. Graves had recently been working in Australia, where he had been heavily involved in the management of change and the technology enablement of business processes at The University of Adelaide; he had come to RGU to help it go down the same road.

Since the arrival of its new Secretary, RGU has embarked on a highly-ambitious Business Process Re-engineering (BPR) initiative, which will eventually involve most of the University, and will bring about 'significant and measurable changes' in the way it works. This will cover all areas of the University's operations, including:
- Student enquiries, applications, admission and matriculation;
- Academic processes, including course development, costing, accreditation, delivery and assessment;
- Student record-keeping, graduation, and relationships with alumni;
- Estates management, timetabling and resource management;
- Human resource management, including staff recruitment and induction;
- All aspects of financial management, including e-procurement.

Specific projects that have been (or are in the process of being) implemented under this BPR initiative include the following:
- Continuing to re-develop the University's Web site, with a view to producing an exciting, visually-attractive 'shop window' where the entries are in a standard format and provide potential students with all the information they could possibly need - and help to convince them that RGU should be their University of 'first-choice'; subsequent on-going updating and maintenance of the Web site.
- Developing robust, effective and efficient systems for the e-enabling of student enquiries, applications, admission, record-keeping, assessment, graduation and alumni relations; these projects are being heavily focussed on improving operational efficiency and customer service through such things as streamlining, automation, and eliminating the need for shadow and paper-based systems.
- Improving the effectiveness of the 'CAMS' system, which forms an integral part of the University's Student Records system (SITS), so that it fully supports the assessment process, both in academic and in non-academic areas.
- Implementing effective and efficient business-intelligence and reporting tools as a strategic means of delivering information where it is needed, and extending the various tools involved to cover the University's key business applications.
- In connection with the above, designing and developing a comprehensive 'Data

Warehouse', which will act as a repository for key management information that can be reported against, linked into Web sites, etc. without the need to create multiple duplicate systems.

• Evaluation of the full capabilities of the University's new e-mail system, and extension of its messaging and workflow-management capabilities to support BPR initiatives, group working, and remote working.

• Evaluation of the possible implementation of a comprehensive Document Management System for the University.

• Implementation of the new state-of-the-art Library Management System currently being introduced.

The first phase of the BPR project was successfully completed by the end of October, 2001. This concentrated on the modernisation of the student matriculation process, and had the following specific objectives:

1. To introduce PC-based matriculation for all centrally-funded students by September 2001.
2. To issue SMART cards at matriculation.
3. To provide a data download from SITS and SMART card systems to automate creation of new Intranet accounts for students.
4. To capture 80% of student enquiry data in SITS at the point of origin, ie in the Information Centre, Admissions and International offices.
5. To produce 'snapshot' class lists within 24 hours of matriculation.
6. To complete matriculation before courses began.
7. To launch a SITS benchmarking programme to support continuous improvement of processes.
8. To ensure organisational change issues were managed and staff capability was developed to support enhancements effectively.

Of these, all but objectives 5 and 6 were fully achieved, with the remainder being '90%' complete' by October 31st; they were both fully achieved later. The success of the new matriculation process was confirmed by an exit questionnaire that was completed by 3125 (44%) of the students who matriculated during the peak September period. This produced the following results:

• 87.1% of continuing students rated the new process 'far better' than before.
• 79.6% said the process was 'very easy' to understand.
• 79.6% said staff at matriculation were 'very helpful'.
• 73.4% completed the process within 15 minutes.

In terms of operational efficiency, the new process reduced the time taken to produce reports on enrolled student numbers (a key performance indicator for the University) by a full two months. A number of areas where further improvements might be made were also identified, and these are to be implemented during the next matriculation round.

At the time of writing (April 2002), Phase 2 of the BPR initiative is well in hand.

THE UNIVERSITY OF THE FUTURE?

What, then, are the implications of all these various IT-related developments for the future of The Robert Gordon University? Here, the author will have to discard the 'historian's' hat that he has worn for the last nine months and revert to being an educational technologist. From this perspective, he predicts with some confidence that the students who enrol at RGU (or at a combined RGU and Aberdeen University) in a few years time will experience something along the following lines.

They will, first of all, decide to study at this particular University largely as a result of what they have learned about Aberdeen, the University and its courses via the Internet. By then, its Web site will have developed into a highly-sophisticated 'shop window' of the type envisaged in the previous section, incorporating audio and video material as part of a state-of-the-art multimedia package. If they require any further information, or want to 'get a feel' for any courses in which they are interested, they will be able to do so by getting directly in touch with a suitable 'contact person' on the course team, or by linking up with one of the student 'chat lines' or conferences.

If they decide to enrol on a course, they will almost certainly be able to do so electronically - either via an updated version of the present national admissions system, or by getting in direct touch with the University. Many aspects of the admission and induction process will also be handled electronically, although it will still be important for students to come in contact with 'real people'. By the time these processes have been completed, they will have been made thoroughly familiar with the University's electronic support infrastructure, and will have been provided with all the authorisations and tools that they need in order to access and make effective use of this - and of all the University's more traditional facilities.

The way in which they work through their course programme will depend on whether they are enrolled on a conventional 'taught' course or are studying on a distance-learning basis. In both cases, however, most of the so-called 'lower-cognitive' elements of the course (the underpinning facts and principles of the subject or area being covered) will be delivered electronically, via self-study or learning-support packages available on the World Wide Web and on the University Intranet. Students will still be able to access these via workstations provided within the University premises, although more and more of them will probably elect to do so remotely, via an Internet-linked laptop (or whatever has replaced this by then), via the next generation of mobile phones, or via their home 'edutainment' consoles. Students will also complete most course-related exercises and assignments electronically, submitting their work via the Internet or University Intranet, and receiving feedback from their tutors by the same route. Their tutors will be able to check their work for plagiarism and other forms of cheating using standard software packages.

Students who elect to come to the University to study will still attend lectures (although these will be far fewer than at present), will still participate in tutorials, seminars and other group-learning sessions, and will still undertake practical work in laboratories and studios, where this is part of the curriculum. In the case of distance-learning students, suitable arrangements will be made to provide them with equivalent learning experiences. In some cases, it will be possible to do this electronically, using appropriate teleconferencing or other communication facilities. In other cases, it will be necessary for them to attend practical classes organised on a 'block attendance' basis, either within the University or at a suitable 'outlier' venue. Both 'traditional' and distance-learning students will, of course, continue to undertake appropriate clinical or other work placement, where this is an important element of their courses.

Electronic systems will also play an increasingly important role in student assessment as time goes on. Both traditional and distance-learning students will be able to keep a check on their progress by undergoing regular computer-administered tests, with their tutors being able to monitor their performance and identify any need for remedial help. As we have seen, most assessed course assignments will be submitted electronically, and will be evaluated online by the course tutors. Some parts of formal examinations will almost certainly also be carried out using computers, and, increasingly, will also be marked by computers, since computer-based-assessment systems are becoming more and more versatile and sophisticated with every year that passes. Work involving high-level cognitive activities such as analysis, synthesis, problem-solving and evaluation will probably always have to be assessed by human beings, however, although some artificial-intelligence enthusiasts may well think otherwise. The same is almost certainly true of practical, clinical and creative work, and of assessed work placement.

Once students complete their courses, their records will be stored electronically, making it very much easier to access them in future years. Records will also be kept of what happens to students *after* they leave the University, with regular communication taking place with all alumni via the Internet. Indeed, many students will probably continue with their studies right through their working lives, making use of e-enabled CPD modules and units to keep themselves up-to-date in their respective fields, prepare for career changes, and so on. Alumni will also use the University's electronic communication systems as a vehicle for keeping in touch with their classmates, allowing 'reunions' to take place on an ongoing basis rather than once every 20 or 30 years.

But what of the *long-term* future of universities such as RGU? Here, the author is reluctant to make any firm predictions, since whatever he says is almost certain to be proved wrong. It may well be that universities as we know them today will eventually largely disappear, as some commentators are currently predicting, being replaced by commercial 'education vendors' that use the Internet to market academic courses and training programmes on a country-wide or world-wide basis. Or it may be that universities become much more specialised than is the case at the moment, with each catering for its own niche market, and only those that can sustain such a market surviving. Almost certainly, they will be very different places from those we see today, but just *how* different is anybody's guess. If he is still around at the time, the author will be very interested in finding out!

Postscript

As we saw at the end of Chapter 14, Aberdeen's two Universities began serious discussions regarding possible future collaboration in the autumn of 2001, with all options up to 'full merger' being explored. The possibility of such a merger had in fact been raised by the University of Aberdeen in the mid-1980's, long before RGU attained full university status. The idea had, however, been abandoned as a result of the report produced by the Scottish Tertiary Education Advisory Council, which recommended that Central Institutions such as RGIT should remain independent of the Universities (see Chapter 7). As we saw in Chapter 13, the merger scenario was revisited in 1991, following the announcement of the imminent abolition of the binary line between the universities and the public-sector higher education institutions and the disbandment of the CNAA, through which all RGIT's degrees were awarded at the time. The idea was rejected by the Governors, however, who decided that RGIT's future would be best assured by applying to become a full University with its own degree-awarding powers.

Following the attainment of university status in 1992, RGU went from strength to strength, more than doubling in size during the following ten years, and establishing itself as one of the very best of the 'new' universities. Indeed, by the end of the 1990's, it had almost caught up with the University of Aberdeen in terms of total student numbers and student FTE, although the latter was still very much larger in terms of total staff numbers and overall budget, mainly because of its much-more-extensive research activities. Both Universities were also extremely strong financially, with healthy surplusses on their trading accounts and large accumulated reserves. Nevertheless, the two Universities felt that the time was now right to look again at the idea of closer collaboration and even possible merger, since they both realised that this could well be the best strategy to safeguard their respective futures as they moved further into the uncharted waters of the new millennium.

Firstly, the two Universities recognised that their currently-strong financial positions would be difficult to sustain in the long term, since overall Government funding for higher education was unlikely to increase significantly in the foreseeable future, whereas delivery costs were certain to continue to rise steadily. Secondly, traditional Universities were likely to be faced with increased competition from alternative providers of higher education and continuing professional development opportunities. Thirdly, the numbers of school children in Aberdeen and the North East of Scotland (major catchment areas for both Universities) were falling alarmingly, with a drop of up to 25% being forecast over the next 12 years. Fourthly, the overall economic prospects for the region were also deteriorating, mainly due to the steady downsizing of the once-burgeoning North Sea oil industry. Fifthly, there was increasing pressure from the Scottish Higher Education Funding Council and the Scottish Executive for increased specialisation and concentration on key strengths, and for increased collaboration, on the part of all Scotland's Universities.

It was for these reasons that The Robert Gordon University and the University of Aberdeen set up a joint working group in October 2001 (see Chapter 14). This had the following brief:

- To explore the range of existing collaborations between the two institutions;
- To examine and identify ways in which collaboration between the two institutions could be enhanced;
- To explore models of collaboration in both academic and support areas;
- To identify any obstacles in pursuing each or any of the collaborative models further.

A preliminary report on these issues was submitted to the two University Principals in December 2001. This suggested 'that greater collaboration between the two institutions would, by adding scale, produce a greater critical mass, in turn allowing better and enhanced strategic positioning'. It would also 'provide stronger protection in adverse circumstances and a greater ability to serve better Aberdeen, the North East of Scotland and the UK'. It was agreed that a more detailed feasibility study should be carried out during the following six months, with five possible options, up to and including full merger, being examined. These are outlined below.

Option 1: General Collaboration. This would involve a continuation or enhancement of the co-operation that had taken place hitherto, with all such arrangements taking place on a purely voluntary basis, and being relatively unstructured and informal. No new entity would be created under this model, which effectively represented the 'status quo'.

Option 2: Strategic Alliance. This would involve the two institutions agreeing to joint working, with a structured approach, in certain specified areas of activity, allowing the two institutions to continue to compete in areas not explicitly covered by the agreement. The two Universities would remain as fully-independent institutions.

Option 3: Federal Structure. This would involve the creation of a single overarching governing body, but retention of subsidiary boards with reserved powers. Each institution would retain its individual identity and much of its autonomy, but competition would be controlled, and a degree of administrative integration would be achieved.

Option 4: Traditional Merger. This would involve integration of all academic and administrative functions under one or other of the governing bodies and management structures. There would be no creation of a new legal entity, with one of the institutions effectively being dissolved, and its activities, staff, assets and liabilities being fully transferred to the other.

Option 5: New Model Merger. This would involve full academic and administrative integration through a new constitution, together with new structures of governance and management. The new entity thus created would enable new cognate groups to be created, but would also enable strong existing units to continue to operate, and to retain their current cultures.

Each of these options was appraised against (a) the merger criteria that had been established by the Scottish Higher Education Funding Council, and (b) the need to safeguard the interests of the two institutions involved, including the preservation of their distinctive cultures and missions. The basic factors that were taken into account included: enrichment of educational provision; complementarity of academic programmes; preservation and strengthening of research traditions; enhancement of quality; improvement of access for students; improvement of financial health; more effective employment of resources; adaptation to change in higher education. In addition, the two Universities carried out a preliminary 'due diligence' exercise, with external consultants being engaged to examine their financial status, legal and constitutional matters, and issues related to human resources, information technology and communications provision, and estates - and to report on the implications for each of the five options being considered.

The resulting report was presented to the two Universities in June 2002, and was unequivocal in its conclusions and recommendations. It rejected the 'General Collaboration' and 'Strategic Alliance' options on the grounds that they did not offer significant added value to the current activities of the Universities, and did not provide the organisational framework for innovative strategic development. It also rejected the 'Federal Structure' option, on the grounds that it was too complex, would be too costly to establish, and was likely to prove operationally difficult. It recognised that full merger between the two institutions could bring about many benefits, including consolidation of resources to create greater critical mass, reduction of duplication and waste, and provision of opportunities for strategic rationalisation and development under a single governance and management structure. It nevertheless rejected the 'Traditional Merger' option on the grounds that the 'valuable characteristics of heritage, culture and *modus operandi*' in the subordinated institution might well be lost, along with 'long-standing relationships and stakeholder loyalty' - risks that would not be acceptable to either institution in view of their high standing in the Aberdeen area and in Scottish Higher Education. The report therefore concluded that the 'New Model Merger' option was by far the most promising, since this would have all the advantages of a full merger without the risks associated with a traditional merger in which one of the institutions effectively took over the other.

The report was discussed by the Governors of The Robert Gordon University on 19th June, 2002 and by the Court of the University of Aberdeen on 25th June, 2002. Both bodies agreed to implement its main proposal, namely:

> 'That the two Universities explore in detail the option of a merger to establish a new - model institution, engage in a thorough risk-management study of the option, and consult widely with staff, students and other stakeholders.'

This further feasibility study will involve wide discussion and consultation, both within and between the two Universities, and with many stakeholders and external bodies, including the Scottish Higher Education Funding Council. If a firm proposal is agreed, it is hoped that a final report, incorporating a detailed implementation plan, will be available for consideration within the two Universities by June 2003. If this is approved by both institutions, the formal approval of the Funding Council and the Scottish Executive would be required before the necessary legislation could be enacted and the merger could proceed. The earliest date by which this could happen would be the start of the 2004-2005 academic session.

In a letter sent to all RGU staff at the end of June 2002, Professor Stevely made it clear that the proposed merger between The Robert Gordon University and the University of Aberdeen would only take place if both institutions were happy with the final detailed plan, and if this was also approved by the Funding Body and Scottish Executive. He did, however, offer his own personal view on the matter, stating that he believed that the proposal offered 'an exciting opportunity for a new institution to be established that would be better than either of the two current Universities'. He further believed that, as a result of such a merger, 'Higher Education in the North East would be enhanced, the Grampian community would benefit, and the contribution we make to Scotland's social, cultural and economic health would be strengthened'.

As the 'official historian' of The Robert Gordon University, what does the author make of what is being proposed? Having studied the June 2002 report in detail, he finds it difficult to find fault with any of the arguments presented or with the conclusions reached. He will, however, be sorry to see the name that was so fiercely fought for in 1991 disappear, since it is being proposed that the new, combined University will still be called the 'University of Aberdeen' - a logical choice given the 500-year history of that institution. He is glad to see that the revered names of Robert Gordon, John Gray and Tom Scott Sutherland will not be completely lost, however, since it is intended that these will be incorporated in the names of major academic units of the new University. All three of RGU's 'founders' can therefore rest safely in their graves!

Appendix A : Key dates in the history of the University

1668 :   Birth of Robert Gordon, founder of Robert Gordon's Hospital, in Aberdeen.

1729 :   Foundation of Robert Gordon's Hospital by Robert Gordon through Deed of Mortification.

1731 :   Death of Robert Gordon; start of work on Hospital building.

1732 :   Completion of Hospital building (the 'Auld Hoose') at Schoolhill.

1746 :   Conversion of Hospital into 'Fort Cumberland' and occupation by Hanoverian troops during march north to Culloden.

1750 :   Opening of Robert Gordon's Hospital; appointment of first 'Master' (Headmaster) - Rev. George Abercrombie; initial intake of 14 boys.

1754 :   First 'dismissal' of 8 boys from Hospital into apprenticeships.

1772 :   Granting of Royal Charter incorporating Governors as 'The President and Governors of Robert Gordon's Hospital in Aberdeen'.

1821 :   Bequest by Mr. Alexander Simpson of Collyhill, resulting in formation of Collyhill Trust, providing funding for expansion of Hospital.

1824 :   Formation of Aberdeen Mechanics' Institution; start of adult education programme.

1833 :   Completion of extension of Hospital building as a result of Collyhill Bequest; addition of two major wings to 'Auld Hoose'.

1840 :   Opening of Mary Emslie's Female Orphan Asylum at Albyn Place.

1848 :   Opening of new Mechanics' Institution building in Market Street.

1855 :   Opening of School of Science and Art in Aberdeen, under aegis of Mechanics' Institution; expansion of adult education programme.

1857 :   Opening of Technical School in Aberdeen, under aegis of Mechanics' Institution; start of Navigation classes.

1858 :   Transfer of School of Navigation to control of local Marine Board.

1867 :   Second Reform Act, extending franchise to working classes.

1870 :   Education Act, establishing Elementary Schools throughout Britain.

1872 :   Education (Scotland) Act, establishing local School Boards.

1878 :   Endowed Institutions (Scotland) Act, enabling institutions such as Robert Gordon's Hospital to be radically reformed.

1881 :   Transformation of 'Robert Gordon's Hospital' into 'Robert Gordon's College'; division into day secondary school and adult education college under Headmaster Dr. Alexander Ogilvie; reconstitution of Governors.

1882 :   Inauguration of evening class programme in Robert Gordon's College.

1883 :   Offer by John Gray to build new School of Science and Art in Aberdeen and to make gift of same to Robert Gordon's College.

1884 :   Transfer of entire adult education programme of Mechanics' Institution (with exception of Art classes) to Robert Gordon's College.

1885 : Opening of Gray's School of Art; transfer of Art classes from Aberdeen Mechanics' Institution to new School.

1886 : Extension of Gray's School of Art; completion of entrance archway to College campus.

1891 : Opening of Aberdeen's School of Domestic Economy at King Street.

1898 : Establishment of School of Pharmacy in Robert Gordon's College.

1901 : Recognition of Gray's School of Art as one of four Scottish Central Art Colleges.

1903 : Recognition of Robert Gordon's College as a Scottish 'Central Institution for specialised instruction'.

1907 : Launch of appeal to establish a Technical College in Aberdeen.

1910 : Formation of 'Robert Gordon's Technical College'; reconstitution of Governing Body as Governors of Robert Gordon's Colleges; establishment of School of Engineering and Chemistry; establishment of Department of Architecture within School of Arts and Crafts (Gray's School of Art); incorporation of School of Domestic Economy at King Street, to become School of Domestic Science; appointment of Charles Stewart as first Principal of RGTC.

1911 : Serious fire in Robert Gordon's College; erection of temporary huts at Schoolhill.

1912 : Completion of major extension of School of Domestic Science at King Street.

1914 : Start of First World War; cancellation of all further building programmes; introduction of war-related work; transfer of School of Navigation from Marine Board to RGTC; Architecture course gains exemption from Intermediate Examination of RIBA.

1919 : Extension of temporary huts at Schoolhill to accommodate new engineering classes.

1920 : Establishment of National Certificate and Diploma systems in UK.

1921 : Resignation of Charles Stewart as Principal; start of '23 leaderless years' for Robert Gordon's Technical College.

1922 : Architecture course gains exemption from Final Examination of RIBA.

1924 : Initiation of first National Certificate courses in Scotland; pressure on RGTC to introduce such courses stimulates Governors into starting new course development and building programmes.

1925 : Appointment of Professor W. Blackadder of Aberdeen University as first Director of Engineering at RGTC; establishment of First National Certificate course - in Mechanical Engineering; establishment of Department of Mathematics and Physics.

1926 : Establishment of Department of Electrical Engineering within School of Engineering; start of work on new main building for RGTC at Schoolhill.

1931 : Opening of MacRobert Hall and original Central Library at Schoolhill; establishment of Students' Representative Council (SRC).

1932 :	Official opening of new Technical Building at Schoolhill; recognition of Diploma in Architecture by UK Architects' Registration Council.
1934 :	Start of research on diets of anaemic women in School of Domestic Science - first recorded case of top-quality research in RGTC.
1938 :	Opening of new extended Central Library at Schoolhill.
1939 :	Start of Second World War; introduction of war-related work.
1944 :	Appointment of Dr. Alexander West as first Director of RGTC; 1944 Education Act stimulates expansion of College.
1945 :	Introduction of Business Training Scheme in College.
1951 :	Completion of new third floor of main building at Schoolhill.
1952 :	Acquisition by SRC of premises in Rubislaw Terrace.
1955 :	Gift of Garthdee estate to Governors by Tom Scott Sutherland; start of work on new School of Architecture; opening of new boathouse for School of Navigation on south bank of River Dee.
1957 :	Opening of Scott Sutherland School of Architecture at Garthdee.
1960 :	Opening of new Electrical Engineering Building incorporating new Central Library at Blackfriars Street.
1961 :	Opening of School of Navigation's new Radar Station at Bridge of Don; start of City and Guilds' course in Papermaking; Government White Paper leads to future concentration on full-time courses.
1962 :	First course in Quantity Surveying started; formation of Department of Business Management Studies
1963 :	Move of School of Domestic Science to new building at Kepplestone; Robbins Report published.
1964 :	Move of School of Navigation to King Street; retirement of Dr. West as Director; formation of CNAA.
1965 :	Appointment of Dr. Gerald Bulmer as Director; Foundation of College Council (Academic Council); change of name to 'Robert Gordon's Institute of Technology'; division of School of Mathematics and Physics into two separate Schools.
1966 :	Acquisition of first mainframe computer; move of Gray's School of Art to new building at Garthdee.
1967 :	Formation of School of Librarianship at King Street; validation of first CNAA degree (B.Sc. in Pharmacy).
1968 :	Formation of Schools of Business Management Studies and Social Studies; division of School of Engineering into separate Schools of Mechanical Engineering and Electrical Engineering; designation of all major teaching departments as 'Schools'; consolidation of service-teaching system; acquisition of St. Andrew Street building.
1969 :	Move of Schools of Chemistry, Physics, Mathematics and Social Studies and Central Library to St. Andrew Street; acquisition of Harriet Street site.
1970 :	Resignation of Dr. Bulmer as Director; replacement by Dr. Peter Clarke;

establishment of Course Committees.

1971 : Division of School of Domestic Science into separate Schools of Home Economics, Hotel and Institutional Administration and Nutritional Science.

1972 : Transfer of College of Health Visiting at Willowbank House to RGIT to become School of Health Visiting; formation of School of Speech Therapy.

1973 : Formation of separate Institute Committee of Governors; first CNAA Quinquennial Visit; formation of Educational Technology Unit; start of offshore survival training in RGIT.

1974 : Establishment of Faculty system; appointment of Executive Deans; formation of Computer Services Unit; opening of new Students' Union at Schoolhill.

1975 : Introduction of Professorial titles; separation of central administration from Robert Gordon's College.

1977 : Establishment of Offshore Survival Centre.

1978 : Transfer of School of Navigation to Aberdeen Technical College; closure of School of Speech Therapy; second CNAA Quinquennial Visit.

1979 : Revision of Faculty structure, with elected, non-executive Deans; revision of academic committee system; re-designation of post of 'Director' as 'Principal'; establishment of full-time Vice Principal post.

1980 : Move of School of Business Management Studies to Hilton.

1981 : Establishment of separate Board of Governors for RGIT; acquisition of new Coat of Arms.

1982 : Move of School of Social Studies to refurbished King Street Building (renamed Merkland Building); opening of colour CCTV studio at King Street; formation of Centre for Offshore Health

1983 : Formation of separate School of Surveying at Garthdee; incorporation of School of Health Visiting into School of Social Studies; first stage of third CNAA Quinquennial Visit.

1984 : Second stage of CNAA Quinquennial Visit.

1985 : Third stage of CNAA Quinquennial Visit; retiral of Dr. Clarke as Principal; replacement by Dr. David Kennedy.

1986 : Fire at Harriet Street delays opening of new building.

1987 : Opening of new Clarke Building at Harriet Street; formation of Viscom.

1988 : Major inspection of RGIT by Scottish Education Department; introduction of new Faculty structure, with Executive Deans; formation of new School of Public Administration and Law; formation of Schools of Applied Sciences and Food and Consumer Studies by amalgamation of existing Schools; formation of Centre for Enterprise.

1989 : Attainment of partial CNAA accreditation (for taught courses); expansion of foreign language teaching; establishment of RGIT Survival Centre Ltd.

1990 : Major revision of management structure; transfer of Schools of Occupational Therapy, Physiotherapy and Radiography from Grampian

Health Board to RGIT to form Centre for Professions Allied to Medicine (CPAM).

1991 : Change of name to 'The Robert Gordon Institute of Technology'; launch of successful campaign for full university status.

1992 : Achievement of full CNAA accreditation (for research degrees as well as taught courses); achievement of full university status, to become 'The Robert Gordon University'; establishment of Department of Nursing within CPAM; establishment of Scottish Higher Education Funding Council (SHEFC) and Higher Education Quality Council (HEQC); involvement in first Research Assessment Exercise (RAE).

1993 : Installation of first Chancellor (Sir Bob Reid); establishment of Industrial Unit as Limited Company (subsequently re-named as Univation); conversion of CPAM into School of Health Sciences; construction of Kepplestone Annexe and Gray's School of Art Annexe.

1994 : Establishment of separate School of Nursing.

1995 : First (and last) HEQC Quality Audit; start of revision of academic quality system.

1996 : Incorporation of Foresterhill College, to become Associate Faculty of Nursing, Midwifery and Community Studies along with former School of Nursing; involvement in second RAE.

1997 : Retirement of Dr. Kennedy as Principal; replacement by Prof. William Stevely; Dearing Report published.

1998 : Introduction of Common Course Architecture; move of Faculty of Management to new building at Garthdee; conversion of HEQC into Quality Assurance Agency (QAA); establishment of School of Nursing and Midwifery from former Associate Faculty: establishment of Centre for Open and Distance Learning .

1999 : Launch of Virtual Campus; formation of Institute for Learning and Teaching (ILT); 'rebranding' of School of Food and Consumer Studies as School of Hotel, Tourism and Retail Management, and transfer to Faculty of Management.

2000 : Establishment of Faculty of Management Intranet; development of electronic business environment.

2001 : First QAA Quality Audit; major revision of academic structure, with reversion to three Faculties by amalgamating Faculty of Design with Faculty of Science and Technology and changing names and compositions of several Schools; involvement in third RAE.

2002 : Discussions with Aberdeen University regarding possible areas of collaboration; decision to carry out detailed feasibility study on possible merger; move of most of Faculty of Health and Social Care to new building at Garthdee.

Appendix B : The evolution of the University's organisational structure

Prior to 1910
No real 'organisational structure' in the sense being used here.

1910 (Robert Gordon's Technical College)
Once Robert Gordon's Technical College had been established, it was divided into the following three Schools:
- *School of Engineering and Chemistry* (incorporating the School of Pharmacy)
- *School of Arts and Crafts* (incorporating a new Department of Architecture and Building)
- *School of Domestic Science*

1932 (Robert Gordon's Technical College)
By 1932, the Technical College had expanded considerably, and now consisted of the following seven Schools:
- *School of Engineering* (with Departments of Civil, Mechanical and Electrical Engineering)
- *School of Chemistry*
- *School of Mathematics and Physics*
- *School of Pharmacy*
- *Gray's School of Art* (with Departments of Drawing and Painting, Design, Sculpture, Architecture, and Building and Surveying)
- *School of Domestic Science*
- *School of Navigation*

1965 (Robert Gordon's Institute of Technology)
By the time the name was changed to Robert Gordon's Institute of Technology in 1965, further expansion had taken place, and the number of major teaching units had increased to ten, as shown below (note that all such units became known as 'Schools' in 1968):
- *School of Engineering* (with Departments of Mechanical Engineering and Electrical Engineering, and smaller units teaching Civil Engineering and Naval Architecture)
- *School of Chemistry* (incorporating Paper Technology Unit)
- *School of Physics*
- *School of Mathematics*
- *School of Pharmacy*
- *Department of Business Management Studies*
- *Gray's School of Art* (with Departments of Drawing and Painting, Design and

275

Crafts, and Sculpture)
- *Scott Sutherland School of Architecture* (incorporating a Department of Building)
- *College of Domestic Science* (subsequently to be split into three separate Schools).
- *School of Navigation*

1974 (ROBERT GORDON'S INSTITUTE OF TECHNOLOGY)

By now, the number of Schools had risen to 17, and, for the first time, these were divided into four Faculties, each with an Executive Dean, appointed on a rotating basis:

Faculty of Art and Architecture
- *Gray's School of Art*
- *Scott Sutherland School of Architecture* (incorporating a Building Economics section)

Faculty of Arts
- *School of Business Management Studies*
- *School of Hotel and Institutional Administration*
- *School of Librarianship*
- *School of Social Studies*

Faculty of Engineering
- *School of Electronic and Electrical Engineering*
- *School of Mathematics*
- *School of Mechanical Engineering* (subsequently re-named as the School of Mechanical and Offshore Engineering)
- *School of Navigation*

Faculty of Sciences
- *School of Chemistry* (incorporating Paper Technology Unit)
- *School of Health Visiting*
- *School of Home Economics*
- *School of Nutritional Science*
- *School of Pharmacy*
- *School of Physics*
- *School of Speech Therapy*

1979 (ROBERT GORDON'S INSTITUTE OF TECHNOLOGY)

As a result of recommendations made by the CNAA in the report on their 1978 Quinquennial Visit, RGIT changed to a three-Faculty system, with Deans now being elected by staff and having no executive powers; the new structure was as follows:

Faculty of Arts
- *Gray's School of Art*
- *School of Business Management Studies* (subsequently re-named as the Business School)
- *School of Hotel and Institutional Administration*
- *School of Librarianship* (subsequently re-named as the School of Librarianship

and Information Studies)
- *School of Social Studies*

Faculty of Science
- *School of Chemistry* (incorporating Paper Technology Unit)
- *School of Health Visiting* (which would eventually become part of the School of Social Studies)
- *School of Home Economics*
- *School of Nutritional Science*
- *School of Pharmacy*
- *School of Physics*

Faculty of Technology
- *Scott Sutherland School of Architecture* (incorporating a Building Economics Section, which subsequently became a separate School of Surveying)
- *School of Electronic and Electrical Engineering*
- *School of Mathematics* (subsequently re-named as the School of Mathematical Sciences and Computer Studies)
- *School of Mechanical and Offshore Engineering*

(Note that the School of Navigation had by now been transferred to Aberdeen Technical College, and that the School of Speech Therapy had been closed down.)

1988 (Robert Gordon's Institute of Technology)

As a result of a major review of academic structure carried out between 1986 and 1988, RGIT returned to a four-Faculty system, each with an Executive Dean who was a member of the Senior Management Team; the number of Schools was also reduced to 13, as shown below:

Faculty of Design
- *Scott Sutherland School of Architecture*
- *Gray's School of Art*
- *School of Surveying*

Faculty of Health and Food
- *School of Food and Consumer Studies* (formed by re-merging the Schools of Home Economics, Hotel and Institutional Administration, and Nutritional Science)
- *School of Health and Social Work* (now incorporating an expanding Nursing Section)
- *School of Pharmacy*

Faculty of Management
- *Business School* (subsequently re-named as Aberdeen Business School)
- *School of Librarianship and Information Studies* (subsequently re-named as the School of Information and Media)
- *School of Public Administration and Law* (formed from sections of the School of Social Studies and the Business School)

Faculty of Science and Technology
- *School of Applied Sciences* (formed by merging the Schools of Chemistry and Physics; it still incorporated the Paper Technology Unit)
- *School of Computer and Mathematical Sciences*
- *School of Electronic and Electrical Engineering*
- *School of Mechanical and Offshore Engineering*

1996 (THE ROBERT GORDON UNIVERSITY)

In 1996, Foresterhill College of Nursing joined The Robert Gordon University to become part of a new Associate Faculty within the Faculty of Health and Food. The overall academic structure was now as follows:

Faculty of Design
- *Scott Sutherland School of Architecture*
- *Gray's School of Art*
- *School of Surveying* (subsequently re-named as the School of Construction, Property and Surveying)

Faculty of Health and Food
- *School of Applied Social Studies*
- *School of Food and Consumer Studies* (this subsequently became the School of Hotel, Tourism and Retail Management, as part of the Faculty of Management)
- *School of Health Sciences* (with Departments of Occupational Therapy, Physiotherapy and Radiography)
- *School of Pharmacy*
- *Associate Faculty of Nursing, Midwifery and Community Studies* (with Directorates of Pre-Registration and Post-Registration Nursing)

(Note that the Associate Faculty was subsequently re-designated as the School of Nursing and Midwifery, with the Faculty of Health and Food being re-named as the Faculty of Health and Social Care.)

Faculty of Management
- *Aberdeen Business School*
- *School of Information and Media*
- *School of Public Administration and Law*

Faculty of Science and Technology
- *School of Applied Sciences* (incorporating Paper Technology Unit)
- *School of Computer and Mathematical Sciences*
- *School of Electronic and Electrical Engineering*
- *School of Mechanical and Offshore Engineering*

2001 (THE ROBERT GORDON UNIVERSITY)

A further major review of academic structure was carried out in 2001, following the early retiral of the Dean of the Faculty of Science and Technology, with the University returning to a three-Faculty system, as shown opposite:

278

Faculty of Design and Technology
- *Gray's School of Art*
- *School of Computing* (previously the School of Computer and Mathematical Sciences)
- *School of Engineering* (formed by merging the Schools of Electronic and Electrical Engineering and Mechanical and Offshore Engineering)
- *Scott Sutherland School* (formed by merging the Scott Sutherland School of Architecture and the School of Construction, Property and Surveying)
- *School of Graduate Studies*
- *Centre for Interdisciplinary Studies*

Faculty of Health and Social Care
- *School of Applied Social Studies*
- *School of Health Sciences* (with Departments of Occupational Therapy, Physiotherapy and Radiography)
- *School of Life Sciences* (previously the School of Applied Sciences but now incorporating a Nutrition and Dietetics Section)
- *School of Nursing and Midwifery*
- *School of Pharmacy*

Faculty of Management
- *Aberdeen Business School*
- *School of Hotel, Tourism and Retail Management*
- *School of Information and Media*
- *School of Public Administration and Law*

Appendix C : Facts and figures relating to the present University

KEY STATISTICS

At the time of writing this Appendix (April 2002), The Robert Gordon University has just over 1400 staff, of whom roughly 500 are teachers or researchers, and over 11,000 students (8385 FTE). Its main campuses are at Schoolhill/St Andrew Street, Kepplestone and Garthdee. The University runs over 180 award-bearing courses, including over 90 honours degree programmes. It has an annual budget of roughly £72 million.

VISION, MISSION AND OBJECTIVES

The 'vision' of The Robert Gordon University is 'to be widely recognised as the premier vocational university in the UK'. Its 'mission' is:

'To provide high-quality, practice-based higher education and training programmes, research and consultancy services'.

The University's key objectives in meeting this mission are:
- to provide initial and continual higher education and training that encourages entrepreneurship and professionalism, and enables students to gain and retain employment and enhance their careers;
- to provide research, development and consultancy in support of industry, the arts, the professions, commerce and the public sector;
- to offer access to educational opportunities to all sectors of the population;
- to recognise the aspirations of staff and to enable them to give excellent services to all customers of the University, through the provision of appropriate personal development in good working conditions;
- to observe high professional standards in all activities.

ORGANISATIONAL STRUCTURE

The University currently has 13 Schools grouped in 3 Faculties, as shown below:

FACULTY OF DESIGN AND TECHNOLOGY
(Dean : Professor Jim Penman; Associate Dean : Professor Ian Bryden)

School of Computing (Head : Professor Susan Craw)
Location : St. Andrew Street
Total number of academic and research staff : 51
Total student numbers in 2001/02 : 704 (601 FTE)

School of Engineering (Head : Euring Professor Norman Deans)
Location : Schoolhill
Total number of full-time and part-time staff : 81
Total student numbers in 2001-02 : 1174 (893 FTE)

Gray's School of Art (Head : Professor Jeremy Diggle)
Location : Garthdee
Total number of full-time and part-time staff : 60
Total student numbers in 2001/02 : 822 (617 FTE)

Scott Sutherland School (Head : Professor Robert Pollock)
Location : Garthdee
Total number of full-time and visiting academic staff : 37
Total student numbers in 2001/02 : 777 (672 FTE)

FACULTY OF HEALTH AND SOCIAL CARE
(Dean : Professor John Harper; Associate Dean : Professor Valerie Maehle)

School of Applied Social Studies (Head : Professor Joyce Lishman)
Location : Kepplestone (Garthdee after August 2002)
Total number of full-time and part-time staff : 26
Total student numbers in 2001/02 : 672 (450 FTE)

School of Health Sciences (Head : Professor Valerie Maehle)
Location : Woolmanhill (Garthdee after August 2002)
Total number of full-time and part-time staff : 27
Total student numbers in 2001/02 : 475 (401 FTE)

School of Life Sciences (Head : Professor Maureen Melvin)
Location : St. Andrew Street
Total number of full-time and part-time staff : 40
Total student numbers in 2001/02 : 460 (422 FTE)

School of Nursing and Midwifery (Head : Mrs Jennie Parry)
Location : Hilton (Garthdee after August 2002)
Total number of full-time and part-time staff : 125

Total number of students in 2001/02 : 2101 (1204 FTE)

School of Pharmacy (Head : appointment pending)
Location : Schoolhill
Total number of full-time and part-time staff : 30
Total number of students in 2001/02 : 717 (564 FTE)

FACULTY OF MANAGEMENT
(Dean : Professor Bill McIntosh; Associate Dean : Professor Richard Mays)

Aberdeen Business School (Head : Mr. Hector Douglas)
Location : Garthdee
Total number of full-time and part-time staff : 50
Total student numbers in 2001/02 : 1781 (1331 FTE)

School of Hotel, Tourism and Retail Management (Head : Dr. Vicky Houston)
Location : Kepplestone (Garthdee after August 2002)
Total number of full-time and part-time staff : 25
Total student numbers in 2001/02 : 338 (328 FTE)

School of Information and Media (Head : Mr. Ian Johnson)
Location : Garthdee
Total number of full-time and part-time staff : 37
Total student numbers in 2001/02 : 548 (426 FTE)

School of Public Administration and Law (Head : Professor Richard Mays)
Location : Garthdee
Total number of full-time and part-time staff : 33
Total student numbers in 2001/02 : 490 (394 FTE)

OFFICERS OF THE UNIVERSITY

Chancellor : Sir Bob Reid
Principal and Vice-Chancellor : Professor William S. Stevely
Vice Principal and Dean : Professor Jim Penman
Vice Principal and Dean : Professor John Harper
Vice Principal and Dean : Professor Bill McIntosh
University Secretary : Dr. Adrian Graves
Director of Finance : Mrs. Patricia Briggs
Director of Human Resources : Mr. David Briggs
Director of Information Technology : Mr. Andrew McCreath

AREAS OF RESPONSIBILITY OF STRATEGIC MANAGEMENT TEAM

Principal and Vice-Chancellor : overall responsibility for all aspects of the work of the University, with all SMT members reporting directly to him.

Vice Principals and Deans

Professor Jim Penman : Dean of Faculty of Design and Technology, with University-wide responsibility for Strategic Planning; also responsible for the following Departments:
- Graduate Studies
- Research and Commercialisation
- Strategic Planning

Professor John Harper : Dean of the Faculty of Health and Social Care, with University-wide responsibility for Academic Quality; also responsible for the following Departments:
- Academic Affairs (including European Office and Faculty Administrative Officers)
- Centre for Enhancement of Learning and Teaching (CELT) - formerly the Centre for Learning and Assessment (CLASS)

Professor Bill McIntosh : Dean of the Faculty of Management, with University-wide responsibility for Academic Development; also responsible for the following Departments:
- Univation Ltd.
- Centre for Open and Distance Learning (CODL)

University Secretary : responsible for the following Departments:
- Corporate Governance
- Student Finance and Administration
- Student Services
- Library Services
- Estates and Physical Resources
- Corporate Affairs

Director of Finance : responsible for the following Departments:
- Financial Management
- Treasury and Accounting Services
- Procurement

Director of Human Resources : responsible for the following Departments:
- Occupational Health and Safety
- Personnel Services (including Employee Relations)
- Staff Development and Training
- Graphics and Printing

Director of Information Technology : responsible for the new, integrated IT Services Department, which comprises the following Sections:
- Customer Services
- Development Services
- Shared Services

STUDENT PROFILE OF THE UNIVERSITY

Student numbers by Faculty and School in 2001-02

Faculty of Design and Technology	Full-time home students	Full-time overseas student	Part-time Students
School of Computing	516	145	43
School of Engineering	519	234	421
Gray's School of Art	584	2	236
Scott Sutherland School	584	71	122
Interdisciplinary Students	31	0	3
	2234	**452**	**825**

Faculty of Health and Social Care	Full-time home students	Full-time overseas students	Part-time Students
School of Applied Social Studies	349	1	322
School of Health Sciences	388	6	81
School of Life Sciences	387	16	57
School of Nursing & Midwifery	1153	1	947
School of Pharmacy	433	30	254
	2710	**54**	**1661**

Faculty of Management	Full-time home students	Full-time overseas students	Part-time Students
Aberdeen Business School	946	143	692
School of Hotel, Tourism & Retail Management	315	10	13
School of Information & Media	349	4	195
School of Public Administration & Law	340	10	140
	1950	**167**	**1040**

All Faculties	**6894**	**673**	**3526**

Student characteristics (excluding students on collaborative programmes)

Gender	Undergraduate students (taught)	Postgraduate students (research)	Postgraduate students	Total
Male	39%	55%	57%	42%
Female	61%	45%	43%	58%

Age on entry	Under 18	18-20	21-24	Over 24
	1.5%	47.0%	32.1%	19.4%

Geographical origins	UK	Other EU	Overseas
Undergraduate students	93%	4%	3%
Postgraduate students (taught)	74%	4%	22%
Postgraduate students (research)	60%	16%	24%

Qualifications awarded (in 2000/01)

Level of award	Number of awards
PG Research Degrees	27
Taught Masters Degrees	282
PG Diplomas/Certificates	345
Undergraduate Degrees	1257
Diplomas	415
HNC/HND Awards	186
	2512

INCOME AND EXPENDITURE FOR FINANCIAL YEAR 1/8/00 - 31/7/01

Income (£000)

	Group	Joint Venture	Total
Funding Council grants	26,472	-	26,472
Tuition fees and education contracts	15,77	-	15,773
Research grants and contracts	1,979	-	1,979
Other income	8,058	18,470	26,528
Endowment and investment income	1,717	86	1,803
Total income	53,999	18,556	72,555

Expenditure (£000)

	Group	Joint Venture	Total
Staff costs	32,032	9,667	41,699
Other operating expenses	15,880	7,148	23,028
Depreciation	5,465	920	6,835
Interest payable	458	96	554
Total expenditure	53,835	17,831	71,666
Surplus for year (£000)	164	725	889

Appendix D : Notes on sources of information used in writing book

CHAPTER 1 : ROBERT GORDON, AND THE FOUNDATION OF ROBERT GORDON'S HOSPITAL

Here, the author was able to obtain all the necessary source material from documents held in the Antiquarian Collection in the Georgina Scott Sutherland Library at Garthdee. The key source document was 'The History of Robert Gordon's Hospital', by Robert Anderson (D.Wyllie and Son, Aberdeen; 1896), which provided detailed information on the life of Robert Gordon, the foundation of the Hospital, and the work of the Hospital until its transformation into Robert Gordon's College in 1881. Another useful source of information on these matters was the 'Bicentenary Record of Robert Gordon's Hospital in Aberdeen', by James Mackenzie (The Rosemount Press, Aberdeen; 1929). Further information on the life of Robert Gordon was found in the chapter on 'Robert Gordon' in 'Lives of Eminent Men of Aberdeen', by James Bruce (D. Wyllie and Son, Aberdeen; 1841), although the author was forced to conclude that this was more of a character assassination than an attempt to produce an objective biography; it made enjoyable reading, however!

CHAPTER 2 : THE TRANSFORMATION INTO ROBERT GORDON'S COLLEGE

Here, the author was again able to obtain all the necessary source material from documents held in the Antiquarian Collection at Garthdee. The key source documents were Robert Anderson's 'History of Robert Gordon's Hospital (see under Chapter 1) and the first two chapters of 'Scientia et Opera', by R.B. Strathdee (Robert Gordon's Institute of Technology, Aberdeen; 1971). Other useful sources again included James Mackenzie's 'Bicentenary Record of Robert Gordon's Hospital in Aberdeen' (see under Chapter 1) and the section on 'Technical Education' in 'The North-East of Scotland', a survey prepared for the Aberdeen Meeting of the British Association for the Advancement of Science in 1963 (The Central Press, Aberdeen; 1963).

CHAPTER 3 : JOHN GRAY, AND THE FOUNDATION OF GRAY'S SCHOOL OF ART

Here, the author was once again able to obtain all the necessary source material from documents held in the Antiquarian Collection at Garthdee. In this case, the key source document was the commemorative brochure that the Governors of Robert Gordon's Colleges caused to be prepared in 1935, to celebrate the 'Jubilee of Gray's School of Art, Aberdeen', (Robert Gordon's Colleges, Aberdeen; 1935). This provided detailed information on the life of John Gray, on the foundation of Gray's School of Art, and on the early work of the School. Another extremely useful source of information was again R.B. Strathdee's 'Scientia et Opera' (see under Chapter 2), which provided further detailed information on the foundation of Gray's School of Art and on its subsequent development. Further useful information was once again found in James Mackenzie's 'Bicentenary Record of Robert Gordon's Hospital in Aberdeen' (see under Chapter 1).

CHAPTER 4 : REVIEW OF THE TECHNICAL COLLEGE YEARS

Here, the author was once again able to obtain all the necessary source material from documents held in the Antiquarian Collection at Garthdee. By far the most important source was R.B. Strathdee's excellent 'Scientia et Opera' (see under Chapter 2), which describes the development of Robert Gordon's Technical College from its inauguration in 1910 till its conversion into Robert Gordon's Institute of Technology in 1965 in meticulous detail. The key chapters were Chapter 3 ('Technical College, 1909 - 1921), Chapter 4 ('Technical College, 1921 - 1944') and Chapter 5 ('Technical College, 1944 - 1965'). Further useful information was once again found in James Mackenzie's 'Bicentenary Record of Robert Gordon's Hospital in Aberdeen' (see under Chapter 1) and in the British Association's 1963 survey of 'The North-East of Scotland' (see under Chapter 2).

CHAPTER 5 : THE INCORPORATION OF THE SCHOOL OF DOMESTIC ECONOMY

Once again, the author was able to obtain all the necessary source material from existing published documents. In this case, the main source document was the extremely informative 'Aberdeen School of Domestic Science - An Outline History', edited by Robert A. Bayliss, that was published by Robert Gordon's Institute of Technology in 1979, a copy of which was found in RGU's Kepplestone Library. R.B. Strathdee's 'Scientia et Opera' (see under Chapter 2) also proved to be an extremely useful source of information once again, with further useful material being found in James Mackenzie's 'Bicentenary Record of Robert Gordon's Hospital in Aberdeen' (see under Chapter 1).

CHAPTER 6 : TOM SCOTT SUTHERLAND AND THE GARTHDEE BEQUEST

Yet again, the author was able to obtain all the information he needed from documents held in the Antiquarian Collection at Garthdee. The key documents in this case were R.B. Strathdee's 'Scientia et Opera' (see under Chapter 2), the excellent seven-part biography of Tom Scott Sutherland by Diane Morgan published in 'Leopard Magazine' in 1976, Tom Scott Sutherland's autobiography 'Life on One Leg' (Christopher Johnson, London; 1957) and a set of copies of newspaper cuttings on the foundation of the School of Architecture donated to the Library by Georgina Scott Sutherland. Further useful information was obtained from other newspaper cuttings, prospecti, commemorative brochures and other documents held in the Archive, and from James Mackenzie's 'Bicentenary Record of Robert Gordon's Hospital' (see under Chapter 1).

CHAPTER 7 : REVIEW OF THE RGIT YEARS

The information needed to write this chapter came from an extremely wide range of sources, including (yet again) R.B. Strathdee's 'Scientia et Opera' (see under Chapter 2), prospecti, annual reports and reviews, Governors', Academic Council and Faculty minutes, reports on CNAA quinquennial visits, the report on the 1988 Institutional Inspection, documentation relating to the 1991 Campaign for University Status, and material from the various staff newsletters that were produced during the 'RGIT years'. A great deal of extremely useful (and often highly confidential) information was also provided by Dr. Peter Clarke, Director and Principal of RGIT from 1970 to 1985, Dr. David Kennedy, Principal from 1985 to 1997, and Mr. Gavin Ross, Vice Principal during the same period. Having been on the staff from 1966 onwards, the author was also able to draw on his own memory of most of the events being described.

CHAPTER 8 : THE IMPACT OF THE OFFSHORE OIL INDUSTRY

Here, the author was able to obtain much of the information he required from his personal archives on the development of the North Sea oil industry and its impact on RGIT. Specific sources included the following: 'Oil and Gas from the North Sea', Shell Briefing Service (1972); 'Scotland and Oil', Teachers' Bulletin no. 5, Royal Scottish Geographical Society (1973); 'Responses of Industry within Aberdeen to Oil-Related Change', by D. Hunt, School of Business Management Studies, RGIT (1975); 'Ekofisk — One of a Kind' Teacher's Guide, by H.I. Ellington and E. Addinall, Phillips Petroleum (1980); 'Case Studies in Game Design', by H.I. Ellington, E. Addinall and F. Percival, Kogan Page, London (1984). He was also able to draw on many of the same internal RGIT documents that were used in researching Chapter 7, as well as on information provided by Dr. Peter Clarke and on his own memory of many of the events being described.

CHAPTER 9 : THE GROWTH OF SOCIAL AND MANAGEMENT-RELATED TEACHING

Here, the author was able to obtain virtually all the information he required from internal RGIT documentation, including annual reports and reviews, prospecti, staff newsletters, and minutes of meetings. One particularly useful source was the excellent 'History of the Aberdeen Business School' written by Dr. Douglas Gourlay, former Deputy Head of the School, in 1995; this highly-detailed account of the formation and subsequent development of the School saved the author a great deal of time and effort! The 'History of Aberdeen School of Domestic Science' produced by R.A. Bayliss and his colleagues in 1979 (see under Chapter 5) also proved useful. The author was again also able to draw on his own memory of the events being described, and on conversations with numerous members of staff over the years.

CHAPTER 10 : THE GROWTH OF HEALTH-RELATED TEACHING

Here, the author was once again able to obtain virtually all the information he required from internal RGIT documentation, including annual reports and reviews, prospecti, staff newsletters, and minutes of meetings. R.B. Strathdee's 'Scientia et Opera' (see under Chapter 2) once again also proved useful, as did the 'History of Aberdeen School of Domestic Science' produced by R.A. Bayliss et al (see under Chapter 5). The author was again also able to draw on his own memory of the events being described, and on conversations with numerous members of staff over the years.

CHAPTER 11 : CHANGES IN EDUCATIONAL METHODOLOGY

Here, the author was able to obtain all the information he required from material in his personal archives, backed up by his memory of the various events being described. Of particular use were : two review papers that he wrote during the mid-1990's - 'Educational innovation - where are we now?' ('Innovation & Learning in Education'; vol. 1; no. 1; 1995; pp 15-20), and 'Flexible learning - your flexible friend!' (Aspects of Educational and Training Technology XXI; Kogan Page, London, 1996; pp 3-13); two of his most-recent books on educational development - 'Facilitating Student Learning', by H.I. Ellington and S. Earl (Universiti Teknologi Malaysia Press, 1999) and 'A Practical Guide to Instructional Design', by H.I. Ellington and B. Aris (Universiti Teknologi Malaysia Press, 2000); and two recent booklets produced for RGU staff - 'Making Effective Use of Electronic Communication Systems' (CLASS; RGU; 2000) and 'Making Effective Use of the Computer' (CLASS; RGU; 2001).

CHAPTER 12 : RESEARCH, CONSULTANCY AND EXTERNAL COLLABORATION

Here, the author was again able to obtain most of the information he required from internal RGIT documentation, including annual reports and reviews, documents prepared for visits and inspections, and reports on same. This was again backed up by material from his own personal archives and by his memory of the events being described. The 'Statement of General Information' produced by RGIT in 1973 proved particularly useful, as (yet again) did R.B. Strathdee's 'Scientia et Opera' (see under Chapter 2). The information in the final section was almost entirely drawn from his own published papers and articles on the various projects being described, and from 'Case Studies on Game Design', by H.I. Ellington, E. Addinall and F. Percival (see under Chapter 8).

CHAPTER 13 : THE ACHIEVEMENT OF UNIVERSITY STATUS

The information needed to write this chapter came mainly from internal RGIT and RGU documents such as minutes, reports, annual reviews, institutional plans and staff newsletters, from CNAA documents, and from reports on visits. Documents that proved particularly useful included : the 1987 CNAA 'Future Strategy : Principles and Operation' document; the 1989 'Institutional Relationship with CNAA - Submission for Accreditation' document produced by RGIT; the 1990 RGIT Quality Handbook; the 1991 'Campaign for RGIT' document produced by Dr. David Kennedy; The Robert Gordon University's 1992 Corporate Plan; 'Chasing the chimera of academic quality', by H.I. Ellington and G.T.N. Ross (Quality Assurance in Education, vol. 1; no. 1; 1993; pp 15-20); and the RGU 'Report on Work of Internal Quality Audit Team 1990-1994', by H.I. Ellington. As in the case of Chapter 7, a great deal of extremely useful (and, again, often highly confidential) information was provided by Dr. Peter Clarke, Dr. David Kennedy and Mr Gavin Ross. Once again, the author was also able to draw on his own memory of the events being described.

Chapter 14 : Review of RGU's first ten years

The information needed to write this chapter again came from an extremely wide range of sources, particularly internal RGU documentation such as minutes of meetings, annual reviews, strategy documents, reports on visits, staff newsletters, and so on. The two statutory instruments through which RGIT acquired full university status - the 'Further and Higher Education (Scotland) Act 1992' (HMSO, London, 1992) and 'The Robert Gordon University (Scotland) Order of Council 1993' (HMSO, London, 1993) - also proved to be useful sources. A great deal of extremely useful (and often confidential) information was once again provided by Dr. David Kennedy and by Mr. Gavin Ross, and also by Professor William Stevely and other members of the senior staff of the University. Once again, the author was also able to draw on his own memory of the events being described.

Chapter 15 : New buildings for a new University

Here, most of the material again came from internal RGU documentation, including the 'Estates Strategy' produced in 1994, the 'Estates Strategy (Update)' produced in 1997, and the design documents produced in respect of different buildings. The article 'Learning Curve' on the new Faculty of Management building by Martin Spring (Building Review; 11 December, 1998) also proved extremely useful. Further extremely useful information was provided by Mr. Roger Bond, RGU's Estates Director, and by Professor Bill McIntosh, who had overall strategic responsibility for Physical Resources and Estates over the period when the Faculty of Management and Faculty of Health and Social Care buildings were constructed. Mr. Gavin Ross, who had been heavily involved in the early development of the institution's Estates Strategy and its subsequent implementation, also provided a large amount of extremely useful information.

Chapter 16 : Moving the University into the 'electronic age'

Much of the information needed to write this final chapter of the book was provided by

Mr. Andrew McCreath, with the IT Strategy documents that he wrote in 1999 and 2001 and the report on the first phase of the University's Business Process Re-engineering Project in October, 2001 proving particularly useful, together with the update on the University's IT strategy that he wrote specially for the author in March 2002. Further useful sources of information included the author's own booklet: 'Making Effective Use of Electronic Communication Systems' (see under Chapter 11), a paper on the history of the Virtual Campus specially produced for the author by the Centre for Open and Distance Learning in March 2002, and the paper on 'The Robert Gordon University Faculties' Intranet - iNET' written by Les Tarr, the Faculty of Management's Internet Development Manager, in 2002 (http://inet.rgu.com). Further useful information was obtained from the RGU Web site.

POSTSCRIPT

All the information needed to write this section was obtained from the Report to the Governing Bodies of the University of Aberdeen and The Robert Gordon University on 'Institutional Collaboration' that was published jointly by the two Universities in June 2002, and from private conversations with Professor William Stevely, Principal of RGU.

Appendix E : List of illustrations and acknowledgement of sources

CHAPTER 1

Figure 1.1 :   William Mossman's 1758 portrait of Robert Gordon; from photograph of portrait provided by Bill Black, Centre for the Enhancement of Learning and Teaching, the Robert Gordon University.

Figure 1.2 :   The original Robert Gordon's Hospital building (the 'Auld Hoose'); from drawing published in 'Bicentenary Record of Robert Gordon's Hospital in Aberdeen', by James Mackenzie (Rosemount Press, Aberdeen; 1929).

Figure 1.3 :   Robert Gordon's Hospital, as enlarged in 1830-33; from drawing published in 'The History of Robert Gordon's Hospital in Aberdeen', by Robert Anderson (R. Wyllie and Son, Aberdeen; 1896).

Figure 1.4 :   The outgoing Hospital class of 1874 with their Headmaster, Dr. Alexander Ogilvie; from photograph provided by courtesy of Robert Gordon's College.

CHAPTER 2

Figure 2.1 :   The Aberdeen Mechanics' Institution building in Market Street; from copy of drawing provided by courtesy of Aberdeen City Council Arts and Recreation Department.

Figure 2.2 :   The teaching staff at around the time of the transformation from Robert Gordon's Hospital to Robert Gordon's College; from photograph provided by courtesy of Robert Gordon's College.

Figure 2.3 :   Dr. Alexander Ogilvie - first Headmaster of Robert Gordon's College; from photograph provided by courtesy of Robert Gordon's College.

Figure 2.4 :   How Robert Gordon's College looked in 1910; from photograph published in 'Bicentenary Record of Robert Gordon's Hospital in Aberdeen' (*op. cit.*).

CHAPTER 3

Figure 3.1 :   John Gray, Founder of Gray's School of Art; from photograph published in commemorative Brochure on 'Jubilee of Gray's School of Art, Aberdeen' (Robert Gordon's Colleges, Aberdeen; 1935).

Figure 3.2 :   Gray's School of Art as it looked shortly after its opening; from photograph discovered by author in box of old documents at Schoolhill (now lodged in Antiquarian Collection at Garthdee).

Figure 3.3 :   The arched entrance to Robert Gordon's College and The Robert Gordon University, showing the School in the background; from photograph provided by Bill Black.

Figure 3.4 :   A 'life class' in Gray's School of Art in the early 1930's; from photograph provided by Jim Fiddes from the Antiquarian Collection in the Georgina Scott Sutherland Library at Garthdee.

CHAPTER 4

CHAPTER 5

Laboratories; from photograph provided by Bill Black.

Figure 9.5 :   A seminar being run in the School of Social Studies; from photograph provided by Bill Black.

Figure 9.6 :   A meal being served in RGIT's Training Restaurant at Kepplestone; from photograph provided by Bill Black.

CHAPTER 10

Figure 10.1 :   One of the School of Pharmacy's general laboratories; from photograph provided by Bill Black.

Figure 10.2 :   Pharmacy students carrying out advanced experimental work; from photograph provided by Bill Black.

Figure 10.3 :   Part of the Pharmaceutical Care Centre in the School of Pharmacy; from photograph provided by Sid Merrakech, CELT.

Figure 10.4 :   A Dietetics student carrying out placement work in a hospital; from photograph provided by Bill Black.

Figure 10.5 :   Mrs Anne Porteous, Head of the School of Speech Therapy, carrying out a clinical demonstration; from photograph provided by Bill Black.

Figure 10.6 :   An Occupational Health Nursing student carrying out an audiometer test on a patient as part of her clinical training; from photograph included in 1993 RGU Prospectus.

Figure 10.7 :   Woolmanhill Hospital, where Grampian Health Board's Schools of Occupational Therapy and Physiotherapy were based in 1990; from photograph provided by Bill Black.

Figure 10.8 :   Mr. Donald Graham, Director of the Department of Radiography in the Centre for Professions Allied to Medicine, carrying out a demonstration for students at Foresterhill Hospital; from photograph provided by Bill Black.

Figure 10.9 :   An Occupational Therapy student working with an elderly patient during one of her clinical practice placements; from photograph provided by Bill Black.

CHAPTER 11

Figure 11.1 :   A student of the former School of Chemistry using a tape-model kit to study the molecular structure of different compounds; from photograph in author's personal archives (originally taken by Bill Black).

Figure 11.2 :   'SODIT' - a simulated planning exercise on the impact of North Sea Oil being run in the Scott Sutherland School of architecture during the early 1970's; from photograph provided by Bill Black.

Figure 11.3 :   The climax of 'The Power Station Game', in which the three teams present their cases to the 'Generating Board'; from photograph in author's personal archives (originally taken by Bill Black).

Figure 11.4 :   Students in the School of Computer and Mathematical Sciences carrying out a group-problem-solving exercise on the properties of knots; from photograph provided by Bill Black.

CHAPTER 14

Figure 14.1 :   The University's name being changed at Schoolhill in June 1992; from photograph published in Issue 1 of 'Alumni' magazine (January, 1994).

Figure 14.2 :   Sir Bob Reid, first Chancellor of The Robert Gordon University; from photograph provided by Bill Black.

Figure 14.3 :   Sir Bob Reid conferring an honorary degree at one of RGU's graduation ceremonies; from photograph provided by Martin Parker.

Figure 14.4 :   Research being carried out in Gray's School of Art during the mid-1990's; from photograph provided by Martin Parker.

Figure 14.5 :   Foresterhill College of Nursing and Midwifery; from photograph provided by Martin Parker.

Figure 14.6 :   One of the 'Garthdee Towers' that were built during the early 1990's; from photograph provided by Bill Black.

Figure 14.7 :   Teaching being carried out in one of RGU's language laboratories; from photograph provided by Martin Parker.

Figure 14.8 :   Baroness Thatcher delivering her Leadership Lecture in 1993; from photograph provided by Martin Parker.

Figure 14.9 :   Professor William Stevely, Principal and Vice-Chancellor of RGU since 1997; from photograph provided by Bill Black.

Figure 14.10 : A nursing student on ward-based work placement; from photograph provided by Martin Parker.

Figure 14.11 : The Altens Headquarters of RGIT Montrose Ltd; from photograph provided by Bill Black.

Figure 14.12 : Environmental monitoring work being carried out by staff of RGU's Centre for Environmental Engineering; from photograph provided by Martin Parker.

Figure 14.13 : RGU Principal Professor William Stevely and Aberdeen University Principal Professor Duncan Rice at 'Offshore Europe 2001'; from photograph published in 'RGyou' in September, 2001.

CHAPTER 15

Figure 15.1 :   An aerial view of the Faculty of Management building at Garthdee; from photograph provided by Roger Bond, RGU Estates Director.

Figure 15.2 :   The Faculty of Management building seen from the ground; from photograph provided by Roger Bond.

Figure 15.3 :   The atrium in the Faculty of Management building; from photograph provided by Roger Bond.

Figure 15.4 :   Part of the Georgina Scott Sutherland Library in the Faculty of Management building; from photograph provided by Roger Bond.

Figure 15.5 :   One of the main lecture theatres in the Faculty of Management building; from photograph provided by Roger Bond.

Figure 15.6 :   Sir Ian Wood, Chairman of Scottish Enterprise, opening the Faculty of

Management building on April 17, 1999; from photograph provided by Martin Parker.

Figure 15.7 : An artist's impression of the new Faculty of Health and Food building planned for Garthdee; from 'Investing in a real future', a publicity booklet on the Safeway/Garthdee project produced by RGU in 1999.

Figure 15.8 : The new Faculty of Health and Social Care building at Garthdee under construction; from photograph provided by Roger Bond.

Figure 15.9 : One of the student activities that will be catered for in the new Sports Centre at Garthdee; from photograph provided by Bill Black.

CHAPTER 16

Figure 16.1 : Mr Andrew McCreath, RGU's first Director of Information Technology; from photograph provided by Bill Black.

Figure 16.2 : The Web home page for RGU's Virtual Campus (April 2002).

Figure 16.3 : The Web page on the CODL Director, Judith Smith (April 2002).

Figure 16.4 : Part of the Web entry on the 'e-business' Programme that is available through RGU's Virtual Campus (April 2002).

Figure 16.5 : One of the IT laboratories in the new Faculty of Management building at Garthdee; from photograph provided by Martin Parker.

Figure 16.6 : Part of the Web home page for the Faculty of Management Intranet Campus (April 2002).

Keyword Index

A.

B.

C.

D.

K.

L.

M.

Professions Allied to Medicine, incorporation of: 125; 164-166
Professorial lectures: 222
Professorial titles, introduction of:114
Public Administration, development of teaching of: 150-151; 168-169
Process skills, development of: 170-174
Publishing Studies - see under 'Librarianship'

Q.

Quality Assurance Agency (QAA): 225; 231-232
Quality assurance/control: 118; 198; 202-205; 226; 218-219; 231-232

R.

Radiography, development of teaching of: 125; 164-166
Reid, Sir Bob: 214; 215
Research, development of: 82; 84-85; 156; 174; 175; 183-189; 189-191; 192-195; 200-201; 203; 216-218; 228-231
Research Assessment Exercise (RAE): 216-218; 230-231
Robbins Report: 107
Robert Gordon (person) - see under 'Gordon, Robert'
Robert Gordon (training schooner): 74; 75
Robert Gordon's College: 33-41
- buildings: 22-23; 24; 25; 38; 39
- development of: 36-41
- establishment of: 33-36
- establishment as Central Institution: 40-41
- evening class work: 38-41
- Governors of : 35; 40; 41; 43; 45-49; 57
- motto, origin of: 36
Robert Gordon's Hospital: 17-27
- buildings: 22-23; 24; 25
- Charter of Incorporation: 23
- development of: 23-27
- foundation of: 20-23
- Governors of: 20; 23; 29; 33-35
- reform of: 33-36
- motto, origin of: 20
Robert Gordon Institute of Technology, The - change of name to: 125
Robert Gordon's Institute of Technology: Section 3 (103-209)
- administration of: 114; 121; 199-200

S.

T.

U.